BEAUTIFUL WITNESS

STEPHEN SCOURFIELD

BEAUTIFUL WITNESS

In a world of travel

First published in 2013 by
UWA Publishing
Crawley, Western Australia 6009
www.uwap.uwa.edu.au

UWAP is an imprint of UWA Publishing,
a division of The University of Western Australia.

A full CIP data entry is available from the National Library of Australia

Typeset in 11 pt Bembo by Lasertype
Printed by Lightning Source

Cover image:
Village children at Mangily fishing village,
near Ifaty, Madagascar, with a *kabosy*.
Photograph by Stephen Scourfield

beautiful

Pleasing the senses or mind aesthetically; beautiful poetry.

Of a very high standard; excellent; she spoke in beautiful English.

witness

Have knowledge of, from observation or experience.

A person giving a sworn testimony. Openly profess one's religious faith.

from Oxford Dictionary of English

About the Author

Stephen Scourfield is an award-winning travel writer.

He has twice been voted Australia's Best Travel Writer in the National Travel Industry Awards.

He is also the recipient of a United Nations media award for fairness in publishing.

Stephen is also a critically acclaimed and award-winning novelist and fiction writer. His current works of fiction include two novels, *As the River Runs* and *Other Country*, and *Unaccountable Hours: Three Novellas*.

Previous titles include
Connected
Travel Etcetera
Western Australia: An Untamed View
Are We Nearly There Yet?

He is also a word performer and public speaker.

Contents

	Map of the world	x
1	ABOUT BEING ELSEWHERE	1
2	CROSSING BORDERS	21
	Over the Lines on a Map	22
	Crossing the Borders of Time in Lesotho	24
	Porous Borders in South Africa	30
	My Friend Pramod in India	34
	Bridging the Gap Between Australia and Papua New Guinea	38
3	TRANSPORTED	43
	On My Feet in Caucasus	45
	On the Road in Oman	48
	Driving the Desert in Qatar	53
	Flying Backwards to Africa from Forwards Dubai	55
	On Horseback in Kenya	59
	A Donkey in Greece	62
	The Island under Siege in Papua New Guinea	63
	Sea Kayaking along Ningaloo Reef	66
	Finding Old Batavia in Jakarta	69

Motorcycling in the Himalayas 71
Travelling on the World's Highest Train 78
Riding the Rails of India 80
Walking Beside the River Thames 84
A Slice of England by Rail 91
Driving to the Heart of Australia 99

4 RAIN 107
The Kimberley in the Wet Season 109
A Soft Shower in Bali 114
Delhi in the Rain 115
Dedication under Umbrellas in Sri Lanka 117

5 QUESTIONS OF BELIEF 119
The Water of Life in Sri Lanka 120
Temples of the Cosmic Dancer in India 123
Sikhism in the Subcontinent 130
Indiana Jones & Cambodia's Temple of Angkor Wat 132
The World's First Christian Country, Armenia 135
Spreading the Word through Turkey 140
Peace on Patmos 143
Sunday in Kenya 146
The Monasteries of Tibet 148
Animism in Toraja Land 152
The Turning of the Bones in Madagascar 156

6 THE FABRIC OF SOCIETY 159
The *Bangdians* of Tibet 161
Lotus Weaving in Burma 164
Making a Difference in Africa 166
Destruction & Creation in KwaZulu-Natal 167
The Natural Colours of India 169
Delicacies & Thai Silk 174
The Fabric of Death in the Indian Ocean 177
Embroidery in Vietnam 177

7 NATURAL WORLD 183
From Hunters to Guides in Madagascar 185
Baobabs & Boabs & a Tale in Common 188
Borneo & a Close Encounter with an Orangutan 190
Falcons & Ships of the Desert in the Middle East 194
A Lion Roars in the Masai Mara 196
An Intimate Moment with Tigers in India 200
Fishing & Paddling in Canada's Yukon 202
Swimming with Whale Sharks on Ningaloo Reef 205
Budgerigars & Zebra Finches in the Australian Desert 207

8 SUSTENANCE 211
Tea in Sri Lanka 212
Zen & the Sustenance of Shopping 217
Yak & Hotpots in Tibet 221
Ouzerias on an Old Greek Island 223
Food & Family in Italy 225
Sustained to 121 years old in Madagascar 229
The World's First Wine in Georgia 229
Ramsay & Onsen in Japan 234
The Poppies of Thailand's Golden Triangle 238
Eating in India Where All Are Equal 240
Silver Scales in Oman 242

9 THE MUSIC OF LIFE 245
A Sitar Lesson in India 247
Kabosy, *Valiha*, *Djembe* in the Indian Ocean 250
The Ancient Music of Greece 253
Lesiba in Lesotho 255

Acknowledgements 259

Other titles by Stephen Scourfield 261

About the Disk 265

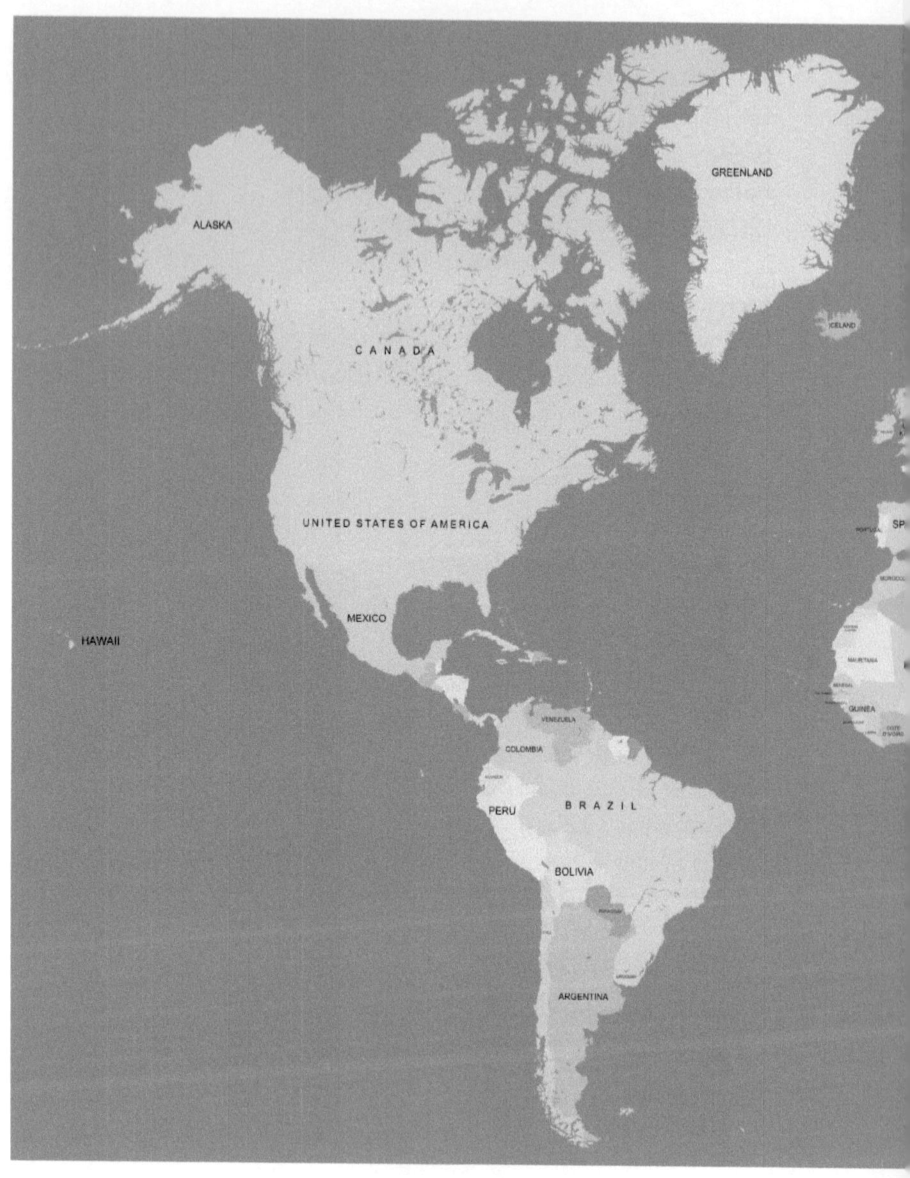
GREENLAND
ALASKA
ICELAND
C A N A D A
UNITED STATES OF AMERICA
MEXICO
HAWAII
VENEZUELA
COLOMBIA
PERU
B R A Z I L
BOLIVIA
ARGENTINA
GUINEA

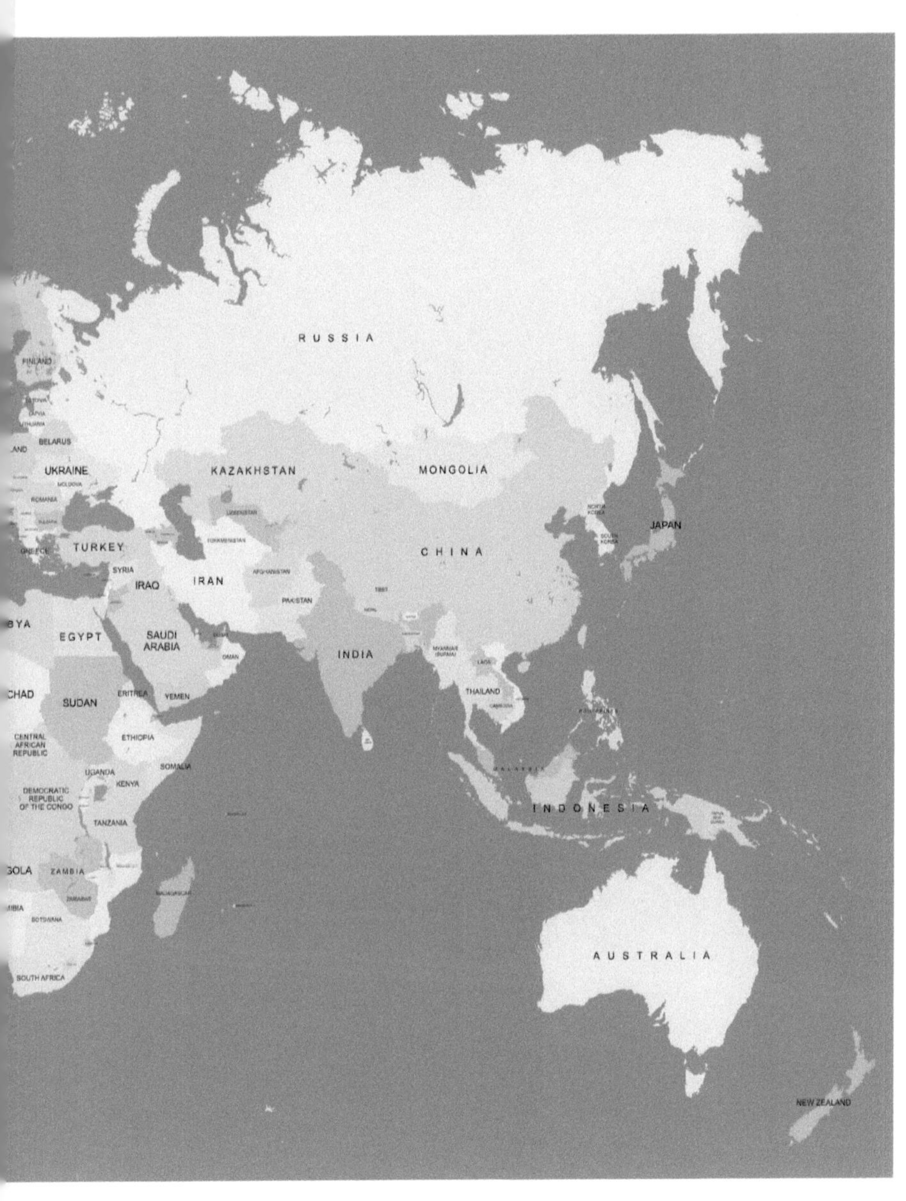
RUSSIA
FINLAND
BELARUS
UKRAINE
ROMANIA
KAZAKHSTAN
MONGOLIA
TURKEY
GREECE
SYRIA
IRAQ
IRAN
CHINA
JAPAN
AFGHANISTAN
PAKISTAN
EGYPT
SAUDI ARABIA
OMAN
INDIA
THAILAND
CHAD
SUDAN
ERITREA
YEMEN
ETHIOPIA
CENTRAL AFRICAN REPUBLIC
SOMALIA
UGANDA
KENYA
DEMOCRATIC REPUBLIC OF THE CONGO
TANZANIA
INDONESIA
ZAMBIA
BOTSWANA
AUSTRALIA
SOUTH AFRICA
NEW ZEALAND

1

About Being Elsewhere

I am often elsewhere, but never really somewhere else. I might have moved physically (my body is not where it was yesterday; not where it usually lives) but I am always here, inside me, fully occupying my self and this moment.

I never feel "away", never displaced. I have long lost the sense of being "over there", out of touch, out of reach; even of being away from home, even when I don't have any contact with it.

I am always in the middle of my life, looking at the world through the same eyes, whichever bit of the world that might be. I am always in the middle of my thoughts. We all are. Literally self-centred, I suppose, in this physical sense, and self-contained in other ways.

I am the hub, with spokes flying off, thin, silver and shining, in all directions, away from me to a glistening rim.

The emotional rim: family, friends, commitments, complexities. Incident and echo, observation and nostalgia, fusion and fission.

The geographic rim: looking over the ocean from my home on the west coast of Australia to South Africa, Madagascar, Kenya, up past Oman and across to India, Sri Lanka, Myanmar (or Burma), down past Thailand and Indonesia to the Kimberley and Ningaloo Reef. The Indian Ocean Rim.

Then to the world beyond this, the rest of Africa and Asia, Europe and the Americas. Back to the rural English town where I grew up, with a pretty ridge of hills that I know better than the undulations of my own spine. At the deserts of Australia, an internal landscape.

Places are like people – sometimes you just click and seem to know them. You are instantly compatible.

I get to know others more slowly, over time and many visits. Circling, digging and letting the spaces in between those visits play their part, too.

These places and people, these landscapes and cultures, form the frame of my self-portrait. Change a frame and you can alter a portrait.

I was a child who wanted to be a writer and I started my writing life on the Malvern Hills in rural Worcestershire; an adolescent walking paths in the footsteps of Sir Edward Elgar and composing lines which, more than three decades later, would appear in my fiction writing.

I wanted to be a novelist more than anything else, but I needed to make a living. That has largely come from travelling and writing, the stories and photographs being published in books, magazines, newspaper supplements, and now in the travel pages and on the website of *The West Australian*, on the west coast of Australia, of which I am Travel Editor.

Clearly it was always going to be this way. A short time after starting work in England as a teenager, I was in Germany on assignment, travelling almost the length of the Rhine Valley with Pearly Kings and Queens from central London, there for charitable work. Me with a shorthand notebook, black ballpoint and a Canon camera (I originally and separately trained as both writer and photographer). Me today, still with a small shorthand notebook, black ballpoints and Canon cameras.

I didn't start publishing fiction until I was in my forties, and now a pair of novels, *Other Country* and *As the River Runs*, both set in the Kimberley region of Western Australia but twenty years apart, sit on the shelves. With them is *Unaccountable Hours*, a collection of three novellas, all written as full novels and distilled into something more viscous. The story of a musical instrument maker, the romantic friendship between an old woman and a young man, and the story of a biologist who retreats to country are all set against the remarkable landscape of the world's oldest continent.

Lyrics from a Kris Kristofferson country song: "I'm a walking contradiction, partly truth and partly fiction."

There are only two people involved in reading and writing. One person writes the words, one person reads them. There is no-one else here, just me and you. It is always this personal, this intimate, and always requires this honesty. That has been the fundamental of every writing day (and every day is a writing day), whether those words have been shorthand jottings or longhand descriptive lists in the notebooks that I have kept and filed all these years; whether they were typed on my massively over-engineered Remington Noiseless in the 1970s or the Scheidegger portable that I carried from country to country for so many years, or the series of Apple Macintosh laptops that I have now used for more than two decades.

It doesn't matter what I write with or where I am. What matters is the integrity of the discourse. Truth and ethic. In my connection to you.

In the pages that follow are some of the people who have inspired me.

From my grandmother's house on the Malvern Hills, I looked out at the Black Hill of the Welsh border, where Bruce Chatwin set his novel about brothers on the land. Chatwin wrote both fiction and literary travel non-fiction. His book *What Am I Doing Here* was described as "anecdotes, fragments, assignments and bits of odd lore", which sounds familiar.

Nelson Mandela said that no white person did more for South Africa's anti-apartheid cause than Bishop Trevor Huddleston, and I met him fleetingly as a child (when he was still Father Trevor) and was struck by his sheer goodness, and by the way that goodness empowered him. The people in these pages – Pramod, Willis, villagers in Borneo and Madagascar, the women working with fabric in Kenya and Myanmar (Burma) – are suffused with ethic, belief, humility and a sense of pilgrimage and quest, just as are Ace and Billy, the brothers on the land in my novel *Other Country*, and Airplane Cuttover, Uncle Vincent Yimi and Henny Breeze in *As the River Runs.*

In the pages of this book, you will also catch glimpses of Casey, my constant travelling companion; my counterpoint. Casey, I should explain, is my suitcase.

The day Casey arrives, his only journey has been to me inside a box. Little does he know what lies ahead. I sling a bit of rope round his waist (it isn't as pretentious as a strap and holds him together when he's being thrown from a wharf to a dodgy ferry or onto the top of a dusty bus) and then we go to Africa.

Not long after I arrive at the baggage carousel at Johannesburg airport, Casey appears. He immediately likes Africa. He feels the pulse. We fly on to Kenya and he likes the sunny, not-too-hot climate of Nairobi, people walking, always walking. A donkey cart, laden; road-verge crews with machetes, swinging at the grass; coffee and acacia trees; rows of concrete block houses, 5 metres by 3 metres, with polite space in between.

But Casey particularly likes being opened at Mount Kenya Safari Club. In the 1950s, Hollywood star William Holden's place attracted big-game hunters but today it's run by the Fairmont hotel group and is more interested in conservation. It's also rather swish. *Casey Does Comfort.* His year has started well.

Trundle Casey into a gorgeous hotel, lay him flat on the wool carpet or ash floor and give him a glimpse of high thread-count sheets and fine French amenities laid out on an Italian marble bathroom counter, and his zip flies open. But drag him round the Australian Outback, where his seams impregnate with red bulldust and his fabric is pinpricked with spinifex tips, and I can almost sense his protests.

In Tibet, I see poor Casey momentarily frozen against the achingly blue high-altitude sky as he is thrown into the back of a luggage truck to lodge alongside a motorcycle and countless boxes and goods being carted away from Lhasa.

In Myanmar (which some still think of as Burma), I catch glimpses of him as the boot of the old car in which we travel is opened and shut. He is in there day after day in the steamy heat; a hostage being taken goodness knows where. Any complaints are muffled. Maybe he tries to remember the twists and turns in the road in the hope that rescuers may follow.

Poor Casey.

But then there are moments when I feel he shivers with excitement, like when he first sees our splendid suite at the heritage bungalow-style Capella Singapore hotel, or the Ava Gardner suite at Raffles Hotel, in the same city at the crossroads of South-East Asia. The ravishing Ms Gardner stayed at Raffles when she was in Singapore for the Asian premiere of her 1954 film *The Barefoot Contessa*, considered her signature movie and in which she starred with Humphrey Bogart. In her suite, Casey is positively enraptured, as he is when we arrive at the Relais de la Riene hotel on the high savannah Plateau de l'Horombe in Madagascar. I am rather interested in the adjacent Isalo National Park and its Bara tribal burial sites, but Casey loves the swimming pool with white umbrellas and the double bed draped exotically with a crimson-trimmed mosquito net.

Casey's love affair with fancy accommodation intensifies when we stay at a couple of Design Hotels in the Greek capital of Athens, but his arrival at the Greek island of Hydra comes as something of a shock. For we are met at the ferry wharf by an old couple with a donkey (there are no cars or motorbikes on Hydra) and Casey is unceremoniously hefted onto the animal's back and secured with a bit of old rope. I walk behind, watching Casey sway in time with the donkey's backside, feeling his ignominy. (It's good to get Casey off his high horse.)

We beg to differ on some things, but Casey is always there for me, and he has the happy habit of reincarnation. When he finally dies (a zip gives up, a handle falls off, a wheel is lost), there is another manifestation of Casey, and the story continues. The new case is just Casey (same personality), and we travel on together.

I don't feel like a travel writer. I just feel like a writer travelling (perhaps a dozen big assignments a year, and quite a number of small ones). The non-fiction and fiction parts of my writing life are balanced – in truth, it is the dream come true, particularly in the moment that my third book of fiction was published. One could be a fluke, two didn't quite seem to seal the deal; there is sanctity in trinity.

When I think I don't really fit as a novelist (not competitive enough, not commercial enough), I tell myself I'm really a travel writer. When I feel I don't really fit as that, I can tell myself I'm really a novelist.

I recently received a communication that began "we thought we'd invite some journalists and you…", so at least I know what I'm not.

(I also recently received correspondence addressed to "Mr Soccerfield". Throughout Asia and a number of other countries, I seem to be known as "Mr Stephen".)

You can't feel you're spending your whole life running around in circles. You have to be still and, even when you're moving, you can be still inside. Movement is measured against the fixed point of the home you go back to. Home is not just the place where I live; it is the one place that constantly lives in me. Being stationary puts motion into perspective. (I look up "perspective" in the dictionary and another definition is "View, viewpoint, point of view, POV".)

In my favourite Indian city of Kolkata (old Calcutta, where I have just jotted down in my notebook the words of a sign, "No parking of outside cars inside apartments") I come across a book stall on the pavement. It is just a sheet of plywood propped on four bricks, with a strange mish-mash of titles, including Adolf Hitler's *Mein Kampfe* and Dominique Lapierre's *City of Joy*, set here in Kolkata. But my eye falls on a book about self-development through the study of Hindu gods. Are there indeed 330 million deities or is this just a number representing the infinite forms of God? Hinduism is complex, and I'll forever seek a better understanding of it. I ask how much the book is.

"Fifty rupees," says the stallholder. He tilts his head slightly, as if in apology at this enormous cost of less than a dollar. I hand him a 100 rupee note. He wraps the book in clean brown paper, tying it with string and forming a loop so that I can carry it easily. When he hands it to me, he gives a little bird-bob, and smiles.

I bow a little too, smile back, and wait.

He waits.

We both smile some more.

And I wait.

There is clearly only one thing missing in the conclusion of our transaction, as he has put the 100 rupee note in his pocket in exchange for my 50 rupee book. I muster the courage and ask, "What about change?"

He smiles rather more sympathetically and raises his hands, fingertips touching, like a chapel. "Ah, my friend," he explains. "Change comes from within."

I like to arrive at a destination wide-eyed and slightly confused. I like to be *not quite sure*; to stand back and work out what's going on, and to then research and fill in the gaps. That process takes me to the story.

The difference between being on holiday and travelling for writing is that the writer needs to come to conclusion. Not conclusion in the simple sense ("is it a good hotel or a bad hotel?"), but conclusion in the sense that I need such a big grasp on a place or experience that I can encapsulate it in the 1,000 words a day that I write on the road, and tell a million people about it.

My laptop might be full of digital maps, encyclopaedias, history books, anthropological, geological and astronomical studies, and flora and fauna guides, but they are all for "backfilling" – for piecing together the leads. For first I stand and watch, looking for nuances and hints, and then I fill in the gaps.

"The problem with deep research is that the more you know the less interested you become in your subject," says Sir Bob Geldof in his *Geldof in Africa* documentaries. "You know too much."

I can only remember one occasion when I did extensive research before an assignment. When it came to finishing the packing of Casey and flying there, I felt I was merely going through the formality of travel to justify writing what I knew.

"*Finishing the packing of Casey.*" That sentence sounds slightly clumsy, but I have worded it with care, as Casey is always mostly packed, ready to go. In the front pocket, there is a survival space blanket, roll-top waterproof bag, a rain suit (good for the cold, good for ocean activities, the pants even good for snorkelling on blisteringly hot days), umbrella, spare strap, handy rope and a photographic monopod. Inside, across the front, there is a row of smaller bags containing, right to left; camera chargers, cables and backup cables; spare spectacles, two worldwide electric power plug adaptors, extra A7-sized notebooks, pens, business cards, big back-up computer hard drives, the dual-SIM mobile phone I take overseas but use mainly as an alarm clock (almost invariably SIM-less); bathroom kit; toolkit including head torch, small LED torch, climber Swiss Army knife, multi-tool, fire flint, sewing kit, boot cleaner; comprehensive medical kit with everything from Gastro Stop to Gastrolyte, an elastic support to serious pain killers, *pau d'arco* capsules to myrrh; and my indulgence, a travel mug stuffed with teabags and sugar sachets. I dislike the little white cups and saucers in hotel rooms and tea is my luxury during the four or so hours every day that I need to keep up with writing and photography work.

All this lives in Casey, ready to go.

Finally, as I "*finish the packing of Casey*", clothes are folded on an ironing board, shirts and pants in three parts, and stacked carefully so they arrive uncrushed. Scarves are rolled, socks and small items balled in mesh bags and jackets folded in half on top.

It is all designed to never be unpacked. So often I am in a different bed each night, and in a new room only briefly. My nightmare is leaving a cable behind.

"I didn't think I'd see you today." I am at home, painting the front wall of our studio on a Saturday morning and a barrel-shaped man in singlet, shorts, towelling hat and double-plugger thongs pads up the street. He stops to speak to me, his barrel-shaped blue heeler dog alongside. I don't know him, but smile and say hello.

He adds, "How can you be in South Africa and India and Sydney and get back here for Saturday?"

He has clearly already seen today's Travel supplement and thinks he's caught me out. He hasn't considered that I might write more than one story on any particular assignment.

"Ah," I say. "But I am."

He shrugs and looks down at the dog. "Come on Harley", and they pad off together.

A few steps later, he turns and explains, "It was my fiftieth birthday present, and it wasn't what I meant."

Travel is about bringing back stories, and it helps to develop our point of view.

"Point of View" is as much an intellectual, emotional and philosophical term as it is filmic and photographic.

On the physical side, it appears throughout film scripts. POV: I look at you. POV: You look at me. Photographically, it is the precise position and angle at which a camera is placed to take a picture.

On the philosophical side, it is what we want to believe, state and defend… "well, if you want my point of view…"

And travel *can* form and inform our point of view…

…I have a plan for today's outing in Myanmar. I am going to buy every t-shirt that I am politely offered, which will be a lot. I am going to buy every postcard (in strings of 10) and every puppet. I am going to spread a little money around and give these young entrepreneurs some income as the curtain around their country falls and they come out into the world. And I am going to do the same every day that I am here. A good quality t-shirt is about $3 (if I don't bargain) and a packet of postcards just a few cents. (A dollar is a good tip here, and I meet some ladies earning under $2 a day in a small workshop.)

But I am not going to take any of this home.

On the last day of the trip, I talk with the hotel's room attendant. Does she know anyone who wants to start selling souvenirs? "Why, my daughter," she says. And so I send everything I have bought, for her to start her business. She has a start in life, I don't stuff Casey full of souvenirs that will languish in cupboards until they become landfill, and I don't stimulate the manufacture of unnecessary goods. Many have had a little of my money and I haven't had to keep saying "no, thank you" to people not begging, not hassling, but politely trying to make a living.

And I must share another entrepreneurial insight into Myanmar. I ask Thandar Aung, who is showing me around (local lady, two degrees, in economics and French), about her family. She tells me that her father is a banker. But in the family, she says, her mother is most definitely the financial manager. "And we children are the customers."

I have been charged by a rhinoceros in Africa, I have been charged by an elephant in India, and I have now been charged by a dominant male orangutan in Borneo.

(I have only ever been overcharged by a human which, come to think of it, is good preparation for the blood-sucking leeches of the rainforests of deepest Borneo. The giant red Kinabalu leech grows to 30 centimetres, or 12 inches long.)

I am in the jungle in Borneo when I am charged by the orangutan. When humans experience something, our instinct is to tell someone. Travelling alone makes for good writing, as the first telling of the story is to you, the reader. After the "orangutan incident", I immediately go back to my room at a rainforest lodge in Danum Valley and write the moment, which appears in 'The Natural World' chapter in this book.

But it can be enriching to travel with like-minded people. On a drive from Perth through the Great Victoria Desert to Uluru, the heart of Australia in more than one sense, I am with my wife Virginia Ward, an artist, and naturalists and botanical specialists Grady Brand and Lesley Hammersley, from Perth's Kings Park and Botanical Gardens. Virginia is drawing and painting, Grady and Lesley collecting plants and interpreting the landscape, and I am writing and photographing. We each bring something to the group and the journey; we each take much away from it. And we have great times together, of course.

But on the way home we get rather caught out in the Goldfields town of Leonora. I plan to not drive in the Australian bush at night, because of the dangers of wildlife and livestock on the roads. But we spent a good deal of time this afternoon exploring a rocky range east of Laverton (red conglomerate encrusted with quartz blocks like giant sugar lumps), and by the time we get to Leonora, on the Goldfields Highway in the northern Goldfields, it is dark. I've seen warning signs for kangaroos, cattle, trains, even wedge-tailed eagles (not one for dingoes, though one has run alongside the vehicle, all but snapping at the tyres), but it is none of these that suddenly appears from the dark on the roadside, caught in my headlights. It is a Shetland pony, suddenly just there on the roadside, in Outback Australia.

At first it seems rather out of context, incongruous; but then, this small breed of horse was taken from the islands off Scotland to mainland Britain to be used underground as coal-pit ponies for some 200 years from the mid-eighteenth century, particularly in Wales. And, of course, the ghost town of Gwalia is just a stone's throw to the south of me. Gwalia is an ancient Welsh name for 'Wales', as anyone who has heard Welsh poet and writer Dylan Thomas's radio drama *Under Milk Wood* will recall. In it, the character Reverend Eli Jenkins quotes his own poem:

Dear Gwalia
I know there are
Towns lovelier than ours,
And fairer hills and loftier far,
And groves more full of flowers…

And, indeed, out east from here, the Great Victoria Desert is full of fairer hills and groves of flowers. (And, indeed, 'Scourfield' is an ancient Welsh name from the Pembrokeshire region.)

I have travelled a great deal with Glen Chidlow, an experienced Kimberley man after more than two decades living in Kununurra and Broome. One Kimberley wet season trip (500 mm of rain may fall in fourteen hours) is particularly hot and humid, the air full of insects. At the end of the red strip of dirt road up the Dampier Peninsula in the West Kimberley, we arrive at Cape Leveque. We're each staying in a cabin with shutters raised and open to a dusk full of insects. Green frogs stick around the walls and hop around the concrete floor. Glen uses the outdoor shower first, as I open my laptop computer's lid to write, its light attracting even more insects. I am hot, sweaty and looking forward to showering, too.

But when Glen comes out, he calls: "The shower's free, but there's a snake in it."

Mmm. Disappointing.

"A python?" I ask.

"Maybe."

Even worse.

So, not shower and display cowardice? Shower with what turns out to be a 1½ metre long snake?

It was one of life's shorter showers and it seems certain it was a king brown.

It is a good test of ethic to write about people you will meet again. Revisiting is part of becoming encyclopaedic.

First I left rural England to work near and in London, then I was recruited to change hemispheres. On my first day working in Western Australia, I was writing for people born here and educated here. Immediately vulnerable, I set about learning the place from the ground up; its geography and geology, its indigenous and contemporary timescales and histories. I researched its fauna and flora, agriculture and industry, culture and humour. I see this as an advantage. It is one thing to absorb by osmosis the place in which we grow up, it is quite another to consciously and technically learn a place. I was fortunate to be travelling with a purpose, with each assignment a full immersion. Among my learnt places, Western Australia is the most encyclopaedic; I feel connected to its coastline, but more so to its arid interior.

I have been writing about people at the Mowanjum Aboriginal community and its Mowanjum Art and Culture Centre, near Derby in the west Kimberley, for many years. Three tribes – Worrorra, Ngarinyin, and Wunambal – were brought together here on a Presbyterian mission in the 1950s. There are now perhaps seventy children, fifty youths, twenty babies and fifty middle-aged people. For all, the Wandjina is the supreme spirit being.

On this day, I am sitting chatting with my friend Leah Umbagai's son Folau and brother Kellum. They are still young boys, and 'Lau has been making Aboriginal totem weavings – yellow, white, black and red wool bound onto a cross he's made by binding two sticks together.

"What do you boys like doing?" I ask.

"Hunting," says Folau. "Bush turkey. Goanna."

By way of joining in, I tell them I shot a fox recently with a .223.

"A fox?" They look aghast. Why would you want to eat a fox? I explain that I didn't shoot it to eat; foxes decimate native fauna.

"So you buried it?" Their Wandjina law says you have to eat it or bury it.

"You eaten barramundi?" Folau asks, moving on.

I nod.

"Wallaby?"

I shake my head.

Kangaroo, crocodile, sugarbag honey? Turtle egg, dugong?

"No," I say. They look a little incredulous.

Kellum asks me what vehicle I drive, and when I say I have an old Toyota Landcruiser, I pass the test. ("Toyota" is another word for "Muddacar" in remote Australia.)

He asks me what Aussie football team I barrack for and there's some argy bargy over the reply.

"What's your totem animal?" Kellum suddenly asks.

"In my tribe, they don't give you one," I explain.

He widens his eyes in horror. "Then I will." He considers it, looking solemnly up and down the stringy length of me. "Giraffe". He explodes with laughter.

So I am now the giraffe of Mowanjum.

But it strikes me that this giraffe might have the last laugh, as under tribal law one must not eat one's own totem, and Kellum's is the barramundi.

Alongside the contrivance of return is the spontaneity of the unexpected moment, and the writer should miss no moment (should hear all notes being plucked).

I've been on the road for a couple of weeks, writing my 1,000 words a day and I'm heading for Cherrapunjee, in the north-east Indian state of Meghalaya, which is reckoned by many to be the wettest place on earth and has averaged more than 12,000 millimetres of rainfall a year – more than 470 inches. Casey is back in a car boot, not enjoying India's roads, getting spiteful. Indian drivers are both fearsome and fearless. They are unfailingly wildly optimistic, believing that, even where there is no discernable gap, a vehicle will still fit through if you honk the horn loudly enough. Honking is not only cultural but demanded, especially on the backs of the colourfully painted TATA public carrier trucks. HORNOK, say some. HORNDO, say others. Or POPOHORN, BLOWHORN, or a vaguely nautical version, HORNBLOW. The tally for this day on the road will end up being one TATA truck on its side, one bus half on its side in a rocky gully, one small car left much smaller after being front-and-rear-ended, a young woman hit by a scooter (she was staring at a giraffe-like, white stranger at the time), and a dog dead.

We drive up into the mountains, past brick factories and quarries where people labour by hand, and wine shops where a bottle of serious rum costs much less than $2, if you buy it on the one side of the road that has no tax. We pass goat farms and rice fields, and hill homes made from poles and split trunks, or woven timber walls. We also pass trucks laden with armed police and soldiers, guns sticking over tailgates, or mounted on the top of Mahindra four-wheel drives. This place is a political hotbed and there is the edginess of having borders with China, Bangladesh, Myanmar and Bhutan. But it proves once again to me that the world works in horizontals. In Australia, Perth fits with Sydney. Broome fits with Cairns. Kununurra fits with Darwin. And these villages fit with those of northern Thailand and Vietnam.

In the village of Mawphlang, the local clothing changes to the dungaree with a long check cloth either worn simply from the shoulders and knotted at the front or over the head, ends wrapped around the neck and knotted at the back. Fast food is rice served on a piece of newspaper, shaming Western packaging.

Tribal groups have distinctive languages and beliefs in this hills region, and no more so than the Khasi in Meghalaya. Local man Pynbudlang Khonghat takes me to the East Khasi Hills and shows me standing stones, placed both as a memorial to the dead and also as places for people from the villages to socialise. Young men select and stand one stone upright and place another flat, and these are judged, as a competition.

Then, on the final section of the road to Cherrapunjee, there is a rhythmical sound like bell-ringers. I stop and it leads me to five men working in a forge – one pumping hand bellows, heating metal to bright red, the other four standing round the anvil, hitting it in turn to shape the metal into the commonly used digging tools. They all have bare feet.

And then Cherrapunjee itself, looking down into big, jungled valleys, with hilltop villages of colourful homes, Khasi hill tribes people, and shrouding clouds. Here at last. (A welcome respite for rather scuffed Casey.)

I am staying with Dennis Rayen at his mountain resort and my 100 rupee dinner is excellent home-cooked dhal, vegetable curry, rice and potato nan. Then, with local tribesman John, I walk along the ridge through the villages. Or, to be precise, a series of villages, though they merge one into the other. Then the road simply stops, and the weather clears briefly to reveal Bangladesh far below. "The last village in India," announces John, and I laugh at the joke. "And this" (he points to a small traditional home) "is the last house in India".

Then the heavens open and we rush from verandah to verandah, "hello-ing" the people inside the houses, and me happy that verandah is, indeed, one of the Indian words introduced into the English language. It doesn't look like easing when, apparently miraculously, a bus appears on the tiny road. "We take the bus," says John and we bundle on, locals staring. It stops a few metres later to drop off, now amid much hilarity, one huge sack of rice, lugged on a young man's back, and, a few metres later, another. And then everyone gets involved in reversing the bus on the track-like road, in the dark and raging rainstorm.

When I arrive back at Dennis's place, he asks me if I'd like to see their bridges. I can almost sense Casey shudder at the prospect of any delay in our departure, and I too am feeling rather exhausted, but the writer should miss no moment.

"Sure," I say. "I'd love to see your bridges."

"You'll have to get up early."

I leave Casey still horizontal and set out at 6 am with John, walking through the villages of Laitkynsew, Sohsarat and Mawluintuin, and then down nearly 3,000 uneven, mossy rock steps in the often muddy valley side, which is close to vertical. One small, wiry, quick, black man. One tall, camera-bag carrying, slow, white man.

Why am I doing this? Remind me. And then I *am* reminded, for near the bottom of this jungled valley I see my first living root bridge. The 20-metre-long bridge was made some 150 years ago by a senior village man, Sri Snaton Chyne Sohsarat, using a method many hundreds of years old. It took at least fifteen years to make, and will last for hundreds of years – the life of the tree.

The bridges are made where the river gorges are narrower. An India rubber tree, *ficus elastica,* is planted in a particular way, usually over rocks so that some of its roots grow back into the mountain, others dangling in the air. A tall, straight betel tree is cut, split lengthwise, the centre scooped out, and then those roots are placed in it and the top is put back on. The pole is lengthened, and the roots are nourished and trained across the valley. Other roots will be trained around this, until a bridge is formed. A bridge may be 35 metres long and it may be twenty years before it is strong enough to be used. There is one double living root bridge, grown as a pair, one higher than the other.

The living tree root bridges are inspiring and a reminder that some people are capable of doing things for the benefit of their children, their neighbours' grandchildren and the great-grandchildren of the village.

All of these travel moments are like notes plucked on a good guitar. The note sustains, lingers, and when another note is plucked (*and another, and another*) they vibrate together and eventually meld into a chord. And so it is with a moment when something is experienced or understood, and other moments added.

My collections of observations and enlightenments on themes become the equivalent of these chords, amalgamating from the single moments of the travel story into the more dense and viscous (hopefully still smooth and creamy) prose of fiction.

I collect in what may seem an odd palette of interests – ethic, belief, agriculture, horses, small boats, timber watercraft, stringed instruments, shadows, issues surrounding suicide, issues of landscape, kayaks, motorcycles. And each glimpse, each thought, each conversation adds to a growing thesis (a *melody*), until it conglomerates into fictitious worlds like those of *Unaccountable Hours*, *Other Country*, *As the River Runs*, and other fiction that will follow. I need a forty-four gallon drum of fact to make a cupful of fiction. It is a distilled essence; the droplet that comes after everything has percolated through my body, this carbon filter.

To bring land and people to life in the non-fiction world of the literary travel essay (*in this book*), real characters and dialogue may be injected into description and statistics; the writer story-telling.

On the opposite hand, for me it is important that novels set in landscape, characters and issues are plausible, possible, even probable. They have to be "right" and combine experience and observation with specific research.

Sometimes there is a crossover – a comment so profound that it is included in a travel story and later comes from the mouth of a character in a novel.

For some years now, I have run a Young Travel Writer competition in Travel in *The West Australian*. High-school-aged writers enter travel stories and photographs, and I take the two winners away on assignment, to travel, research, write, photograph and shoot videos, all to be published.

On one of these trips I take two young writers to an Aboriginal community in the Kimberley. One morning, one of the young chaps who lives there is wearing just one thong, on one foot.

"Have you lost a thong?" I ask him.

"Nah," he says. "I found one."

His cup is half full, and I have used his words in both essay and novel.

I was a child who wanted to be a writer and, having this book on the shelf alongside the works of fiction, I feel like a boy who just found a thong.

2

Crossing Borders

I am on the border between two countries. It is a definitive line on a map, but there is nothing in the dirt I'm looking down at. I take one stride forward, pause (half here, half there), and then simply step into another country. I am in remote Africa, a long way from official border crossings or checkpoints, but there are plenty of other places in the world where I could do this.

Physical borders shape our world, our politics and our prejudices. In our attitude towards them, we display our common sense and pragmatism, our fears and humanity, and so it has been for most of human history.

But in contemplating edges and boundaries, we stray into the cultural, philosophical and emotional – crossing borders in a wider context. Armed with an open mind, we can pass through these invisible but tangible barriers between societies, mores and values, just as we cross a no man's land. Societies may be at odds, but when two people meet, they are simply two human beings. They recognise one another; they cross a border.

For now, I step through the dirt, over this border, and look back and realise that Casey, just behind me, is still in another country.

Over the Lines on a Map

Laptop on my back, camera bag slung over my shoulder, eating a breakfast of bread and towing Casey, I wander over the border from Armenia to Georgia.

I have just had my passport stamped as I left Armenia and I'm in no man's land, crossing the bridge over the river Debed, vaguely wondering what the reception will be at the other side. I have been in no man's land many times, with this feeling.

Some border crossings are difficult. There are bundles of forms, language difficulties – questions you can't understand, answers they can't understand. It can take hours.

But this time I join a short queue, the benign but unsmiling young lady behind the glass screen scans and stamps my passport and that's it. I'm in Georgia and my journey through the Caucasus region continues.

I am so often amazed by the complete difference as soon as I cross a border. Language, culture, clothing is understandable but so frequently it is an instant change not only in attitude but also in landscape and climate.

Armenia and Georgia are chalk and cheese. Armenia has a complex past – the world's first Christian nation, a victim of genocide, caught between aggressive neighbouring countries, much invaded – but the capital Yerevan is ordered and cultured and safe. It rained a bit and was cool.

Here in Georgia, just over the river, it is hot and sunny. I am soon in rolling green grazing hills and the people are louder, looser, relaxed. Just the other side of the river.

The same happens to me crossing the Friendship Bridge border over the Sun Khosi river between Tibet and Nepal. Behind Tibet you feel the pressure wave of China. In Nepal you feel, not far in the background, the complexity and craziness of India.

The night before crossing from Tibet to Nepal I leave my laptop on in the bathroom, with the screen on bright, to make sure it runs out of battery. I pack the charger in my suitcase, knowing it will be transported across the Friendship Bridge separately.

I have historic reading on the exploration of the Himalayas, various recordings, a lot of photographic images and also plenty of research and background information on Tibetan Buddhism, resistance to the Chinese presence in Tibet and writings by the Dalai Lama. I also have electronic maps, and know that maps are often contentious, depending on their labelling and the borders they show.

All of this is a good way to have your laptop confiscated or, at very least, your files deleted.

I back up everything thoroughly on to separate drives and disperse them throughout my luggage, just in case.

When the Chinese immigration official demands to see the contents of my laptop, I get it out, press the power button hard and show him that nothing's going to happen. I shrug, offering no solution.

Sometimes you just have to stand there and let things play out.

Nearby there is a kerfuffle as the officers go through a man's bag and find a book by George Mallory, an English member of the first three British expeditions to Mt Everest. Mallory went missing on the 1924 British Mount Everest expedition.

The young Chinese officer spends ages going through the book until he finds a reference to the Dalai Lama and promptly confiscates it.

Once over the bridge, it is as if someone has flicked a switch – on one side it says Tibet/China, on the other Nepal/India. The whole spirit this side of the bridge is totally different. I look behind me, and see the line I have just crossed.

Crossing into the southern African kingdom of Lesotho, at a remote border post, I duck under the slightly raised swing-bar, with no fence either side, and amble up to a wooden hut with a window. There are two young men inside, looking bored.

"Botseno," I ask, using the Sotho word for "entry" – about the only thing I can think of.

The man at the main desk looks up at me with disinterest. The white man in me finds this puzzling, because he is an immigration officer and I am likely to be one of few people asking for his services today.

He might at least pay me some regard.

Then he looks up, with languid eyes and asks, "What football team do you support?" A low, sing-song voice and the familiar sub-Saharan African pronunciation of foot-u-(pause)-ball. Well, that one came out of the blue.

He means soccer, of course, and the other young man in uniform chimes in (as if his colleague can't hear) with, "If you say Manchester United, it will be quicker."

Being a George Best fan from childhood, this would have been my first option anyway.

"Manchester United," I say.

"*Rrreally*?" he replies happily, rolling the rrrr almost the length of a soccer pitch. It is as if he hasn't heard his colleague. "This is *verrry* good."

He's cheered up and, without even looking at the name or photograph in my passport, stamps it.

The two men are looking down again and I leave. Walking away, laptop on my back, camera bag slung over my shoulder, I look behind me but the line I have crossed is lost in the mist.

Crossing the Borders of Time in Lesotho

I have driven up the Sani Pass, up the Drakensberg Mountains, up folds like green velvet spread over a reclining body, out of South Africa, vertically, up towards the clouds. Up here, on the plateau, completely surrounded by South Africa, is the Kingdom of Lesotho. The roof of Africa, shrouded in mist, etched into my childhood, running through my life, like an artery.

When I was nine years old, I promised myself I'd come to Lesotho one day, a romantic pledge by a country boy in England to himself. That day is today, nearly four decades later.

It's raining. My goodness, it's raining. Not just 'good for the garden' rain, but running down the sheer dirt track towards me, in a river, almost like a waterfall. I don't think the Land Rover can make it.

But a promise is a promise, and when the person making that promise is the person receiving it, it lodges in the gut, niggling, unavoidable. I jam the vehicle into low-range, and drive on, up and up and up and up, over the rocks, up the stream, doubling back, don't look over the side, (oh my goodness, don't look over the side), up and up and up, into the clouds...

I grew up in a nice house on a sharp hill next door to an English church. Its cool mustiness, reverence and formality were comforts to me. Evensong hymns, coloured light sharding from low sun, a blackbird sings.

("*The day though gavest Lord is ended...*")

If Lesotho was somehow invisibly preparing itself to figure throughout my life, it was one man who completely installed it. Father Trevor Huddleston was the guest speaker at a church function. Bringing the anti-apartheid message from South Africa to the world, he had a particular and intense interest in Lesotho. I spent hard-saved pocket money on his book *Naught for Your Comfort*. I had never read anything quite like it.

The impact of his sheer goodness was enormous. The empowerment of being ethical was inspirational.

Africa caught my attention; Lesotho caught my heart. I thought my interest in Lesotho had come to me by chance, but I now see it was a place selected by the person I had already set out to become. We do not find ourselves – we make ourselves.

I managed to get a big map of Lesotho for my bedroom wall.

Nelson Mandela says no white person did more than Trevor Huddleston in the struggle against apartheid.

Huddleston died in 1998, after becoming Bishop and then Sir, and – quite by coincidence – as I write this, celebrations are being held to mark the centenary of his birth. Quite by coincidence they are centred on St Martin-in-the-Field church in Trafalgar Square, London, where the Swan Bells, in the Bell Tower on the Swan River foreshore, in the Western Australian city of Perth, where I now live, rang for nearly 300 years…for England's victory over the Spanish Armada in 1588…for the coronation of every British monarch since King George II…for the homecoming of Captain James Cook after his voyage of discovery…ringing in every New Year for more than 275 years.

Connections.

Some nicknamed Father Trevor the Red Bishop, a moniker he didn't like. But if he objected to the slur of communism, he might have taken pleasure in being likened to a visually startling and flighty finch. Red Bishops are native to Africa but were introduced to Australia more than half a century ago. I've seen Red Bishops in the Kimberley, where I have set my two novels, *Other Country* and *As the River Runs.*

These brilliant red dots offer dramatic punctuation to even the massive Kimberley landscape.

Connections.

From the day I met Father Trevor until somewhere in my mid-teens, I saw a choice of only two paths ahead – in part of me, to do good works overseas, to enable people to grow spiritually, to thrive physically, to have a voice – in part of me, to be a writer. (And maybe, I hope now, in some small way, they have melded.)

Honesty, integrity, belief, ethic. I often trace my life's themes back to that momentary encounter with Father Trevor Huddleston. Such people live in my novels. Dylan Ward, Uncle Vincent Yimi, Airplane Cuttover, even Kate Kennedy, all in *As the River Runs.*

My mother and I ran stalls at fetes, made fabric covered doorstops and frilly coat hangers, raised money, and sent it to projects in Lesotho. The work in schools and St James Hospital were almost constantly in my thoughts. I promised myself I'd go to Lesotho one day.

There is, of course, risk attached to taking an almost-mythical place and making it real.

The heavens open, the temperature drops 10°C in a few minutes, and the stair-rod rain cuts deep channels across the dirt road. Ahead is 8 kilometres of switchbacks, seemingly straight up.

It seems hopeless, and then, round a bend, bizarrely, the sun is out and there is no more rain. Two more bends and there are sweet alpine meadows, the earth completely dry. Things change quickly in the mountains.

The place is blooming. Yellow Sutherlandia, Lesotho red-hot poker, Suicide Gladiolus in cliff crevices, Watsonia, endemic, precious to the local people.

And then I am at that border – that single horizontal pole in the middle of nowhere, talking soccer with the guards. The country then called Basutoland gained independence from Britain in 1966.

England won the World Cup.

Lesotho is a sovereign kingdom, proud of its heritage. They love their ruling king Letsi III.

A single stamp in the passport. "Lesotho Immigration. Permitted to enter and remain."

(Well, I promised myself I'd be here one day.)

I am blanket-wrapped in cloud. The Sani Top Chalet is "the highest pub in Africa". A rack of old wooden skis, faded photographs of Lesotho white with snow. The old hotel has windy corridors, solid walls and wooden beds. The kitchen is filled with the constant laughter, singing and chatter of women. And I sit now in my room, with Casey open and partially unpacked on the old dresser beside me, and wind and rain beating on metal lattice windows similar to those of my grandmother's cottage in my childhood. All night long, the windows are lashed by rain but I am warm in the reminiscent texture of flannelette sheets under old-fashioned blankets. I lie awake through the night and savour it, and let the feelings of childhood back in. I am visiting Lesotho, and revisiting the boy I was.

The morning is damp and misty. We are living in the clouds. I should set the scene for our journey onward by saying that Lesotho is rated the third poorest country in the world. It has a population of around two million people and between seventy and 100 die every day as a result of HIV/AIDS and poverty. Rampant disease, low life expectancy, a declining population. The numbers of street children and orphans is increasing. There is still a basic need for food, clean water, shelter and sanitation, and a decent education system...despite all those doorstops and frilly coat hangers...

The people here – Basotho – are known for wearing big blankets wrapped around themselves and for the home-woven conical hat that is the country's symbol, and for their accompanying gumboots.

It has the highest lowland of any country on earth, and is the highest place you can drive a vehicle on the African continent.

Dry stone walls, round, thatched huts, Angoran goats in the mist. Lesotho's mountain ponies are tough and nimble, Basotho are excellent horsemen. People here have a talent for suddenly appearing in the landscape (and, equally quickly, disappearing again) and a horseman appears, feet sticking out, toes pointing down. Our eyes meet and he frowns fearsomely. I smile and he smiles back – a big, booming smile that shows bright teeth.

Shepherds watch for the jackal buzzards. Lesotho makes money from high quality mohair wool, as much as from its labour for the mines.

Near the two big government shearing sheds is a village. There are seventy people in the village, twenty of them children. Flags fly above some huts, white meaning beer has been made and is for sale, green for vegetables, red for meat. There is a blue flag, but when I ask what this is for, I get only mysterious answers.

"They come for the shearing and we make food for them," says Aleni Sebilo, in her hut. She lifts the lid of the camp oven in the middle of the floor. There is only one triangle left of the huge loaf she bakes every day. Breakfast, lunch and dinner are bread and *moroho*, an endemic mountain cabbage. By the two-shelf unit which comprises her kitchen are a plastic barrel of wheat flour, and a sack of *mealie* (maize meal). "Sometimes meat," she adds. If an animal is injured, it will be quickly and skilfully butchered, but it is worth more alive. Sometimes eggs, occasionally chicken. On very rare and special moments, a pig, but still with *moroho* and maize, She walks a kilometre to fetch water from a mountain stream; washing is done in the river. The prevailing wind is from the south and the light from the north, and the hut has a small door facing that direction. For the weather can be savage at this altitude. Winter, spring, autumn, and even summer, can see the land quickly covered in snow. The temperature can plunge to –14C, plus wind chill factor.

"How do you keep warm?" Aleni points to the fire. In the ground below the floor, big boulders were carefully placed, filled around with sand. The fire warms these rocks – "underfloor heating".

Back at the border, when I eventually leave Lesotho, I hold out my passport and a young man takes it, barely shifting his gaze from the soccer on television. He stamps it. It clearly is irrelevant to him who I am, what I think about Lesotho, what it means to me. And that is probably how it should be. It is his reality, my dream. It was my promise and it was private.

I am thinking about all of this, about patterns, syncopation, about connections in every sense, about the coincidence of Father Trevor Huddleston's centenary, of the exhibition at St Martin, 'Trevor Huddleston – A life called to Justice and Freedom'.

I think about his Prayer for Africa, which in its way is as appropriate today as it was then, "God bless Africa, guard her people, guide her leaders, and give her peace."

And as I finish writing this, sitting in a peppermint-scented park in Margaret River, in the South West of Western Australia, in winter sun, a Scarlet Robin darts in, his chest vermillion, and lands on the end of the timber table. They're usually timid, but he cocks his head over and looks at me out of one eye. Just like the Red Bishop, he looks straight at me and straight into me.

Porous Borders in South Africa

It is just a meeting in a market. It is just a moment when I am browsing carved giraffes and weird wooden walking sticks, a life-size tin mother holding her baby in the air, and even a glistening gold-beaded replica of the FIFA World Cup. Of tablecloths with bushman figures more-than reminiscent of the Kimberley's Bradshaw or Gwion artworks, and artefacts carved from buffalo bone. Of beads and baubles and even the ubiquitous world scourge, the fridge magnet.

It is just a meeting in a market; Willis Muirimi looks like just another young stallholder at the Chameleon Markets in Hartbeespoort, forty-five minutes north of Johannesburg, South Africa.

With his striped beanie, open smile and glistening dark skin, he greets me as the others in orange sellers' sashes do, with a smile and politeness, a quiet question or two to try to engage me enough to stop me and sell me something, but no sense of hassling.

But with Willis, it isn't quite like that. His stall, just on the edge of this market near Hartbeespoort Dam, has much the same as others. Tablecloths, beaded sculptures, stone carvings. He is an artist and he is keen to tell me the stories behind them, he says.

"Where are you from," he asks when I stop to look. A good opener.

"Australia. And you?" Expecting him to say "here".

He holds a slim black hand to his heart. "Zimbabwe," he says. "That is my country. That is where I am from. Zim." Lyrical.

For Willis is part of the tidal ebb and flow of people across and up and down Africa. Of people displaced, seeking and seeping through porous borders. Part of a global movement looking for better, fairer lives.

"It is very bad there, sir," he says. We launch into the politics of Africa.

I have been very interested, I tell Willis, in China's growing influence in Africa in recent years. Of its presence in Zimbabwe.

Shame on me but I think I am telling Willis some deep political secret that he will know nothing about, that ruthless governments are being propped up all over Africa.

That it has been reported that Zimbabwe's President Robert Mugabe's vast personal fortune has come, in part, from a deal struck in 2005 under which he handed to China his country's mineral rights. That London's *Daily Telegraph* also reported in 2008 that he received arms including guns, jet fighters and military vehicles. Similar stories have been reported from the Democratic Republic of the Congo and Angola. The oppressive government of Sudan is said to have been given support by China in return for a monopoly on its reserves of oil.

"It is very difficult because we can do nothing about it," says Willis. With the word "we", he touches his chest again, as if touching his whole, troubled people.

"But you are doing something," I say. "We are standing here talking about it. Like that, it exists. It has a life. That's doing something. Look at this place, South Africa. Every day it is writing a new history. For all the difficulties of that – the good and the bad days – it is writing a new future."

Willis is educated. He went through what we might think of as scant schooling but he has educated himself and will continue to do so. Education is the answer; Willis knows that.

He is unhappy about much of Africa's lot but adds: "I feel like everything is happening in Africa. It is the place to be."

He is enthusiastic, full of ideas and discussion.

"You are young and you have a voice."

"You are young, too," he says. I tell him I am over fifty.

"Wow," Willis says, instantly correcting himself. "Over fifty? You are gone."

He roars with laughter and throws his arms around me in commiseration.

By this stage, the items on his stall are forgotten between us.

"How many children," he asks me. It is often the second question here, where family is a fundamental.

"One son," I say.

"Just one?"

A mix of sympathy and outrage. Whoever heard of anyone having just one son?

"And what do you do," asks Willis.

"I am a writer."

"I want to be a writer," he bursts, as if it is some strange twist of divine fate. As if we are brothers, meeting in this market – the only two writers on the planet, brought together by some destiny.

We talk about it a little. He is an artist but he has ideas for films, for books. "I want to be a writer."

I give him a little lecture on not needing permission. How he should just start writing every day. Just fifteen minutes a day, a few words, get things going. Get ideas running in the back of your head; get momentum. I show him the tiny notebook and pen that I always carry, always use. "That's all you need. That and no permission from anyone but yourself."

And then I realise that time is pressing and tell Willis that I want to buy some of his little pieces to take home with me. A beaded V, my wife's initial, a key ring for my son's new car, a handmade wire cross for my mother. I haven't any South African rand on me and tell him this. Any currency is good, Willis says. No problem. Australian dollars or dirham, whatever. In my pocket, I finger the US$50 that I have decided to swap for some token trinkets.

And then, approaching just at this point, I see the black African driver who is taking me back to Johannesburg airport down roads lined with orange sellers and rows of shiny tin jugs, work parties of up to 40 people swinging machetes, cutting the invasive and prodigious roadside grass, a laden cart pulled by five donkeys, a woman pumping water by hand, a handpainted sign: "Traditional Healer, house 9". Acacia trees, thorn trees.

"You really want to buy these things?" The driver prods them, dismissively.

"How much you asking for these," he shirt fronts Willis.

Willis gives him a figure, in rand.

"You really want these?" The driver has turned to me again.

I am supposed to say "not really" and shrug dismissively in this little play act aimed at pushing the price down.

"Yes, I do," I say.

I can see the driver's disgust. Stupid visitor. He decides to assert himself, take over. There is no way Willis is getting what he asks for. The driver cuts it in half, spits the new figure and takes a step forward.

"Sure," says Willis, that sum will be fine.

We are both intimidated now and I hand over a roughly equivalent ten dollar note.

Willis turns to put the items in a bag and I go to tell him it's not necessary. The driver walks away, inflated; he has saved the silly white man from being ripped off.

I slip Willis the US$50 note. "Get books, paper and pens," I whisper. "And don't let the driver see." He laughs.

I ask Willis to write down his address in my notebook. "I will send you a book I have written."

"Yes. Yes," he says. "What is it called?"

"*Connected.*"

"Yes," Willis says. "Like us. We are connected." And we shake hands in three parts, the African way.

It was just a meeting in a market, but it was as if Willis had crossed over the border from all his was, and I had too, and we had met in some happy no man's land in the middle. That no man's land of just being human. It was as if our cultural borders had become porous.

My Friend Pramod in India

Nine years ago, in a railway carriage in India, Pramod brought me morning tea on a silver tray. Gradually, over a week on that train, I got to know him a little, and I never forgot his pride, professionalism and kindness.

And here, today, in April 2013, Pramod again brings tea on a silver tray.

A different carriage, a different decade, but when Pramod greets me and introduces himself, I am flabbergasted. "Pramod!"

I show him a picture I took of him in 2004. I say he looks exactly the same, but he notices hair without the very slight dusting of grey that it now has, and perhaps thicker. My hair is unchanged, in its complete absence.

In 2004, I was here on the 2,650 kilometre *Deccan Odyssey* route from Mumbai to Sindhudurg, Tarkarli and its backwaters, Goa, Panaji, Pune, Ellora and Ajanta caves, and back to Mumbai.

I was, of course, writing for you.

Pramod Pandey was looking after train passengers.

These two men at work who met briefly, connected politely, have met thousands of others in the course of their duties in the years in-between and now, on a twenty-one coach train on a different route in India, are thrown back together, by chance.

So many of our greatest travel memories – the stories we tell – come from chance meetings. It is people like Pramod who live on in you.

And in India, the traveller can't help but come into contact with people. Hesitate slightly and look confused, and there's a good chance that someone will ask if they can help direct you.

But I wasn't looking confused at all in the car park today, when I met Spicy Boy.

"Not a Spice Girl," he laughed, reassuringly, though I had already noticed that.

Spicy Boy's real name is Rajkumar Soni, and he sells tea, saffron and spices in his shop at Galta Gate in Jaipur. But he just happened to be in the carpark under the Amber Fort, too.

"I like your cap," he said, pointing to my black Akubra hat. I smile and lift it slightly to reveal my bleachingly white, shaven head. "I need it." It sends him and his mates into convulsions of laughter.

"And I like your black hair," I add – for Spicy Boy has a thick, coal-black mane.

"Where are you from," he asks.

"Australia."

"You want to talk about cricket?"

"No." And we all laugh. What else can you do?

And so we end up in an amusing, warm, backward and forward conversation, much like the one I just had with the newspaper seller inside Jaipur's wonderful Amber Fort.

He had yesterday's London's *Daily Telegraph* and *Daily Mail* among his armful of worldwide mastheads.

"Newspaper?"

"No thanks," I say.

"Ah, Australian. Pity."

I raise my eyebrows questioningly.

"Yesterday, I had a *Sun Herald* and *The West Australian.* I could have sold you one of those. Bad luck for me."

Hold on a minute. *The West Australian* in Jaipur, deep in Rajasthan in north India, the day after publication?

He reels off some headlines from that paper and when I later check (slightly embarrassed at doubting him), he is correct.

"How do you get *The West Australian* here?" I ask him.

He smiles broadly. "I can't tell you. It's my secret. I tell you my secret, I lose my business."

And he walks off jauntily, whistling.

Musician salesmen play their knocked-together instruments, men sit painting miniatures, and there are plenty of sellers of colourful umbrellas – red, orange, green, inset with mirrors the size of a fingernail.

A woman near me buys one for 400 rupees, which starts a flood of other sellers.

One is particularly persistent and, at one point, I see the woman simply standing, head cowered, besieged by his heckling – her husband with a flat hand up saying in a fine English accent: "No. No more. Definitely no."

Not words Indian sellers tend to acknowledge.

Amber Fort is up on a hill. Visitors are taken up and down in Mahindra four-wheel drives, and I end up in one with the couple, some time later, the seller in hot pursuit.

"Two for 500. Two for 500." He throws two of his silk paintings into her lap and she tries to give them back. By now he is in the vehicle with us.

And then we reach some invisible boundary, and he gives up, grabs his wares and jumps off, nonplussed, and walks away.

"When you get back to your room and open the door, he'll be there...two for 500," I say, and for a moment the woman looks scared to death.

"In the wardrobe...under the bed...two for 500..."

If you go to India, pack a sense of humour alongside the Gastro Stop. Along with belief and aesthetic, Indians can be just plain funny.

They can also be disarmingly insightful, and these beguilingly intuitive moments come out of the blue too.

I step into a Jaipur spice shop (no, not Spicy Boy's unfortunately) to buy tea, and end up not only with Garden Black Tea ("a taste of India"), but Tea Spice ("a perfect blend of cinnamon, cardamom, ginger, black pepper and clove") and Winter Tonic – "use for warming body and sex," I later read.

They are rather pushed forward by the man behind the counter, who says he was a teacher in Melbourne for a while, but now back home. "I am a *kundalini*."

Kundalini yoga combines physical, mental and spiritual discipline to develop not only strength of body, but of character and consciousness. Its practitioners call it "the yoga of awareness" as it so enhances intuition.

And with that he tells me that I have healing powers, and should learn to use them more for others. Not the sort of thing that's dropped into the brief conversation at the checkout in Coles.

Though his assessment of another woman in the shop is to avoid dairy products, I have seen her show a better instinct than me for helping others. She was in the street with, on one side, a man desperately trying to sell her a box of bangles for 100 rupees – about $2 – and on the other, a little boy begging for ten rupees for food.

And so she bought the bangles without negotiation, delighting the man, and turned and handed them to the boy to sell, delighting him, too. Then she simply stepped on to a tour coach, leaving goodness behind.

Back on the train, Pramod brings tea on a silver tray and we chat a little. He's still happy here, he says. He has responsibility, like that for the key for each cabin, and has been with the company a long time.

Pramod shows me a picture of his young daughter Amrita, who is doing very well at the good school he is managing to send her to, renting a house nearby for the family. "She is coming top of her class and is often the monitor," he said. His son Vaibhav is seven; his wife, Shaila, is looking after them while he is away working.

But not for the next few weeks. For my friend Pramod, from Varanasi, has leave and, after a thirty-two-hour train ride home – on one of those packed Indian Railways trains – will be spending time with them before returning to the *Deccan Odyssey*. To work.

He's still doing pretty much what he was when we first met. I'm here to do pretty much what I was doing then.

Pramod smiles at me. "Life goes by."

In Mumbai, after the train, we meet up again – Pramod turning up in a striped polo shirt and jeans. We go to a local Khadi Ghandi shop, as Pramod wants to buy a long shirt and pyjama set for a friend in Australia, and I'm going to take it for him. Mahatma Gandhi ("Ghandhiji") started the Khadi movement to boycott foreign goods, emphasising the need for Indians to make, buy and wear their own cloth.

Pramod is on the way home.

Just before I board the plane home, I get a text message from Pramod. "Dear sir, wish you safe journey."

He might be of the high Brahmin caste, but calling me "sir" is just too ingrained in him.

"Thanks, friend," I reply, pushing his social boundaries.

Another text: "I keep in touch."

Bridging the Gap Between Australia and PNG

I think back to the map that shows what is often described as the old land bridge between Papua New Guinea and Australia and across which homo sapiens are said to have first arrived on what is now the Australian continent in numbers, possibly about 47,000 years ago.

But the two land masses of today seem more like one piece and not joined by a "bridge". Indeed, it was only at the end of the last ice age, some 12,000 years ago, that saltwater divided the two parts of what was known as the Sahul continent. I have been looking out for their remnant links and today I saw some.

On an expedition ship anchored off Lambom, I am greeted by the beautifully calm and welcoming villagers of this remote, jungled island off the south-west side of the New Ireland coast of Papua New Guinea.

We are here to watch cultural songs and dances being performed, and I am told this is the first time the people of Lambom Island have done this for outsiders. Three ghost figures enter with tall headdresses that have "the fire" in their tops and are smouldering. The village's children have already lined up to sing. After the fire ceremony, women perform their welcome dance and then the men come in noisily with theirs. Each song and dance takes between fifteen and thirty minutes, and the length of the chant becomes the most enjoyable part of the morning for me. We are used to three- or four-minute songs and here is a palpable example of a different sense of time. To sit and listen to eight to twelve bars of simple music repeated for half an hour becomes a meditation.

Is it ridiculous to contemplate in these words how time can seem shorter and longer? There is more time in the New Guinea islands – the commodity we Westerners often seem short of – and this is an example of something being allowed to fill a bigger pocket of it. It reminds me of time spans in Aboriginal communities. But it is the headdresses that have the strongest echo. I was recently given a book of photographs by anthropologist Baldwin Spencer, taken in northern and central Australia between 1894 and 1923. The tall tribal headdresses are reminiscent of those in the dances at Lambom. This is reinforced the next day on Duke of York Island, where we anchor in a deep water, curving bay and go ashore to watch a performance of a fish trap dance. It is said that genetic research shows the common DNA of New Guinean tribes and Australian Aborigines, but after the land bridge was submerged and Australia became drier and hotter and New Guinea became wetter, differences developed.

I have previously sailed the Kimberley coast from Darwin to Broome. There are Australian Aboriginal art sites such as the galleries on Bigge Island and at Raft Point, where I climbed the side of the rocky hill to sit in a natural gallery with the final depiction of the Wandjina story of the fish chase across the Kimberley, with striking images of the creation figure, Namarali, and the Wandjinas, mouthless and with their staring eyes and powerful auras. Fish, dugong and yams. And in this memory, I feel the strongest connection of the two trips.

Every day we have been greeted by villagers on outrigger canoes, who have often sat around the ship, fishing with handlines. Yesterday, on a snorkelling trip to Matatai Beach, near the southern tip of New Ireland, some had seen dugong pass.

Matatai is the creation place of people living around this part of the Papua New Guinean islands. They believe that in their ancient history, a mother had two sons, one white and one black. The original people. The woman knew a secret – where there was a saltwater spring, where she got the vital addition for food. The sons followed her to it and startled her, causing a rock to fall out of the spring and filling the world with saltwater.

I am interested in the link that yams form, and it is said that yams up to 3 metres long and weighing 70 kilograms have been grown here. In fact, there are 600 species of yam produced in forty-seven countries but only ten are cultivated and they have been so since 50,000 BC.

They can be stored for up to six months in the islands' well-ventilated yam houses.

In the Sepik River region of Papua New Guinea, some people believe they embody ancestors, and the Trobriand Islands (also known as the Kiriwina Islands) have an important yam festival from June to August.

Yams are also depicted in Australian Aboriginal Gwion Gwion, or Bradshaw, art in the Drysdale River region of the Kimberley and I feel another piece of the jigsaw falling into place.

I look again at the old map, when Papua New Guinea and Australia were one piece, and see the distinctive shoulder of the Kimberley, just a walk away from where I am now.

3

Transported

One game I like to play is to start writing when the train starts and finish when it stops: on a laptop on the carriage's table as I rattle through the back gardens of England; in India, travelling behind net curtains.

Another game is to write descriptive lists in the little notebooks that I always carry, fill and file (A7, 105 mm by 74 mm). I list a few words on each line; as I pass, in a minibus with rain on its windows, a queue of people in Sir Lanka who are waiting to see Buddha's holy relics; like a poem, driving through the Sitka spruce forests of Alaska in a big pick-up truck; in shorthand on the dusty roads of Madagascar.

Being transported is physical and practical, of course, but when the mode of that transport enhances the moment, I am taken back to a hymn from my childhood.

And O what transport of delight,
From thy pure chalice floweth.

Oh, my transports of delight. I think I actually said those very words aloud when I was riding a Royal Enfield motorcycle through the Himalayas, surrounded by the white sharks' teeth of 8,000 metre peaks. I could sing it aloud just about any time I am on long, turquoise swells in my sea kayak, or cantering on a decent horse. (It ends up with a country music twang; but then, everything I play or sing seems to.)

Being transported is not about a vehicle – *a machine* – but about a way of moving across the planet's surface and through the world. It is about approach and flow. It is about having the momentum of a poem's spoken words, as they stream into the air. It is about moving along a songline embedded into your very essence; about creative pace.

Driving from my front door in Perth to Uluru is not just about pressing the accelerator with my boot. It is about driving to the heart of Australia.

It is a culmination of decades of travel in Australia's arid zones. It is about sense of place just as it is about sensible pace in a vehicle that's taken me through so much country that it feels like home. The four-wheel drive feels like part of the cast of characters around me, just like Casey.

Casey, of course, has his own set of wheels, but other modes of transport are inflicted upon him. I often think of Casey down there in the aircraft cargo hold, shivering his handles off. At a big aircraft's cruising height of 38,000 feet (more than 11,500 metres), the outside temperature may be below −50°C – even below −70°C. Most commercial passenger airlines heat cargo holds, but they can still be pretty chilly.

Yes, I do think of Casey – and particularly on two occasions. The first was when I was in an aircraft taking off from Kununurra in the East Kimberley. Directly beneath my feet, I could hear a dog barking. Not a manic bark, but a slow, rhythmical bark, something like the beeping of a reversing vehicle. (It reminded me of a fibreglass dog that I once saw bolted into the tray of a ute on Parramatta Road in Sydney. When the ute was being reversed, the fake dog barked like this. When it braked, the dog's eyes lit up red.) The second time was when I was looking round an airline's animal handling facilities at their hub airport in Malaysia. "On many flights from Perth, we have goats in the hold," they told me. And I'm sure Casey loves that.

On My Feet in Caucasus

I spend the morning on foot alone, wandering without an agenda, gradually piecing the city together, in every sense. Tbilisi, Georgia – between Russia, Iran, Turkey, Armenia. I am not in a group, I do not have an itinerary, I am not trying to make some taxi driver understand me – I have nowhere in particular to go. I am on the ground, moving at the speed humans were truly built for, walking pace. Walking speed matches thinking speed.

These are the most gorgeous moments. The free-flowing walking that lets a place unfold, and allows for whim and serendipity.

I watch tour groups pass in single file – day packs, cameras, each clutching a water bottle lest they might die of dehydration, here in the middle of the city. Cameras around their necks, slightly crushed holiday clothes, following the guide.

There are no spaces between sentences – no silences to allow a place to just whisper and seep in. For once given space, I am no longer in the process of visiting or seeing or even feeling a place but absorbing it by osmosis. The process of gradual assimilation. That organic process by which molecules from a less concentrated solution pass through a semi-permeable membrane of a more concentrated one. Me concentrating hard on nothing in particular.

Then, suddenly, it all connects – not just the sites or districts but the geographic and emotional fabric of it. I just get it.

And I think again about the young Georgian guide that I've met. I've been trying to put my finger on what it is about her.

And it strikes me (now there is space enough to let the thought come) that, at 21, she is traumatised; conceived in war, brought up in the upheaval that followed the Soviet occupation of her country. The Soviet Union dissolved in 1991, the year before she was born. Tbilisi's Georgian National Museum brings home the politics. Outside, there is a poster for a permanent display: "Soviet Occupation Museum, 1921–1991".

But the animosity remained, and remains. In 2006, the Russians banned imports from Georgia. In 2008, her country's history came alive for her during the Five Day War with Russia over the region of South Ossetia. As I write this, Georgia claims that Russia has moved the border by 300 metres.

"Will there be another war?" she says, shrugging; tears not far behind that shrug, I think.

She says intellectuals have still been jailed in Georgia, just like under the Soviet neurosis.

She is a devout Christian.

I sit on a wall outside a church in the capital Tbilisi and watch passers-by stop and make the sign of the cross on themselves, turning towards Kashveti Church of St George in Rustaveli Avenue.

With thumb and two fingers puckered together to represent the Holy Trinity, top of the head, tummy button, top of the right shoulder, heart. Repeatedly and fast. A holy devotion.

There is a particularly Georgian way of doing this – a big movement; a larger cross. The authoritative *Studia Biblica Et Ecclesiastica: Essays Chiefly in Biblical and Patristic Criticism*, written and compiled by University of Oxford intellectuals and published in 1903, traces this back possibly to fourth century Georgia.

St Nino, a female saint, brought Christianity to this, the world's first country to make it its official religion. She is said to have performed miraculous healings and then converted Georgian Queen, Nana, and subsequently pagan King Miriam. *Studia Biblica* says, "St Nino began to pray and entreat God for a long time. Then she took her (wooden) cross and with it touched the Queen's head, her feet and her shoulders, making the sign of the cross and straightway she was cured." A larger cross, indeed.

And just then, I watch a young man put down the bucket he is carrying, turn to the church and do much the same. Top of his head, belt buckle, top of the right shoulder, left bicep.

The famous Georgian hospitality and Christian kindness seem to stop on the kerbside. Georgians are savage drivers. Pedestrian crossings merely mean you have a slightly better chance of getting across the road alive. There are underpasses but they are few and far between and on one road I have no choice but to take my life in my hands and cross all six lanes.

I have noticed pedestrians crossing themselves before doing so and consider doing the same. Halfway across, with cars whisking past me, I hear an angry voice through a loudspeaker. I turn. Now what? "He is supporting us," says a Georgian woman, also crossing. For the voice is blaring from a police car, and he is apparently telling motorists to not run us down.

The police do this here. Without stopping, they shout at drivers who have stopped their car on a clearway, bark at people to get moving, to slow down, to get out of the way. And, in this case, to be more considerate.

Stand at the kerbside and wave at drivers. No, not to cheer them up but to ask them to stop. Nearly every car in Tbilisi can be used as a taxi. Dropped the children off at junior sport and got a couple of hours to kill? You can pick up a fare and ease the transportation situation. No meters – just agree on the charge before you set off.

The land that smiles almost forgot. And then, in a shop full of gold religious icons and brass incense burners, I discover they're not so far beneath the surface.

I am rather intrigued by this little shop and spend ages in here, fossicking around. Eventually a young woman comes up, holds her palms out wide, in the religious manner and beams at me. "No Inglisss." I beam back. "No Georgian."

And then we make ourselves understood.

On the Road in Oman

There's a moment of blinding clarity on my first day in Oman. It comes as the afternoon call-to-prayer is chanted from minarets and I stand in the fish souk in Old Muscat. It is very hot. The sweat is streaming off me. And there, among the marlin and shark, the anchovies and pitiful little crabs, in a pile of sweaty fish, one of them jumps. It just takes off from underneath the dead others, kicks up with its tail, arcs in the air, twists and flicks, then flops back down.

Yes, I think. A fish out of water.

It is as prophetic – as mystical – as any happening in the stories of the *Arabian Nights*, which I've been reading on my way to the Middle East. Stories where an animal might speak and genies appear at an appropriate moment. A fish out of water. HA!

In coming here, driving myself, finding my way around Oman's villages and markets, exploring its coast and running along the edge of the Empty Quarter's Wahiba Sands, home of the Bedouin, and in crossing its formidable Hajar Mountains, that is just what I want to be. You're right, my dear fish, that is the point.

(And I am still sure that at the top of his arc, he looks at me with a big, black, glassy eye and winks.)

There are many ways of doing things. The popular way of "doing" Oman is as a luxury destination, and I've done that, too. Fantastic hotels, epic foyers, infinity pools, fine food, spa treatments, souks, date palms and pastel sunsets. But it struck me last time I was here (doing that) that it would feel adventurous but not be too daunting to just fly in, jump into a hire car and head off. I had visions of me in a yellow Hyundai Getz crossing the Empty Quarter with just a camel-skin water bottle, a little Omani bread, a cloth wrapped around my head, the books I have owned for more than three decades by writer and Arabist Sir Wilfred Thesiger in a carpet bag, and only a map of dubious integrity to go by.

The vehicle has turned into a Toyota Landcruiser, which is probably a good thing, as you will read, but it still feels adventurous being footloose in Arabia. Being independent affords freedoms. It takes away the filter – the guide, the someone who can speak Arabic and knows exactly what's going on all the time, the someone between you and the place.

I have to navigate roads and language barriers, make contact with people, read, research, pick up clues. In groups, it's too easy to park your brain and your sensitivities.

Muscat is captivating. Yesterday I marvelled at the Islamic architecture, wandered the souks of Old Muscat and took an evening stroll along the corniche of Muttrah Bay. Men, young and old, in *dishdashas* – ankle-length, long-sleeved, usually white gowns – and embroidered *kummar* (caps) in soft colours. Women in long, black *sirwal* and the *lihaf* headdress. Groups of girls in the Aladdin's caves that are backstreet jewellery shops, streaming gold. Little cups of Omani coffee ground from date palm seeds, poured from the long-spouted pots that Bedouins value.

But today I get up early, hum the Indian Jones theme tune, and plunge the Landcruiser into the morning rush hour. "Be kind to me, I'm new here." And they are. No road rage, no rude signs or aggression from other drivers.

Muslim Arabic belief: "Were it not for misdeeds there would be no forgiveness."

By some divine will, I take a correct turn off a roundabout and I'm heading south down a deep, rocky valley. The morning sun on my left shoulder. A good sign.

In 1970, there was only 10 kilometres of sealed roads in Oman. Indeed, until the late 1970s, the country was largely isolated from the rest of the world. The previous Sultan was less progressive; there were no cars, just donkeys and camels. It was only when his son, His Majesty Sultan Qaboos, took over from his father, that things started to change.

By 1999, there was 8,000 kilometres of sealed roads. Today, most of the country is connected. Oman has been investing its resources income in fundamentals for the future.

This first day takes me south and then east and plunges me into old Arabia. Arabic music fills the vehicle. Ninety kilometres from Muscat, I walk the streets and laneways of the small, quiet town of Qurayyat. Carpenters and metalworkers, perfume shops and "shoe sewers", launderers and many small restaurants where six is a crowd.

From there, on to another small coastal village, Fins, where goats stand in slivers of shade. I am looking at a row of fishing boats when a young man comes to greet me. "Muhammad." We shake hands. We chat – he knows a little of Australia and is practicing his English. He's from the bigger nearby town of Sur – he's just come to this mosque with his mates to pray today.

He asks, "You just looking around?"

"Yes."

"You'll be alright," he says. And then he smiles broadly.

And then on to Sur itself, shimmering charmingly across the water. Long famed for builders of the Arabian dhows which sailed between here and Zanzibar and India, around the Middle East and as far as China, it still has a fleet of 100, and forts perched on the rocky headlands.

And soon I am heading for Nizwa, tracking along the edge of the Wahiba Sands of the Empty Quarter. The Friday goat market. Bedouin women in black. Nizwa is a stronghold of culture.

And then, with an Arabic lunch of hummus, flatbread, and rose milk, packed beside me, I head off and up, into the Hajar Mountain range, the 3,000 metre high spine of Oman. Up a narrow track to Jabal Shams, the highest peak. This south-east corner of the Arabian geological plate is being pushed northward as the Red Sea widens; the force that created the Hajar Mountains.

The track is steep and winds along mountain sides, with shale and gypsum dust.

I meet a man called Ali, who tells me to travel on through Hat. I like the Omani way of giving directions...just a big sweep of the arm showing the general bearing. North and then to the east, the arm says. It suits me nicely. And when all else fails, navigate by the sun.

Crossing the Hajar Mountains is not for the faint-hearted.

I have never seen these mountains before, but they have figured throughout my life. I read my first book by Wilfred Thesiger when I was a youngster. He lived for years with Bedu tribes in the Empty Quarter, just as he lived with the marsh Arabs in Iraq and with tribal people in Ethiopia, to which I will travel soon.

He didn't just study nomadism; he was a nomad. He spent his life travelling and writing beautiful, clean prose, and taking wonderful black and white photographs. I looked up to him. I still look up to him.

Thesiger had lived in Arabia for years when he came to the Hajar Mountains in 1949, hoping to venture into, and over, them. But his Christian life was at serious risk, and he never made it.

"It was disappointing to have failed," he wrote. "I realised that my journeys in Arabia were over. There was nowhere left where I could travel..."

When Thesiger returned briefly in 1971, he found the new world created by Sultan Qaboos. Roads, schools, hospitals, airports.

The sultan offered to have him flown to the top of the Hajars in a helicopter, but he preferred to go on foot. "A last gesture of the past."

Thesiger is important to me. He's one of my chaps. One of my team – the company we all assemble, of writers, musicians, actors, historical figures, sports stars, whoever – to populate our internal, intellectual world.

Thesiger is one of mine, as are, for example and more contemporarily, Bruce Chatwin and Colin Thubron. Inspirations and yardsticks.

There is something fundamental in the quest of travel that has not, and maybe will not, change for some of us. It is as simple as looking for connection, searching for understanding, seeking enlightenment.

In his *Anatomy of Restlessness*, which was published in 1997, Chatwin wrote, "Travel does not merely broaden the mind. It makes the mind. I like to think that our brains have an information system giving us orders for the road, and that here lie the mainsprings of our restlessness."

Yes, I like the chaps on my team. I like Thesiger, even with the sure knowledge that he wouldn't have liked me. Me in my fancy rental Landcruiser.

I jump back down from my high, rocky lunch ledge, ready for the rest of it, and land in a cloud of gypsum. Time puffs up over my boots.

I drive on slowly. Make it last.

On my last day in Oman I return to the fish souk in Old Muscat and stand in precisely the same spot that I did at the beginning of this Arabian tale, having crossed the Hajar Mountains.

I await the next moment that God, Allah, serendipity, a genie, or even a fish jumping might bring. But there is nothing. I have come all this way and the scene around me seems completely normal. And that really is something.

Driving the Desert in Qatar

"Ah, the desert is silent, so some music would be good," says Shah Gehen, with a logic that alludes me. He reaches forward to the Toyota Landcruiser's sound system as we head towards Qatar's beige dunes and then Khor al Adaid, its legendary 'Inland Sea', which is connected to the Arabian Gulf by a narrow, deep channel. There is no comparable lagoonal system of this type elsewhere in the world.

This, at last, is not the construction-site Middle East, but the desert on the south-east coast of Qatar, close to the border with Saudi Arabia – the foundation upon which Arabian culture was built.

This is the gasping interior where Arabian horsemen sat proud in their swirling clothes, a falcon on one fist.

I am in the desert, surrounded by sand, space and a sense of Bedouin life. And with that Shah turns on some hip-hop. Black American urban tones...kuchoo-kuchoo-kuchoo..."I like the way you burn...you burn..."

"Hip-hop?"

Shah smiles.

"I like *oud* music..." (And clearly, in brackets, "any chance of that?")

He smiles back. Clearly not.

Shah had picked me up in the Qatari capital of Doha and we have driven 58 kilometres south from the capital, through the coastal towns of Al Wakrah and Umm Said, past oil refineries and fertiliser plants where once, and quite recently really, there was just a village with a handful of houses, a grocers and a tyre shop.

Shah is wearing the Qatari national dress of a *dishdasha* – a long white shirt over white pants – and a white head fabric called a *gutra*, held on with a black agal rope. He looks the business.

"Were you born near Doha?" I ask.

"No," he says. "Pakistan." He smiles again: "But I have been here twenty-five years."

That counts, I say.

"And my grandfather came here under the British," alluding to a phase of history shared by both countries.

But Qatar has been independent since 1971 – and independence runs deep through the interior of this 160-kilometre-long peninsula which juts into the Arabian Gulf.

Much of the country is a low, barren, sand-covered plain. In fact, the highest point of the whole country, Qurayn Abu al Bawl, is only 103 metres above sea level.

Khor al Adaid natural reserve – this 'Inland Sea' area – is such a good example of Qatar's natural landscape that it has earned UNESCO World Heritage status. Archaeological sites have shown that it supported Bedouin people and their grazing stock.

Desert foxes can be seen. There are still Arabian Gazelles in Khor al Adaid, and plans to reintroduce Arabian Oryx.

I spot cuttlefish skeletons and sanderlings around the edge of the big inlet surrounded by these rolling sand dunes. Each has a name. Perhaps the prettiest I see today is Necklace Dune, which runs tall along the edge of a flat, sandy valley, its top in perfect undulations.

For Shah has deflated the Cruiser's tyres and taken off with great aplomb and obvious experience, up a big dune and along its crest, the great wall of it sheering away to our left.

We scoot round the bowls of some, and then he stops rear-to another, and lets the car slide down the 30m of it, backwards.

And all of this with…kuchoo-kuchoo-kuchoo…hip-hop.

But Shah's a good chap, good company, and turns out to be a good instant-friend, too.

For we are deep in the dunes when he spots a black Landcruiser stuck up to its bellypan in sand.

The two young chaps don't wave for help, but when Shah drives along a crest of a dune and finally drops down to them, we find them sitting beside the vehicle, clueless but clearly not panicking.

Shah produces a snatch strap, jerks them out of the sand and then hangs around until they get going again.

"They have no idea," he says, smiling, storming another dune with the Landcruiser flat-chat.

We stop by at a camel camp for lunch and I have the chance to walk off on my own and stand on the top of a dune and feel the full force of the hot desert wind. I like the way it burns.

Flying Backwards to Africa from Forwards Dubai

I am seeking the sense of quest; the point to this journey (I like a point to my journeys). I am looking for the end of the ball of white string, so that I can tease it out and follow it hand-over-hand (an amalgamation of Indiana Jones and Jacques Tati) from where I am to where I am going.

And there it is, on this very morning, as I am waiting to board an Emirates plane, to leave Arabia and fly to Africa – a revelation that may rewrite the books about what was humankind's most significant migration. Our greatest journey of all. The start of our travels.

For the US journal *Science* has published a report that ancient stone tools excavated in the Arabian Emirate of Sharjah suggest early humans may have migrated from Africa about 50,000 years earlier than previously thought. Until now it was thought our ancestors moved north from Africa about 70,000 years ago but the new findings now put that migration at about 125,000 years ago.

Moving the date back that much is momentous but so too is the proposition that early modern humans may have migrated straight across into Arabia, rather than up through the Nile Valley, as has been most commonly thought.

All this is the result of eight years of excavations in Sharjah under Hans-Peter Uerpmann, from Germany's Tübingen University.

Sharjah neighbours Dubai, but it feels more like an adjacent suburb. It has a most fascinating museum.

Professor Uerpmann and his team have unearthed Palaeolithic stone axe heads, scrapers and denticulates (tools with teeth) in the limestone of Jebel Faya. The tools have been dated using luminescence techniques which define when materials were last exposed to light. Their age challenges the previously accepted dates of migration; the style of tools challenges the route, and it may all lead to a rewriting of the history of human migration.

The shortcut to Arabia – from eastern Africa to Jebel Faya – may have only been possible for a short time, about 130,000 years ago, when the sea level was about 100 metres lower than today, and the Nejd Plateau was passable.

I feel like I am travelling backwards, up here in the air heading almost directly along what may be the most significant human migration route, but backwards, from Dubai to Nairobi, and at great height and speed.

I am leaving sparkling glass towers built on sand, including Dubai Mall, the world's biggest, and Burj Khalifa, the world's tallest at 828 metres, and more than 200 storeys. It is a dry place where the only water is desalinated.

I am arriving in Nairobi, the capital of Kenya, and a city that got its name from a Masai phrase Enkare Nyorobi meaning "the place of cool waters" – 1,600 metres above the sea level I have just left and occupied by the Masai adjacent to the eastern edge of the Great Rift Valley.

And here, on its doorstep, is the Masai Mara, in the green of which pastures ends the greatest migration on Earth – that of two million animals which cross the Serengeti from Tanzania. The migration is an obvious journey for us to grasp, but the wildebeest are always moving, seeking nourishment. As photographer Jonathan Scott, who has spent 30 years chronicling the Masai Mara and Serengeti, writes, "The only beginning is the moment of birth." Death is the only ending.

I feel the powerful current of these migration routes. I feel the animal urge to keep moving before I lay down and die.

Behind me, modern man…

Dubai has the world's biggest building, the world's biggest shopping mall, the world's biggest indoor aquarium and the world's biggest dancing fountain.

The tallest building….

The ravishing spire of Burj Khalifa glitters in differing moods as the day's light progresses.

Before dawn, it is a dull pink. Then sharp silver in the morning sun, before bleaching to white so that it almost vanishes into the pale Arabian sky. And in the late afternoon, it turns yellow, then gold. There are plenty of facts and figures about Burj Khalifa. It took 1,200 workers five years to build and they used more than 28,000 glass panels. Empty it weighs 500,000 tonnes, and it is designed to withstand winds up to almost 200 kilometres per hour. There are fifty-seven elevators and from the top on a clear day, you can see 95 kilometres.

The world's biggest shopping mall…

Dubai Mall has 1,200 shops and inside is the world's biggest indoor aquarium, the 10-million-litre Dubai Aquarium tank which holds more than 33,000 aquatic animals.

The world's biggest dancing fountain…

Dubai Fountain sprays water more than 150 metres into the air and "dances like 100,000 belly dancers". Set in the manmade Burj Khalifa lake, it is illuminated by 6,600 lights and twenty-five colour projectors and shoots up to more than 80,000 litres of water at any one moment, to 275 metres in the air. It cost more than US$200 million to build. Its performances, every half hour through the evening, are choreographed to pop, classical and contemporary Arabic music – from Michael Jackson's 'Thriller' to dance music of Hassan Abou El Seoud, against which the water chutes do, indeed, belly-dance erotically.

Dubai has world-class restaurants and high-end bars. It is new, modern – a phenomenon. But it also feels like it has come of age.

When I look back at photographs I take in Dubai, some of them seem more like Computer Generated Images. CGI snapshots of a perfectly constructed city in a digital quest game. Highest quality graphics and rendering.

And it strikes me that this is another way that Dubai sits in the modern world. It is the reality of the virtual reality in which many people spend some of their lives, particularly the online-young.

They may spend as much time in the virtual space of the digital world as they do in the actual world, and Dubai is where the two meet. It is a manifestation of the human imagination – a real-life rendering of a perfect, dreamed city.

This immaculate, visionary, glittering and crimeless city is newly created, building by building, pond by pond, shopping mall by shopping mall, on the dusty crust of Arabia – perhaps, one might parallel, rather like Las Vegas was built in the desert when Cuba, the American playground, was put out of bounds. A bit like that – but more elegant.

Dubai is the product of human imagination, ingenuity, creativity and hard work. And, of course, as much of migrant labourers as financiers. It is an environment created to suit modern humans, and it may well now be the natural environment of many modern homo sapiens.

For here we can live inside in the perfectly controlled climate. We can hunt out super meals and gather artefacts in malls. We can exercise in the gyms, be entertained in cinemas, pursue outdoor activities indoors.

It is all in here for the new humans who edit their own lives so that they just get what they want – who listen to specific songs, not whole albums, who stream specific shows they like rather than sitting through an evening of TV, taking the good with the bad.

It is interesting to be in Dubai for a few days with my son – a young man who is highly intelligent, highly computer literate (and literate, come to that). To see the place, a little, through the sensibilities of a man who appreciates quality and clever design. Who likes things (in this case, a place) that work well. Immaculately, efficiently, like an elegant computer program.

I have seen Dubai grow over a decade and a half, and seen many of the buildings around me as infants in building sites, and desert before that, but for him it is a brand-new place.

And I do see that he appreciates the coherent planning, clean lines, the thought behind the reality.

And it is a good time to be with him in Dubai as it is as if the city has finally "come together". Perhaps reached some critical mass. Moved out of its adolescence and come of age.

And there is no doubt in my mind that the global financial crisis has played its part in the slightly different mood in Dubai. It was not just a financial correction, but a fiscal brake that has made its development perhaps more considered, but nonetheless dramatic. It changed the mix and mood in some areas, as rents dropped and workers could live closer in – rather than spending an hour and a half each way to their accommodation, there was more sense of ethnic neighbourhoods forming around Dubai.

I am more of a natural environment type – usually more at home in country than city, in original desert landscape than in some sterile modernism imposed on it – but I see a beauty to Dubai now that might have eluded me a little before.

It has become an artwork. It has an elegance.

On Horseback in Kenya

It was often big-game hunting that made big names hunt in Kenya, but it was conservation that kept Hollywood star William Holden here.

Holden was one of the biggest box office draws of the 1950s, and his Mt Kenya Safari Club, which was established in 1959 exclusively for members and guests, was once a home away from home for hunters.

The walls still have some mounted trophy heads, and photographs of big-game hunting. White men with rifles in the crooks of their arms and a boot on some hapless dead beast.

Holden won an Academy Award for best actor in 1954 for his role in *Stalag 17*, and is famous for his parts in *Bridge over the River Kwai* and with Gloria Swanson in *Sunset Boulevard*, although he had parts in seventy-three films.

Mt Kenya Safari Club drew the international jet set. Marlon Brando, James Stewart, Humphrey Bogart, Clark Gable, Gene Kelly, Grace Kelly, John Wayne, Clint Eastwood, Kim Novak and Ernest Hemingway came to stay, to name but a few.

There's still part of an old studio on the property, from when *The Lion* was partly filmed there in 1962.

But it also drew English zoologist Jane Goodall, who from 1970 conducted prolonged and intimate chimpanzee studies at Lake Tanganyika.

And actor Stefanie Powers, perhaps still known for the television series *Hart to Hart*. Holden and Powers began a relationship in 1972, though Holden died in 1981.

After his death, she set up the William Holden Wildlife Foundation, which runs alongside and supports the work of Mt Kenya Wildlife Conservancy, which Holden had started with friends Don and Iris Hunt. Mr Hunt is still there and involved.

Powers still has a cottage at Mt Kenya Safari Club, visits a couple of times a year and is actively involved in the orphanage.

The Mt Kenya Wildlife Conservancy has so far rescued and released 1,500 animals to the wild under wildlife manager Donald Bunge.

But it is wildlife guide James Kinyua who shows me the pigmy hippo, eagle owl, the crowned crested crane, the colobus and Sykes' monkeys, the African lynx, dwarf antelope and rock hyrax.

I see three cheetahs and, perhaps more importantly, bongo. They are native to the area but this conservancy is now the only place they exist. There are just sixty or so, but its successful breeding program has seen many births and some animals are being conditioned to be returned to a secure area in the wild. "We have to train them how to adapt to the wild," says James Kinyua.

I join an early morning horseride on feisty Casper up towards Mt Kenya, through forest and past zebra, waterbuck and aardvark holes, to find a breakfast table all laid out and champagne and cooked breakfast under way.

Now run by Fairmont hotels, Mt Kenya Safari Club has maintained its somewhat clubby feel and each room has a fireplace, glass doors that open to let in the fine, high air, and a view of the second-highest peak in Africa.

The light grows over Mt Kenya. At 5,199 metres, the stratovolcano created some three million years ago in the Plio-Pleistocene is second only to the 5,895 metres of Kilimanjaro, and a UNESCO World Heritage Site. I woke with the first light of dawn, just before the lion on the adjoining property started his morning roaring ritual. I opened the doors under a clear, dark velvet sky and let the cold air rush in.

Mt Kenya's celebrity status was revitalised when Prince William, the Duke of Cambridge, who will one day be king of England and the Commonwealth, proposed to the then Kate Middleton, now Duchess of Cambridge, by a secluded lake on the mountain. He flew them up to the remote, secluded spot at 3,810 metres in a borrowed helicopter and the big name hunters missed out.

The couple was staying in a log cabin during a Kenyan holiday. Mt Kenya stands above Lewa Downs, the wildlife conservancy owned by the family of Jecca Craig, Prince William's friend.

The Prince spent several months working there during his gap year after finishing at Eton.

Kenya holds special meaning for the British royal family. Prince William's grandmother made history here in 1952 when, as the young Princess Elizabeth, she was told she had become queen following the death of her father, George VI.

Mt Kenya holds even more meaning for the Kikuyu, Ameru, Embu and Masai – the four main tribes that live around it.

The Embu believe it is God's sacred place, and build their houses so that their doors face it. The Kikuyu believe the mountain is God's throne on earth.

The Kikuyu name for Mt Kenya is Kirinyaga – quite literally, "God's resting place".

A Donkey in Greece

There is a donkey outside my window. Framed by thrown-open louvred shutters and thick stone walls, it is tethered to an orange tree. I kept many donkeys as a child, so this is an added pleasure – a delightful echo – in being on Hydra, a beautiful Greek island a two-hour ferry ride from Athens.

Other donkeys clop past on the marble path, tied nose-to-tail, piled high with goods, including a fridge. An old man in a black wool Greek fisherman's cap rides the first side saddle. Then they are gone up a narrow alleyway, the donkeys skipping nimbly up steps.

There are no cars or bikes on this island where donkeys live comfortably alongside big dogs and healthy-looking cats.

For me today, it's shanks' pony as I walk into the hills, following an ancient path to three high monasteries, and return to the pretty harbour on the Aegean Sea; the heart of Hydra. Mainly white houses, with bright doors and shutters, climb in stacks up the hills, and stare into it.

Cafes and restaurants ring the harbour.

A waiter brings me a dessert I haven't ordered – one of many "gifts" given in these restaurants – "for a sweet memory of your last evening". Yes, sadly, it's my last evening.

I don't often feel so sorry to be leaving a place. It sounds soppy to write that Hydra is not only beautiful but has a beautiful spirit – but I think it true.

It is no surprise that Leonard Cohen found Hydra conducive to creative thought and bought a house here.

The donkey outside my window at the Hydroussa Hotel – once a family mansion, the setting for a Sophia Loren film and now a small elegant hotel – is tethered to an orange tree in Five Prime Ministers square. This is what little Hydra has contributed to the Greek parliament and in easier economic times than these.

Some Greeks are affronted by what in recent years has been said about their collapsed economy and bail-outs; a female shop owner offers a stinging sermon, hands gesticulating wildly. They are saying Greeks are lazy but she works seven days a week, often until 11pm, and they keep asking for more tax. Another says the money coming into the country is being "stolen" by politicians. "Like-eh always, allaways." And, right on cue, a donkey brays wildly. Eeyore, eeyore, eey-always.

And beyond, the spectacular Aegean Sea and the ferry back to Athens.

The Island under Siege in Papua New Guinea

Way off in the distance, a plume rises hundreds of metres into the sky, like scoops of grey ice-cream. It is pushed away to the left, broadening over the span of the sky and above the lights of Rabaul, which begin to twinkle at dusk.

The expedition cruise ship moves steadily towards this Papua New Guinean island's volcano, pushing the silky-warm Solomon Sea silently before it. Finally, it edges up so close to the volcano that in the darkening night I not only see its heart glowing red and molten rocks the size of vehicles being spat up and out of this vent through the planet's 35 kilometre thick crust, but I can hear it. It is something I hadn't expected. Mt Tavurvur rumbles with a dreadful, echoing sound.

And the other thing I hadn't expected was the lightning. Not everyday, stormy sort of lightning but *The Lord of the Rings* Mordor sort of lightning. This awesome stuff that feels as much to do with evil as a natural phenomenon. It is caused as electrons are literally stripped off atoms. Just knowing that can send shivers down your spine.

Mt Tavurvur vents on the edge of the Rabaul Caldera, which was formed in AD 540 on the convergent boundaries of two geological plates. It is part of the so-called Ring of Fire of volcanoes in this area, part of which is the Bismarck volcanic arc. The caldera is the big bowl in which the town of Rabaul sits and which has given way to the ocean on one side to form Simpson Harbour.

The Rabaul Caldera was formed when 110 cubic kilometres of tephra (rock fragments and particles) were thrown up from the earth's guts. And what does that mean? Well, by comparison, Mt Vesuvius threw out three cubic kilometres and Krakatoa eighteen.

The pyroclastic flow (the hot ash, lava fragments and gases ejected) of such a massive venting can hit up to 140 kilometres per hour and over 1,000°C.

In the past 140 years, there have been four more major eruptions.

It is all the result of subduction volcanic activity, caused by sideways and downward movement of the lip of a plate of the Earth's crust into the mantle beneath another plate. All around the ship are the signs of this explosive past: Mt Tavurvur, Rabalanakia, Mt Vulcan and Vulcan Island. Mt Vulcan had exploded in 1937, forming a ninety metre high volcano literally overnight. The lightning created was incredible. Four days later, Tavurvur, meaning "nest of hornets" in the local language, erupted. More than 500 people died.

But through all of this, Rabaul has survived, in one way or another.

It has survived the eruptions, and it survived the stationing of nearly 100,000 Japanese soldiers during the Second World War, and Allied bombing.

By the early 1980s, it had reverted once again to being the Pearl of the Pacific, but in 1983 and 1984 there were 94,000 individual earthquakes in eighteen months. Ash lay up to 3 metres deep, it threw up a cloud of it that could be seen from space, and every tree died.

Ash is pouring into the sky. The ship's anchor is weighed and she is motored slowly past the volcano and the dugout canoes that surround us, and is tied up at a wharf in Rabaul itself. This town that once had an elegant main street lined with mango trees – a place with an intense history now under siege.

The Rabaul Hotel was only saved after the eruptions because the owners regularly climbed up on the roof and cleared the ash. But today, as I stand in its back courtyard, it is still covered in ash, and I watch it gathering on a sharply canted tin roof, and run down like water and cascade off.

The bar has bombs and machine guns, photographs of the volcanoes erupting, a pair of buffalo horns so big that the body of the thing must have been the size of a vehicle. A marlin weighing 173 kilograms was once caught here.

It is all covered in a fine ash and photographs on the wall are being eaten by the acrid atmosphere. With the wind now turned towards the town, a gritty, grey cloud covers it. The floors of the shops, cars, houses, every leaf on every tree. It is pushed back along the roads, to form black mounds.

It is a place under siege and soon the sulfurous ash is dusting the ship. There is an intimacy to expedition cruising – for a short while it seems to become "your" ship. And now the gritty ash is covering my ship, eating at it and I get just a brief, personal glimpse of what living in the shadow of a volcano must be like.

Sea Kayaking along Ningaloo Reef

Soft, turquoise swells come from behind and the sea kayak slides on to them, running a little before they fade and the next comes. We are running with the wind, this yellow Barracuda Beachcomber kayak and me, over the top of the complete, cosmopolitan underwater world of Western Australia's Ningaloo Reef that I glimpsed yesterday in three magnificent snorkelling sessions…

…black-and-white-tipped reef sharks circling, an old turtle as big as a coffee table ambling along, unperturbed by humans, and small ones with cappuccino-coloured shells, flying like saucers through the clear water, fish from tiny neon blue to the rainbow tones of the coral crunchers. And the coral itself, in fans and brains and staghorns…

We are running with the wind over it all today, on a swell that is the remnant of an unseasonal overnight storm, with gale-force winds that whipped the white dunes into a gritty sandblaster, drove them into every crevice, and then added fire-hose rain.

But nature always rewards you. In my experience, for every test outdoors, there is a blessing.

The snorkelling might be murkier today but then there is this energised, spring-cleaned world and the rollers driving us northwards. Paddling in this rhythmic ocean has a mesmeric, sing-your-favourite-song list quality that leaves me almost comatose, lost in the zen of it. It takes on a dreamlike quality.

Cape Range to my right, silky lagoon below, outer reef to my left.

The contrast is striking between the red rock and soft green foliage of the range and the massive white pearl necklace of the outer reef, where 5 metres of swell is breaking, throwing up a long, white, candy-floss line of spray that catches the morning sun.

I am on a three-day, two-night paddling trip along Ningaloo Coast, in this World Heritage Listed area, heading north from Osprey Bay, where I am soon greeted by dolphins, swimming close. There's a kayak mooring off the coast – one of many along the Ningaloo Marine Park – and the kayak ties off easily and I slide over the side into tepid water, and I'm soon following a reef shark. This Osprey snorkel site is amazing.

Paddling back to the coast, I see a big emu on the beach, standing in the water, staring at the horizon.

And today I'll also snorkel at Bundegi and the offshore Blue Lagoon, where a big stingray lies on the bottom, pumping sand until it almost vanishes into a big bowl on the ocean floor.

I have paddled probably only 10 kilometres in this first day but it has been full and interesting.

And then the weather comes in. Camping in the dunes south of South Mandu becomes a bit of an epic.

I'm in a good tent, but the wind is so strong that it blows sand under the flysheet, through one tent wall and out the other side. Where it hits my gear in the tent (and me), it forms drifts.

When I feel the first few drops of rain coming through and falling on me in the dark, I put on my head torch and look up to see the makings of a rainwater shower. I get out of my sleeping bag, take off all my dry clothes and pack everything into my waterproof dry sacks. I put on all my kayaking gear (including my personal floatation jacket, as it's cold now), lie down with my head on the dry sack and sleep happily in an ever deepening puddle of water.

When I get up in the morning, my fingers are wrinkled.

And then I am back out on the ocean, running with the wind.

This second day takes me past Oyster Stacks (where Cape Range is closest to the reef), Turquoise Bay, where I drift-snorkel in surprisingly good conditions, and on to a second camp, overlooking Lakeside Sanctuary Zone.

Still with a stiff breeze through the evening, I suspect the possibility of a second rough camp, but the night settles to peace, and there is just stillness around me, with the distant but distinctive sound of the breakers on the outer reef to lull.

And not only in this does nature reward us.

For in the quiet morning, the gentle sun on my back, I stand with a pop-up bowl full of breakfast, watching reef sharks in the marine sanctuary zone having theirs. Their fins appear briefly and fast as they fish.

Dining, onshore and off.

After snorkelling I prepare to move on. It is surprising how much a sea kayak can hold, and the mountain of gear is quickly packed through hatches into the hulls, and I set off heading further out to sea, toward that line of outer reef breakers, and then on to morning tea at Neds Camp, before heading towards South Passage.

Even power boats are staying inside the reef today. The swell outside is still big, with confused waves breaking through the narrow passage. I paddle quite close, but safely, until the outgoing tide sucks at me and I turn and scarper.

But I am soon captivated by a close encounter, as a dolphin swims close to the kayak as I head in to Mangrove Bay – a trajectory I wouldn't have had but for the paddle out to the South Passage.

It seems to me, when you're outdoors, there's always a gift.

For just a few days in the sea kayak, I have felt the swell and the surge the waters of the Ningaloo coast through my body. I have ritually submerged myself in that water, and moved, albeit clumsily, with its creatures. I have slept in its dunes and accepted its sand as a constant.

And I have come to feel the place as I never before. To fully experience it.

And that's a real reward, isn't it?

Finding Old Batavia in Jakarta

I might be in the old Batavia of my imagination, walking along the quayside by square riggers from Europe, but this is better. For Sunda Kelapa harbour, in the Indonesian capital of Jakarta, is lined with *phinisi* – big-prowed Makassar schooners; boats showing the lines and designs of the fabled sailors of Sulawesi who plied to Australia, and whose presence is evident along the Kimberley coast, and sailed as far as Africa.

"They are known as tough sailors," says Arie Saksono, a journalist, television documentary producer and student of Indonesian history and heritage, who is showing me around the Indonesian capital.

These heavy timbered *phinisi* take goods and produce particularly to Sulawesi and Kalimantan, but also to other parts of the great arch of the Indonesian Archipelago. For, beyond Bali, Indonesia is comprised of more than 17,500 islands.

Today, it is products from Jakarta, supplies for the islands and palm sugar. Once the ships were loaded mainly with timber from Sulawesi and Kalimantan, but logging laws have changed that.

They sail out for between two and four days to Surabaya and Sulawesi.

The *phinisi's* gangplanks are solid tree trunks, cut to a rough log, ridged across and tied to the boat with hemp rope. On some boats, the safety rails are of roughly cleaned-up tree boughs. The hulls are solid timber, too – all tumblehome and low swept decks. The sailors' families live and sail on board, and there are large wooden structures, with balconies and some with turned rails.

Families invite passers-by on board, and for a small sum will paddle them along the line of seagoing craft in the timber canoes that are their tenders.

Loading is going on. Cement, snacks and big bales of cloth, all carried on shoulders up gangplanks that seem precarious to me. Barefooted, surefooted and in white clouds of cement dust, the men signal me aboard, just to look around.

"This is the place where Jakarta's history began," says Arie Saksono. This was long the hub of South-East Asia. "There was no Singapore."

Jakarta was the Queen of the East.

This is from where the *Duyfken*, the first European ship to arrive on an Australian shore, set sail. (The replica built in Fremantle set sail there in 1999.)

This is the city for which the *Batavia* was named – Western Australia's most famous wreck from the Dutch era. In 1629, the ship was sailing to the Dutch East Indies to collect spices when, after leaving Cape Town, it was steered too far south and shipwrecked on the Houtman Abrolhos Islands off Geraldton. The ensuing mutiny and murder of at least 110 men, women and children is the stuff of horrible legend.

But long before that, Sunda Kelapa harbour had seen ships heading to the horizon.

For ships all along the archipelago, and as far afield as India, China and Vietnam, have been docking at this mouth of the Ciliwung River since the fifth century. Sunda Kalapa was the main port of the Hindu Kingdom of Sunda, which was already a century old. At one time, it was said to be the most important port in the Hindu world, and Buddhism gained influence in the ninth century. Over the centuries, the city port became a busy international trade centre, exporting pepper, spices, rice and gold.

Then, in 1513, the first European fleet arrived. Four Portuguese ships arrived in Sunda Kelapa in search of spices, especially pepper.

The found a busy and well-organised port and, in 1522, they signed a treaty of friendship with the King of Sunda.

They took control in 1619 and Jayakarta was to be called Batavia for more than 300 years.

I am not far from the red brick house Kaliber 11, which is recorded as Haram Losman, where Captain James Cook stayed during his explorations of the Southern Hemisphere. It was a hotel then, but later became a maritime academy.

And during these centuries, Batavia left its imprint on Western Australian history. As J. S. Battye recorded in his history of Western Australia, published in 1924, the French Admiral D'Entrecasteaux left France in 1791, and sailed to the East Indian Archipelago, then turned southward down the coast of Western Australia.

And here I am now, after all these eras, in a port full of manual labour and echoes.

Motorcycling in the Himalayas

I am considering collisions, in both geological and political senses. And who wouldn't, here in the Himalayas – this colossal, jagged vertical scar caused by the Indian and Eurasian plates colliding with unfathomable force. Still colliding, in fact, with India pushing north at a geologically speedy 50 millimetres a year.

Politically and in parallel, I am considering the rub of Tibet and Nepal, with the relentless weight of the Peoples' Republic of China behind Tibet, which it forcefully established as an autonomous region in 1965, and the cultural, spiritual and practical Indian influence on Nepal. Indeed, after the invasion of Tibet by China, India tightened its ties, and Indian and Nepalese people still travel across that border without passport or visa.

Unlike the difficult border between Tibet and Nepal that I have just crossed. For in the middle of the Chinese-built Friendship Bridge arched high over the Bhote Kosi river (the only gateway between the two countries), there is a yellow line – one side are Chinese soldiers, the other Nepalese, their shoulders just a metre apart.

A sense of collision, indeed. I am on a motorcycle and considering this when, around the hairpin bend in front of me on a bumpy road only just wider than one vehicle (but actually a major highway), appears a packed bus, flat out, with a single goat on top, rack surfing. The goat is leaning impressively into the bend and all four hooves leave the roof together as the bus hits a torso-sized bump and then lurches full-speed from the potholed tarmac and on to dust and stones.

I instinctively duck my head, throw my 500cc Royal Enfield Bullet motorcycle towards the enormous vertical drop on my left, feel its wheels shift from shale to grass, and close my eyes. Closing my eyes clearly works as, though I feel the brush of bus, I pop out of its cloud of blond dust and diesel fumes into the Nepalese sunshine.

It all leads me to the opinion that one should be careful what one thinks about. Manifestation may well be a possibility. Indeed, I may, for all I know, have just almost pulled one off. Think about collisions and, well…

But the Lord Shiva has shone upon me, for here in Nepal I am instantly swaddled in a Hindu mysticism with which I am already comfortable and the oversight of Lord Shiva, the country's guardian deity.

In the days just past, before crossing that border on this motorcycle ride across the roof of the world from Lhasa in Tibet to Kathmandu, Tibet re-suffused in me the familiar Buddhist ethic and tenet. Monasteries perched on mountain sides, prayer flags shot from party poppers and monks' prayers chanted from ancient strips of scripture. It has all reverberated and resonated within me, stimulating the echoes of a religious childhood and the widening ethical thoughts of manhood, just as the chanting itself is said to stimulate the pituitary gland.

And so now I am considering collisions, in both geographical and personal senses. And who wouldn't, here in the Himalayas, following this river that quickly becomes the Sun Kosi, into which drains the Dudh Kosi, which itself drains from 8,848 metre high Mt Everest.

The Dudh Kosi is the world's highest river and in 1976, under the leadership of Englishman Mike Jones, who was still in his early twenties, a party of kayakers was the first to paddle it.

I was a keen teenage paddler, and soon after they returned triumphant, I went to a room in Crystal Palace in London to see Dr Jones give a slide-show talk about it. It is not only the image of the tumbling water of the Dudh Kosi that is lodged in me but also the sight of the young, be-sandalled, rather British paddlers rolling into Kathmandu in an old Ford Transit van with a homemade rack full of fibreglass kayaks on top.

And here I am, almost unbelievably to me, following the Kosi river system, heading for Kathmandu. After all these years of following rivers, paddling kayaks and heading somewhere or other. A collision of my teenage past and this present moment.

I have in my case the film, recently tracked down, of that 1976 kayak expedition – an almost mythical storytelling. Dr Jones was outdoorsy and intellectual and the leading expedition kayak paddler of his generation. He drowned two years later when trying to save a friend on the Braldu River in Pakistan. And for that I admire him, too.

The Royal Enfield vibrating beneath me – the one that just got me through that sticky bus situation – is the tangible connection to this geography, its big single cylinder thumping out a steady beat.

And the very sound collides with my past, too.

For Royal Enfield, based in the small town of Redditch in Worcestershire, in rural England, introduced the Bullet in 1949 as a 350cc bike, and stepped it up to 500cc in the 1950s.

As a young motorcycle enthusiast growing up just a few kilometres away in Worcestershire, you can imagine that Royal Enfield was very much the local bike. I started riding motorcycles soon after the company was dissolved in 1971, when Japanese motorcycles invaded, but there were plenty of Bullets around. That single-cylinder sound resonated around the granite-walled laneways of my youth. The shape and sound of this classic British design are wired into me.

And around the time I was born, Enfield of India, which is based in Chennai, started assembling Bullets from British components, and by 1962 was making complete bikes. In 1995, it purchased the right to use the Royal Enfield name. This all makes Royal Enfield the oldest motorcycle brand still in production, with the Bullet having the longest production run of any bike.

A love of India is part of my story too, and the echoes of it are all around me on this narrow road coming down the Sun Kosi valley.

They call the Royal Enfield "the bike of the Himalayas", and now I know that is true. For it has handled everything that has been thrown at it – unpredictable bitumen with lumps, bumps and lurches, gravel and rock, stream crossings, passes of more than 5,000 metres elevation that left me breathless in every sense, and soon my transit through warm, traffic-choked Kathmandu.

Somehow all of this – the Himalayas, British exploration, heroic ethic, the rub of countries, history, belief, scripts and scriptures – comes together in the austere immigration room as I leave Tibet to walk out across the Friendship Bridge, towards that yellow line, and cross into Nepal.

One of my travelling companions has a book about George Mallory, an English mountaineer who, in the 1920s, was a member of the first three British expeditions to Mt Everest. Mallory is the man who, on the 1924 British Mt Everest Expedition, went missing with climbing partner Andrew Irvine on the North-East Ridge.

Mallory was also the man who, when asked why he wanted to climb Mt Everest, replied: "Because it's there."

As I have mentioned, a young Chinese officer studies the book intently for many, many minutes, until he finds a reference to the Dalai Lama in it, and confiscates it. I had already been warned that maps are often confiscated, depending on the borders they show and their labelling.

All these thoughts have multiplied into a complex collision when, round the hairpin bend in front of me appears a packed bus, flat out, this one with a herd of goats on top, rack surfing. They lean impressively into the bend and I close my eyes.

I have ridden motorcycles half a million kilometres in Australia, Africa, Europe, Asia and America. On the road, on the track, in the dirt – but I reckon riding across the roof of the world was the best ride of all. Take just this one day. With my fellow riders, I have stood before Mt Everest and crossed the roof of the world through an arch of Tibetan prayer flags streaming in the biting wind at an altitude of 5,050 metres, surrounded by the saw-tooth Himalayas. Then, after sharing lunch with a sheep-herding family in a remote high-mountain home which relies on a yak-dung heater, I have dropped nearly 2,000 metres in 32 kilometres, riding more than 200 bends. Hairpins that you tip into and peel out of, a big 500 cc single cylinder thumping between your calves and the great spread of the planet beneath you. We have left the frigid Tibetan Plateau moonscape of the last two days behind to plunge into a deep green valley, heading from Tibet into Nepal. And, after a sizzling meal in a lively local Tibetan restaurant, I lie here in a comfortable hotel, warm and still buzzing with the day, waiting to ride on. (At this moment, I feel like I just want to ride on forever.) Just one brilliant day and 244 kilometres of motorcycling, Himalayan style, on, of course, Royal Enfield bikes. For the group spends nine days with these classic motorcycles, riding from Lhasa, the capital of Tibet, to Kathmandu, the capital of Nepal.

The bikes set the theme of the trip, but it is the close connection to local cultures which sets the deeper flavour. I dine at local restaurants, on everything from yak burgers to the rare and specialised mushrooms of high-altitude Tibet. Lhasa beer, Everest beer and banana buttermilk lassis. I visit monasteries perched on mountain sides and hear their Tibetan monks chant, and watch them debate in a courtyard in the sun. For an even more intimate view of Tibet, I have visited an orphanage and met city folk and villagers.

I travelled from Xining in China to Lhasa in Tibet, up on to the Tibetan Plateau, on the Himalayan Express train. This is a good way of reducing the effects of gaining altitude, as Lhasa is 3,600 metres above sea level. And it is there – as we arrive at the very comfortable and rather interesting Brahmaputra Hotel, which incorporates a Tibetan museum – that I see the sight I have rather been waiting for. For out the front is my black and chromed Royal Enfield.

The plan to spend the first four nights in Tibet in Lhasa is good. Riders need time to acclimatise to the altitude and get used to the bikes. I ride in company to Drak Yerpa Monastery and up an unsealed hairpin track to Ganden Monastery, perched on a mountain 40 kilometres from the city, Tibetan prayer flags covering the mountain like the contents of a party popper. I join the morning pilgrims visiting Lhasa's Potala Palace and see monks debate at Sera Monastery. I see Tibetan Buddhists faithfully prostrating themselves before Jokhang Temple and explore old Lhasa. And all the while, I am gaining an intimate view of the place through real Tibetan food at carefully chosen restaurants. And then, with my riding companions, I head out of the city, west, towards Nepal. This is real motorcycling. I leave Lhasa in warm sun under blue sky to ride the Enfield 260 kilometres to the traditional town of Gyangtse. The old Tibet. I ride up a spaghetti of hairpins to Gampa La Pass, for a lunchbreak just under the peak of almost 4,800 metres, overlooking the intense aquamarine of Yamdrok Lake, surrounded by friendly yaks. But for me, the highlight of the day is not the going up but the coming down. For after a serpentine ride on bitumen along the side of this splendid lake, I come to the Karola glacier, at an altitude of 4,960 metres. It perches, gnawed by the sun, and from it there come rivulets. And as I ride on through the Himalayas, these turn into a tumbling stream that splits into silver fingers weaving down a widening, rocky valley. Soon they become one flat, thin body as the valley broadens, rolling river stones to rounds. And then, at a specific moment, it becomes deep and shiveringly blue.

Only in recent years has hydro-electric power been harvested from it but, as it flows into the wide, flat valley below, this river, born of a glacier, brings life. It is harvest time and people are winnowing grain in the wind – seed separating, falling first, collected in piles. I saw this river born of a glacier, high in the Himalayas. I've seen it grow and nurture this valley. And all under the high light of the Tibetan sun.

I stay in comfort at Gyangtse Hotel and the next morning walk through this old town, some of it unchanged since medieval times, and see Kunbon Stupa. And then I ride on 90 kilometres, following the Nyang Chu river to Shigatse, and then 230 kilometres, over the 5,220-metre-high Lhakpa La Pass, to Tingri. This is it. I am surrounded by the 8,000 metre snow-capped and saw-tooth highest mountains on Earth – Cho Oyu at just over 8,200 metres and Mt Everest itself are the most distinctive. And at one point in the road there it is. After a lifetime of reading about the mountain and human exploits on it – of knowing its shape – there it is, at the end of the road, set against the pale blue sky, snow blowing off the top in a plume. For it is a day of riding beside these mountains – of riding into them. Of appreciating their massiveness. Of feeling exposed, of concentrating on the road, watching for lumps and bumps and potholes in the bitumen, and gravel cast across it. Wandering animals and wayward vehicles. It's brilliant. Tibetan villagers, yak herds, Buddhist temples and prayer flags, horses pulling laden carts, yak dung being dried in patties as fuel. After a night in the Zhangmu Hotel, I pass perhaps 200 trucks waiting to cross the border into Nepal, and do so myself. I walk across the Friendship Bridge and I am in Nepal, submerged in its more Indian atmosphere, following the Sun Kosi river to Kathmandu, where I will ride triumphant into the city.

Travelling on the World's Highest Train

The *Himalayan Express* is the highest railway in the world and many experts said, quite simply, that it couldn't be built.

A train running 4,000 kilometres from Beijing in China to Lhasa in Tibet, climbing up onto the Tibetan Plateau and reaching an altitude of more than 5,000 metres, over inhospitable and inaccessible permafrost landscapes, made massively difficult by winter conditions, was impossible. But, as I write this, lying back on my comfortable bunk, the *Himalayan Express* is quietly and smoothly scaling its serpentine track to the roof of the world. We have crossed the low grasslands in the afternoon and started the overnight climb to the Tibetan Plateau.

And, after a night rhythmic with the train, I wake to piercing blue sky, raw sun, sharp snow-capped peaks and yak herds. The land is a blond, sandy colour, with rivers frozen to mirror stainless steel.

We pass solitary homes with animal enclosures, yak herds and shepherds with sheep flocks and hawks.

A man in uniform salutes the train as it passes. Another man does the same. Then a boy.

On Cona Lake, the world's highest freshwater lake at 4,800 metres above sea level, there are wild ducks as big as geese.

For the line, 550 kilometres of which is laid on permafrost, was completed with its 675 bridges of a combined length of 160 kilometres, and opened on 1st July, 2006, a year ahead of schedule. The railway's average altitude through Tibet is 4,600 metres above sea level, with temperatures dropping to –30°C. The air oxygen content is just half of that at sea level.

Interestingly, less than two months later, on 28th August, a 75-year-old Chinese man reportedly became the first passenger to die on the train, and there have been more since. It is said he had suffered heart problems beforehand, but insisted on travelling.

Indeed, everyone on the train up to Lhasa must fill out a Passenger Health Registration Card. It mainly warns against travel for those with severe heart, lung or respiratory diseases, but adds other conditions like "diabetes out of control, the hysteria" and "highly dangerous pregnant women".

In fact, no-one in the group I've joined seems to notice the altitude much, as we dine at 3,400 metres and a steady 64 kilometres per hour. In the dining car there is soup and rice, a whole fish, shredded omelette and tomato, mushroom and bok choy, and potato, pork and beef dishes. Yellow River beer for some, sweet hot coffee to follow for others.

The cabins are four-berth, with storage space for small cases and bags, and quite comfortable. I sleep like a baby to the hushed rhythm of the train and its gentle rock.

The diesel locomotives were designed and built specifically for high altitude and can travel up to 120 kilometres per hour where there is no permafrost, and 100 kilometres per hour where the track is laid on this permanently frozen ground. Signs throughout the train are in Tibetan, simplified Chinese and English. I don't spot any to advise against smoking, though officially it is a non-smoking train, and people do smoke. There are no outdoor areas or opening windows, so the smell of cigarette smoke does rather pervade it.

The train reportedly has oxygen-enriched air, and there are personal air supplies, with individual masks, which travellers can plug in to.

To travel all the way from Beijing to Lhasa is forty-seven hours and just over 4,000 kilometres, but I have flown to Xining and joined the train there. One day and night on the train is enough, and the spectacular scenery is all on this second day.

The train leaves Xining just after 3pm and arrives in Lhasa, 1,960 kilometres later, just before 3pm the next day.

There are forty-five stations along the line from Xinging to Lhasa, not that the *Himalayan Express* stops at many. It passes the Chu'erma River Bridge, near the northern source of the Yangtze River, which is just over 2,500 metres long and built for Tibetan antelope to migrate through, as the track crosses their natural path. It passes the Tuotuo River, which is the source of China's longest river, the Yangtze, and it climbs to just over 5,000 metres above sea level at Tanggula Pass. Tanggula is the highest station in the world.

It passes the 400 square kilometres of the Cona alpine lake, revered as holy by people in this area. It passes Asia's biggest salt lake, Qarham Lake, and the Kunlun Mountains, which are an important pilgrimage site for Buddhists.

And the Geladaintong glaciers, snowy Dangla Mountain range, and northern Tibet's Young Tun Basin, a refuge for Tibetan antelope, wild yak and Tibetan wild donkey. It crosses the Qingshuihe Bridge – nearly 12 kilometres long and 4,600 metres above sea level.

And, travelling from Xining to Lhasa, the train rises from the great expanses of grassland scenery and ranges that rise around the horizon slowly at first, golden in the afternoon sun of the first day, to the enormous and white-capped mountains that rise in the sharp morning light the next day.

To the roof of the world.

Riding the Rails of India

A young woman walks along the rail lines in a pink sari with silver trim, carrying an empty silver water bucket. She is beautiful. She steps delicately; more an elegant glide, feet in line, pushing her toes forward, her free arm swinging, the wrist supple. Like a model.

She smiles to herself, and lifts the corner of her head-dress over her face as a man in an immaculate white, collarless shirt passes on a small Hero Honda motorcycle. Following him, two women in saris are riding side-saddle. One in bright turquoise, one in brilliant orange.

Next, a man on his mobile phone, taking his two boys to school on the back of his motorcycle, both with backpacks.

Another man in purest white, head wrapped, standing stock-still, leaning on a stick.

It is morning, somewhere along the rail track between Udaipur and Aurangabad, and the morning is passing.

I'm here in India, travelling on trains...

Not the trains I have just seen in Udaipur or Jaipur or in New Delhi or in Mumbai – the blue trains with people cheek by jowl, or the two-tier sleepers or, goodness me, the three-tiers where people seem packed on shelves. Not the early morning train I've just passed with a dozen people hanging out of each door, and hundreds sitting along the roof as if in neat rows of side-by-side chairs.

It is estimated that 30 million people travel on trains every day in India, over more than 110,000 kilometres of track, passing through 7,500 stations, in 60,000 coaches (up to twenty-six on each train) pulled by 9,000 locomotives.

But not like this.

No, I'm on the *Deccan Odyssey*, a very comfortable train for tourists from all around the world and, certainly, from India itself – which travels from Mumbai to Sindhudurg, Ellora and Ajanta cave temples, Pune, Goa and back to Mumbai.

It has decent-sized cabins with two single beds, a writing desk and a separate bathroom with shower, toilet and basin. Meals are in the rather elegant dining carriage. A bar and lounge with comfy chairs, and a spa.

I travelled on it before, in 2004, shortly after it started service on both some of the oldest and newest tracks in India. And I've travelled on others, like the *Golden Chariot* in South India, from Bangalore to Mysore and the incredible and indelible historic sights of Hampi and Badami. Then there's the *Palace on Wheels* and *Royal Rajasthan on Wheels*.

I've travelled many times in India, and mostly on the ground, on my feet, on buses, in private cars, in taxis and tuk-tuks, on Royal Enfield motorcycles.

But I like travelling on these trains in India very much. They tend to move at night, and you get off to explore somewhere new every day, with sightseeing and guides arranged for you. It is an easy way to dip into a lot of India. Dive in, submerge yourself, then retreat to your comfortable cabin and familiar food at tea time.

As good as the getting off is this staying on board, watching India pass by, framed by the train's window is better. India viewed; India through net curtains, drawn back by day.

In a station, we stop briefly, with the window of my carriage directly opposite a water tap and trough. It feels slightly corrupt to spy like this, knowing my window is tinted so that I can look out, but no-one can see in, but I can't help watching an elderly woman who comes to the brass tap, shiny from so many hands over so many years.

She turns it on so that it runs just a little, catching the shaft of morning sun falling across it. Treating each drop as precious, she cups first her left hand and washes her face, then her right hand and washes her neck, and then, with an index finger, cleans her teeth. And then she turns away towards that sun, places those hands together, and holds them up, her lips just perceptibly moving in a prayer of thanks for this small and enormous gift.

A ritual in this place of complexity – of perhaps millions of Hindu gods and goddesses, where Lord Krishna alone has 108 names.

And then we move on from this small-town scene and back into agricultural lands. Two white cows pull an old timber cart, their horns painted glossy red, and decorated. Wheat cut by hand and stacked in child-size stoops. Corn and bananas in this black-soil part of Rajasthan, not like the dry zone we've just travelled through.

The crop is harvested, the grain threshed into a big pile on the earth, and after it's been bagged up in cotton or hessian sacks, the goats or cattle come in to clear what's left on the ground. Something for all.

What has struck me so on this particular visit is just how much agriculture there is through Rajasthan and Maharashtra states. Even through the dry zone.

Does that sound silly? Do we think of India more as jam-packed full cities, honking traffic, Bollywood bonhomie and slums than as farming communities, clearly co-operative and knowledgeably productive, harvesting by hand sizeable piles of grain from each tiny field?

Yet here there are wheat and barley, pulses, oilseeds, sugar cane and cotton. Two cropping seasons and irrigation water from wells.

And even here, so much colour, across the fields like God (whatever your god) dipped his brush in a childish palette and dotted the landscape. It is a sweeping statement, for sure, but there is an intrinsic aesthetic and artistic intent to so much of India's everyday life. India is varicoloured, psychedelic.

And so the scenes unfold…

Children play in a pool of water, running in and out, muddying it up, as their mothers wash and scold. Cloth spread around on the ground to dry, the raw colours of a rainbow, a big cotton sheet covered with pink Hindu swastikas hanging over a wire fence.

A Hindu temple, Raisoni Fun School. Tin roofs on tiny homes, with rocks to keep the sheets on.

Cow dung drying in round pats, ready to burn. And rubbish. Just so much plastic in some places – lining the side of the tracks, with the trains' straight-through toilets browning the sleepers between.

At Manmad Junction in Maharashtra State, a crucial junction where seven rail lines converge, the hot wind whips paper and plastic into the sky and it wheels against the sun like a massive flock of birds, throwing dancing shadows on the ground.

Railways were introduced to India by the British in 1853 and by 1947 – the year of India's independence from Britain – there were forty-two rail systems.

Travelling in trains in India is part of this complicated nation's history. It is doubtless part of its future. And it is the theme of this warming morning, rolling by.

Walking Beside the River Thames

The Thames is the longest river entirely in England. At least twenty tributaries flow into it, and it has more than eighty islands.

But, flowing through the heart of London, the Thames is perhaps best known as the foreground for photographs of London's Houses of Parliament, the reason for Tower Bridge, the front yard of the Tower of London, something that the London Eye is set against, and for cruise boats to float on.

All that touristy stuff.

Yet it is a dramatic waterway. A real, gutsy, characterful and dangerous river. Years ago, I knew the mother of a Thames waterman – a young chap who accidentally fell off the barge he was working on, was immediately sucked down into the powerful, swirling beige waters of the tidal Thames and was only spat back up to the surface days later, a long way down the river. (The moment he vanished, she said, the Weeping Jesus plant in her lounge room started to drop tears, only stopping the moment his body was found. The only time it ever wept.)

The River Thames has an artistic life. Canaletto, J. M. W. Turner, Claude Monet and James Abbott McNeill Whistler all extensively painted it.

It has a literary life. Julius Caesar's writings on his second expedition to Britain in 54 BC contain long accounts of the Thames.

Far more contemporarily, it set the theme for Jerome K. Jerome's *Three Men in a Boat* in 1889 – three chaps on holiday on the river in a small boat. Its smaller reaches were the setting for Ratty, Toad and co to simply mess about in boats in Kenneth Grahame's *The Wind in the Willows*, which he wrote in 1908, and Charles Dickens thoroughly described it, and the lives of those working on it, in *Our Mutual Friend*, which he finished in 1865. And many of these books may suit Ben McCann – a sixth generation Thames waterman.

"I read books about London and books about boats," he says as he skippers the tourist cruise boat *Millennium Dawn* between the London Eye and Greenwich. "We watermen are very proud of our history – and proud of the history of London and the Thames."

The first bridge was built over the Thames in AD 43, says Mr McCann, and it was the only bridge until the 1700s. Westminster Bridge was built in 1746.

Today there are twenty-nine bridges over the tidal Thames, and seventy-five across its non-tidal reaches, but previously people had to use watermen to cross the river – they'd wait on the bank, and the river workers took them along and across it. The human history of the River Thames is strong and long, dating back to Neolithic times, but it is the natural, environmental, nothing-to-do-with-you life of the tidal Thames that I am particularly interested in. For the Thames has a massive, natural life and has a great influence on the North Sea. Its tide can rise 8 metres and run at more than 11 kilometres per hour.

The average human walking speed is 5 kilometres per hour and a good, strong paddler in a fast sea kayak can maintain a speed of perhaps nine.

But the river's first path wasn't through here at all. For nearly 60 million years until the great ice sheet of the Quaternary Ice Age formed, some 450,000 years ago, the Thames flowed through what is now Oxfordshire, then bore north-east to drain into the sea near Ipswich. But the ice dammed the river in Hertfordshire, creating ice lakes which eventually flooded, with the thaw, pretty much on to the river's present day course to and through London.

For 89 kilometres, from Teddington Lock to the mouth of the Thames Estuary, the North Sea brings its influence. And for some of this, the Thames Path follows the bank.

The Thames Path is a 294 kilometre National Trail footpath, running from the Thames Flood Barrier at Woolwich, just over 7 kilometres downstream from Greenwich, to Kemble in Gloucestershire.

But I am particularly interested in the tidal Thames and today I am just tackling the 12-kilometre leg from Greenwich to the London Eye.

I easily take public transport to this favourite place – home of Greenwich Mean Time, the Royal Observatory, the National Maritime Museum, and the only surviving British tea clipper, *Cutty Sark*, which was launched in 1869.

I easily pick up the Thames Path, which leads through Deptford, Rotherhithe and Bermondsey, after which I look across the water to the huge development of Canary Wharf, with industrial riverside buildings, many of which were primarily used for trade to the Canary Islands, being converted into accommodation.

I have previously passed this on *Millennium Dawn's* river trip from the London Eye to Greenwich, Ben McCann commenting that this development has taken thirty years so far, with thirty to go.

All well and good, but I keep my eye on the water, brown as the result of up to an estimated 300,000 tonnes of sediment a year, not pollution.

The dawn of the flushing toilet might once have turned this into a sewer but river authorities say that the Thames today is cleaner than at any time in the twentieth century, and recognised as one of the cleanest metropolitan estuaries in Europe.

And on my day walk, I spot a raft of birdlife, most commonly cormorants, oystercatchers, mallards, shelducks and those bulky and hook-beaked herring gulls, but also herons and a crested grebe.

Under the surface, the tidal Thames has some 115 species of fish, including thin-lipped mullet, flounder, smelt and perch, and is rich in invertebrates. It is reported that colonies of short-snouted seahorses have also recently been found in the river.

And it is the river that mesmerises me. I turn my eyes from the buildings and keep them on the pull and swirls of the water.

Soon I am past Tower Bridge, City Hall (which looks like a motorcyclist's helmet) and at the London Eye on the South Bank.

But I carry on, still caught by the tide, through the riverside gardens of the Albert Embankment, Lambeth, and over the Vauxhall Bridge turning left towards Pimlico.

At the Westminster Boating Centre in Grosvenor Road, three sailing dinghies are moored, like ducks in a row. And it is here I have to leave the river, peeling off towards my hotel, but with a vague dream. The whole 294 kilometres of the Thames Path National Trail?

Now, that's an interesting thought – a transect through the English landscape and history of my childhood.

London is famous for its art collections but you don't have to go indoors to see them. For many of the most interesting sculptures are strewn around the city.

This is accessible art.

In fact, it is so accessible that I watch a succession of tourists haul themselves up on to the lions surrounding Lord Horatio Nelson's column in Trafalgar Square, to have themselves photographed.

It seems so strange to me to see three women riding one of the lions, and another few hauling one another up to be photographed mock-snogging another, that it sparks the thought of taking particular note of the art around London's streets.

My approach is haphazard. I just bump into things, though not literally. (And that makes the point that, in London, you can just walk out of your hotel, without a plan, and fill the day with interest.)

I am struck in Whitehall by the statue of *Clive*. Not by the sculpture itself, but more by this nomenclature. For it strikes me as frightfully cool to be remembered in such a formal way, in such a massively important venue, just by a single name. Like Sting or Sade. Or Pooh. Ha!

Only, of course, this is a surname.

"Must be Clive of India..." a woman, standing near me, says to her husband. And I suspect it is just a phrase that rolls off her Cockney tongue, and not a real explanation, and probably no exact understanding of the fact that Robert Clive, first Baron Clive of Plassey, was both a British general and colonial administrator and served as governor of Bengal, India, from 1765 to 1767. Or that he was implicated in corruption scandals surrounding the East India Company and suicided.

Bengal's growing reputation and position attracted Portuguese, Dutch, French, Danish and English traders. In 1740, it became practically independent from Mughal rule of India, which gave the East India Company, with its lust for power, an opportunity for political interference. Still, Clive got a terrific statue, on a substantial plinth.

"My uncle was called Clive," the man replies to his wife. Strange – so was mine.

In the Natural History Museum, a sculpture of Charles Darwin sits at the top of the stairs in the main entrance hall, overlooking the hundreds of thousands of people who pour in to see this wonderful storehouse's artefacts. The English natural historian, of course, sailed on HMS *Beagle's* voyage around the southern hemisphere from 1831 to 1836 and was a proponent of the theory of evolution by natural selection. He published *The Origin of Species* in 1859 and *The Descent of Man* in 1871.

The daily tide of faces flooding into the Victoria and Albert Museum from all corners of the world surely proves his theories.

Look up in the museum and its pillars are adorned with climbing monkeys which look ready to spring to life (easily an inspiration for a *Night at the Museum* movie).

In the Victoria and Albert, art students sit on fold-up chairs, sketching sculptures. Art on art. Interesting, if not a little confusing. Classic art reconstructed by contemporary art.

And contemporary sculpture, surely, also in the shop window displays, particularly at Christmas. Selfridges, Harrods. All the usual suspects. Characters set in freakish winter scenes; human forms made of twisted plastic.

At the offices of the International Maritime Organisation, on the Albert Embankment of the River Thames, facing the Houses of Parliament, there is something more didactic. The bow of a cargo ship rams out of the building, and a man standing on its bow stops me in my tracks.

The International Maritime Organisation is truly international, with 158 member states, and the sculpture is the work of Michael Sandle, serving to remind us of the important role seafaring plays in global trade and development. About 95 per cent of world cargo is still moved by sea, and not without cost. The sculpture also serves as a memorial to sailors lost at sea.

British sculptor Sandle says, "I have attempted to transform a ship into a cathedral. Visitors looking up at it at close range would experience resonances similar to being in one; it is not for nothing that the longitudinal axis of a cathedral is called the nave."

But, despite this, it is not this – or any other of the sculptures I have mentioned – that leaves "that echo" in my head. It is a statue stumbled upon, again by chance, in Pimlico Gardens, near Vauxhall Bridge, overlooking a wide, mud-flanked thigh of the tidal Thames.

The big statue is of a man wearing a Roman toga, right shoulder and breast bared. Nothing remarkable in that, but when I walk towards it, the writing on the plinth reads, "William Huskisson. Statesman. Born 1770. Died 1830."

It doesn't sound very Roman, and the anomaly prompts me to look into the life of Mr Huskisson. A natural serendipity reveals that he was born in Malvern, Worcestershire, where I grew up (I am too old and experienced to be surprised by this).

He was a British statesman, financier, and member of the British Parliament for several constituencies. Including Liverpool.

All well and good, but this, unfortunately, is most definitely not Mr Huskisson's claim to fame. For, for all his good works, Mr Huskisson is most remembered as the world's first widely reported railway casualty. And what a casualty. He was run over by George Stephenson's *Rocket* locomotive.

Now, here's an odd thing. The previous day I was standing before Stephenson's actual *Rocket* in London's excellent Science Museum, wondering at the fact that it was there, in front of me. The actual 1829 Stephenson's *Rocket* locomotive. The real deal; pivotal in setting about a change in technology and manufacturing and freight that is so obvious in the world around me today.

And I was as much bemused by the sight of two Eastern European women dramatically, purposefully and stylistically photographing one another in front of it.

I was bemused by the shift in the world and "borders" and by the new global currents and drifts of people and trade which now seem so normal.

Stephenson's *Rocket*, and its implications, occupied my mind so much yesterday – and today I stand before Mr Huskisson (in a toga), who was mown down by it. It severely damaged his leg and he died some days later. (Stephenson was said to have been distraught.)

The statue I stumble across in Pimlico Gardens is similar to one in a monument in Chichester Cathedral (another of those coincidences, as I was born in Kent and spent childhood days at Chichester), which also depicts Huskisson as a Roman in a toga.

And, to this moment, here beside the Thames I can't explain the toga.

A Slice of England by Rail

London's Paddington Station is rather like the shunting shed in the *Thomas the Tank Engine* books. As I stand looking at two trains poised side by side, ready for their runs, they look for all the world like Henry and Gordon. So much so that I can almost hear them exchanging pleasantries and advice.

"Now, don't go too fast down that hill, Henry…" instructs Gordon, who feels himself the most important engine.

And just then a modern train manager – the equivalent of the Fat Controller – comes and stands next to them, back to me, legs spread wide in an inverted V, fists on hips.

As if to say, "Now, come on you two. Go about your business."

I hear the echo of the stories conjured up by the Rev. Wilbert Vere Awdry to amuse his son, Christopher, in bed with measles, and first published as *The Three Railway Engines* in 1945. *Thomas the Tank Engine* followed, one of twenty-six annual books about the trains' mild adventures.

I am not a train buff. I rarely travel on trains. I am not particularly interested in them. I most certainly have never sat on sidings or bridges in the rain in a parka with a small notebook collecting their numbers. Trainspotting? Whoever thought of that?

Though I appreciate the environmental benefits of the modern high-tech train, run on sustainably created electricity, they rather lost my attention after they stopped puffing steam, not that I actually remember it, but scarlet engines puffing white cottonwool balls as they climbed through emerald hills is imprinted into me, as it must surely have been into so many children of my English generation.

Here at Paddington, it is another era. I key my booking number into a machine to collect the pre-purchased, seat-allocated ticket I've bought over the internet for the trip from London to Worcester, in the West Midlands, which will take just under two-and-a-half hours. As if to emphasise the change of epochs, next to me is a statue of Isambard Kingdom Brunel who built Paddington Station's main train shed as Great Western Railway's London terminus in 1854. Indeed, I will leave from one of the eight platforms still under the original three spans of his shed. I feel Mr Brunel would have been thrilled by the internet and rail travel's technological advances.

The great engineer is rightly acknowledged at Paddington, as is a small bear invented by Michael Bond, who was found here by the fictional Brown family. In *A Bear Called Paddington*, Bond wrote, "Mr and Mrs Brown first met Paddington on a railway platform. In fact, that was how he came to have such an unusual name for a bear, for Paddington was the name of the station."

Digital information board, automatic barriers, automatic doors. And then the train slides almost silently from the shed.

Considering London is so big-city, it is surprising how quickly we are flushed down this shiny steel artery and out of the heart of it. Past the backs of sheds and workshops. Soccer pitches, empty on this autumnal morning. Past the industry, walls topped with razor wire, rows of vans parked in compounds, and soon at Slough.

Slough should be pronounced with an "ow", rhyming with bough, but it is an old British joke to call it "sluff", rhyming with rough. Slough, of course, is also the noun for a swamp.

And then we are moving again. The train is quiet, smooth. No rocking, no clickety-clack.

Train travel gives you a slice of country. It takes you into places you'd never otherwise be. It takes you past the end of gardens. Washing on the line, children wrestling over a bike, a couple, hands on hips, having it out, face to face. An old man on the back step blowing smoke rings into the cold morning.

It takes you past allotments – those neat, orderly blocks of land which are shared and gardened by local people. They are bastions of community, where not only the land but knowledge and friendship are so often shared. Where one man's ability to grow broad beans is happily exchanged for another's expertise with cabbages.

Allotments are havens, in many senses.

The train's route gives glimpses into the back windows of homes, not just their neat, presented front facades.

Televisions flickering, children being fed, ironing being done. It shows you wallpaper and mass-produced prints. It draws back curtains and reveals the intimate.

Twenty-eight minutes from Paddington we have roughly followed the River Thames not only in Reading, but a long, long way from London. We pass a new high-rise housing estate with vivid blue sloping roofs, which someone who wasn't going to live there probably thought was a clever idea.

After Reading, we are in surprisingly open country – lots of fields and bouncy hedgerows which I imagine full of chaffinches and great tits. Blackbird song, long, languid summer evenings. Cowslips in spring.

There is just the occasional council estate but these rural curves of all-alike brick houses looked purchased-by-the-renters and spruced up, not inhabited by the CHAVs I have been hearing about in Britain – "Council Housed and Violent".

Under "right to buy" legislation introduced in Britain in the 1980s, two million council houses have been sold to tenants. The scheme went cool but discounts to allow people to buy their council homes is back on the agenda.

There is a chatty announcement over the speakers. The train manager says there are hot bacon baguettes in the buffet car. Baguettes? Whatever happened to the British Rail bacon butty? But he adds that the buffet car is next to First Class, which is a long way from my reserved seat A33 in the first Standard carriage, at the other end of the train. I fancy a bacon baguette, but don't fancy wriggling through all those doors.

I didn't pay for First Class in the First Great Western train, but I sort-of wish I had, as it has bigger seats and they're leather, and just at this moment I rather fancy being a toff.

There's light rain coming across the windows and we've slowed to walking pace. It gives me time to consider these windows, which are so heavily amber-tinted that they look nicotine stained.

Does anyone else remember that? When people smoked so heavily that windows became encrusted with the yellow of nicotine? Perhaps some clever designer somewhere is making an oblique historical reference – a visual nostalgia for the past era – or perhaps it was just deemed more cheering than the usual steely blue-grey.

It gives a rather jaundiced view of the world, as if I was incapable of developing that myself.

Actually, that's not true. I feel very cheerful today. After all, I have good news. I am solving the world's population problem. It has passed seven billion humans. I heard this morning on the BBC News that "somewhere in the world, every eighty seconds a woman gives birth", so I am going to track her down and ask her to stop.

And now we have stopped completely, at an undetermined spot somewhere on Great Britain's more-than 16,000 kilometres of national rail network.

"We are just waiting to cross over on to the other line," announces the train manager. "We are just waiting for a high-speed train." This seems a good plan and, pushing a cushion of wind that rocks us, the high-speed train soon comes flying past, busy-busy-busy on his way to London and back to the shed. (Gordon in a rush?)

I am sitting in a cluster of four chairs, around a table, with two power sockets. I'm on my own and there are just a couple of chaps near me, in the double seat opposite, a young Japanese lady yawning a couple of rows down and two youngsters chatting in respectably low tones.

But then, I booked into this Quiet Carriage, knowing that the use of mobile phones is not allowed. (It is such a pleasure knowing I won't have to listen to what "Sharon and Chazzer" did last night). The sign says, "Welcome to this carriage. Please keep noise levels to a minimum in this carriage. Thank you."

There isn't even that low ch-chacha-ch-chacha-ch-chacha-ch of not-so-personal music system percussion that leaks from headphones and seems to pervade most parts of the world.

We pass the blunt tower of a Norman church (it reminds me of a Tom Sharpe novel which describes such a scene, early in the morning, and comments that the only discernible sign of pollution is a solitary jogger) – and, twenty-five minutes from Reading, arrive at Oxford Station. Suddenly there's a lot of action. At least twenty people I hadn't even noticed in this carriage's high-back chairs, and certainly hadn't heard a whisper from, rise like zombies from the earth, and file off. Businesspeople, students, backpackers – all among the almost five-and-a-half million passengers that will arrive or depart this station.

No one gets on.

"This is the Hereford service," chimes our train manager, as if to explain. (There are less than a fifth as many arrivals and departures annually in Hereford.)

He has more to offer, as we embark on the 139 kilometres of what is now The Cotswold Line, between Oxford and Hereford. The line between Oxford and Worcester was built under an 1845 Act of Parliament and opened in 1851 as part of the Oxford, Worcester and Wolverhampton Railway (OW&W), but originally nicknamed "Old Worse and Worse", for its regular derailments and construction tribulations.

The train manager announces a contemporary one, "All the stations from here on have short platforms." This doesn't sound commensurate with our long train…

"You need to make your way to the front of the train and alight from carriages A and B only."

Clearly good advice. It could be a long way down from C, and seeing as the toffs are now in the back of the train and will have to wriggle through all those doors I mention, I feel rather chuffed that I am here in Standard.

"Only the Standard class carriages will be next to the platform," confirms the announcement.

Ha! I feel sure this would meet with the approval of the line-laying navvies who arced up in 1851 against work conditions in what is remembered as the Battle of Campden Tunnel.

Hanborough Station. The full stop at the end of another conflict but one which still pervades so many corners of the English psyche. World War II is over but it lives large, particularly through November's remembrances, where there are surely more red poppies in the lapels of the British than ever there were in Flanders Fields. In 1965, Hanborough Station was the destination for "Battle of Britain class locomotive No. 34051 *Winston Churchill*" – appropriately enough, bringing home the body of Sir Winston Churchill, the wartime prime minister.

Hanborough. I've never been here before but now I am here, and then I am gone, but not before I see, from my window, a pretty young lady who is there waiting, beaming, to greet a man with a big suitcase who is clearly her father. She rushes forward to kiss him but he looks furtively around before doing so.

A row of cypress trees on a ridge, a farmhouse, three black horses on vivid green grass. Between Hanborough and Charlbury, the fields turn from green to brown. From pasture to neat, ploughed corduroy. We are in the Evenlode Valley, following the river of the same name, in the charming Cotswolds across land that has been farmed for hundreds of years. Across the parliamentary constituency of Prime Minister Cameron.

Someone at Charlbury Station got a job lot on railings. What's more unfortunate is that they also got a job lot on putrid pink-beige paint but, as we move on again, they blur behind and the world becomes pastoral again. The train is higher up and I look across fields where crows scatter like black confetti from oak trees and there are sheep – fluffy white, black-faced Cheviots so unlike Australia's scrawny, droughted specimens.

These fields have been farmed for hundreds of years, crops rotated, hedgerows kept. A sprawling stone farmhouse with a slate roof sits among them.

The leaves have turned. It is autumn, and rows of gold edge the fields, and soon there will be snow. Soon the squirrels I have been watching, diving into piles of leaves in the hope of fallen nuts, popping their heads up, noisy with leaves, will hibernate. By Kingham, it seems impossible to me that on such a small island, with a mainland population of 60 million, I have spent the vast majority of the last ninety minutes passing through open countryside, seeing so few homes. Indeed, a panel of the revered English journal *Country Life* once judged Kingham to be "England's Favourite Village".

England is still a green and pleasant land.

By Moreton-in-Marsh, we have passed the Roman town of Dorn, and pits where Jurassic clay was mined for the adjacent brickworks.

More importantly, here we move from one geographic and social zone to another, for The Cotswold Line leaves Evenlode, which drains into the River Thames, and crosses into the catchment of the River Severn.

By Moreton-in-Marsh, I feel I am coming home. Crossing the boundary; over the line onto the map of my childhood.

I grew up in these parts and, to a small child, places like Moreton-in-Marsh were the end of the world. As far as you could get on a day trip. As far as my Uncle Clive's white Ford Consul with a red bench seat and metal sun visor could get there-and-back in a day, children asleep on the way home, in the back. As far as you could go without dropping over the edge of the world.

These were the boundaries of my childhood and they gave me an intense sense of belonging, of localisation, of specialisation, of pleasure.

I knew these parts. This landscape, its dimensions, the animals and birds that inhabited it. With England's wild range of local accents, as a child, the people in such places felt as exotically foreign as people of Africa or the far-flung corners Asia do to me now. But, if I listened carefully, and with a little sign language, I could make myself understood.

The only man to join our carriage at Moreton-in-Marsh is wearing a green tweed coat, brown brogue shoes and a herringbone country trilby hat, which he raises slightly as he passes.

Through the Cotswolds, under bridges covered with brambles, and then into a long tunnel, the countryside lost, the windows "blacked out" by its brick walls, reflecting the interior to the carriage back on itself. From my reverie of childhood, I see a stranger. A bald, middle-aged, turkey-necked, bespectacled man stares back at me for the long, long ten seconds. He looks like a distant relative.

Honeybourne (which actually consists of two villages: Church Honeybourne and Cow Honeybourne) then Evesham.

The Vale of Evesham is lush and good-soiled. It is famous for its fruit, and there are rows of big produce sheds, quiet now but busy in season. Plums have been grown in Britain for 2,000 years but the Vale of Evesham has lost 80 per cent of its plum orchards since the end of the World War II, picked off by invading cheaper foreign fruit. But you can still find traditional varieties, like Pershore Yellow Egg, and all manner of other produce…leeks and beetroot, beans and broccoli. Rhubarb and pumpkins.

A sparrowhawk performs a thrilling twirl over electricity pylons, where swallows sit on the wires like musical notes. They wisely stay put. Birch and beech trees. Willows by a winding river; another scene from my literary childhood, a light wind ruffling the water's surface.

The carriage is now empty, and I head to the gents, which is spacious, with a shaver socket and decent-sized mirror.

The doors open automatically – no jangling between them and struggling through them, like in the old days. No danger or the possibility of embarrassment, at all. And it's easy to walk between the rows of seats; no jogging elbows and apologising. I now regret the baguette.

Pershore Station.

It was about this particular place that poet laureate Sir John Betjeman wrote of a love left behind, in the verses of *Pershore Station, or A Liverish Journey First Class*; "Evesham, Oxford and London. The carriage is new and smart/ I am cushioned and soft and heated/ with a deadweight in my heart." He had paid the extra, of course, but it strikes me that Pershore's short platform provides a rather interesting analogy to being left high and dry.

A lady who looks a little like my sister gets in, sits near me, smiles and says "good morning" in an accent I recognise. I'm almost home; in the homeland of my childhood, with the family I miss, the weight in some mostly ignored corner of my heart lifting a little. Most of me exists wherever I am in the world, and in the moment, but a little part of me is lodged here, in this place and in the echoes of a blessed rural childhood.

Worcester soon. The train manager's voice comes over the speakers again, "The next station is Worcester Shrub Hill." Shrub Hill is still something of a hub, connected to commuter lines heading for busy Birmingham New Street Station. The voice continues, "This train continues to Great Malvern, Colwall, Ledbury and Hereford. Change for the rest of England."

But it seems to me that the essence of England hasn't changed much at all. And it seems that a small part of me hasn't either.

Driving to the Heart of Australia

I walk up to Uluru and touch it. I put my hands, fingers spread wide, on the big, red, warm skin of it. I am here. I have finally driven to the heart of Australia, my home for most of my adult life.

Towering above me, what some still think of as Ayers Rock is like a heart – as much like a great, livid, pulsing body part as a piece of geology, left rising nearly 350 m from the flat central desert as the land around it eroded away over hundreds of millions of years.

Driving to the heart of Australia has been as simple as packing the four-wheel drive and heading north-east from Perth, through Kalgoorlie, Kookynie, Laverton, Warburton, Warakurna, Docker River and finishing at Yulara. It has been as easy as camping along the way, warming myself by mulga fires, navigating the gravel road, seeing the country pass and change.

As simple as stopping in at roadhouses for diesel and a chat. At Laverton's Great Beyond Visitor Centre for excellent cappuccino and maps galore. At Tjukayirla Roadhouse for more great coffee and to buy authentic Aboriginal woomeras and spears made by

Mr West in Warburton. At Warakurna Roadhouse, a shop that has raspberry cordial opposite a row of vehicle tyres, and a gallery where we buy local Aboriginal art, the money going straight into this community.

Rather unexpectedly, the drive turns into an authentic indigenous experience. I say "unexpected" because there is no string of indigenous tourism operators along the road – just Warburton Art Centre and, more importantly, people living at communities, in their country.

Outside Warakurna Roadhouse, before visiting nearby Giles Weather Station, I end up leaning against a windowless vehicle, chatting with the four locals inside, who've just been helping their elders prepare for a walk along a traditional line through the Rawlinson Range, and have come down to the roadhouse for an ice-cream.

"You just wandering round," the bloke in the back asks.

"Yeah."

"Good on ya. I reckon it's a better pace here than in the city."

"Me too."

"Yeah. Well, see ya, bro."

There have been the simple wonders of seeing budgerigars flying like a madly fluttering flag (green, yellow, green, yellow…) and having a dingo run out and canter alongside the vehicle, his two ochre-haired fellow dogs lurking back in the bush.

There has been a string of *gnammas* – holes in the rock full of fresh water – and the broad lunar landscape of Lake Throssell, a significant salt lake.

It has been as easy as setting out from Perth at 6.30 am on a Saturday morning, taking it easy every day, and rolling into the Voyages Ayers Rock Resort early on the Friday afternoon, for four nights of comfort before driving home. A two-week mix of outback travel – with one night at Kookynie Grand Hotel and five nights camping; four nights of luxury resort holiday; then more outback travel and four nights camping, and a last night back at Kookynie.

I also decided to drive "there and back" along the Great Central Road – giving a chance to spend time on the return trip at places sighted on the way there, and for a two-night camp and explore at a particularly interesting spot. "There and back" works – I like it. Everywhere looks different travelling in the opposite direction, in different light.

You feel like you've totally absorbed a place. A route.

It all ends up feeling like I've been away a month.

Those are the practicalities.

And yet driving to the heart of Australia has been as complex as working over many decades to really learn and understand this land – its geology and geography, fauna and flora, its birds, its ancient and modern cultures, the humour, the clothes, the vehicles.

To finishing up feeling at home here. It has been as complex, intellectually and emotionally, as coming to the point where I want to make this pilgrimage, if you want to call it that…to drive from the rim of the continent to its hub. To its core. To what literally is its red centre. Of wanting to drive to the heart of Australia, in every sense.

And in all that, I have been alone. Some journeys have to be undertaken that way – from the practicalities of research to the peculiarities of emotion, they have to be a singular business.

We all undertake our own journeys, in that sense. But on the Great Central Road itself, between Perth and Uluru, I am not alone.

In the passenger seat of my old Landcruiser is artist and wife Virginia Ward. Alongside in his Hilux is Grady Brand, senior curator of Perth's Kings Park and Botanic Garden and partner Lesley Hammersley, who is director of horticulture and conservation at Kings Park and Botanic Garden.

Great botanical specialists, naturalists, interpreters of the environment; friends-for-life.

Grady and Lesley are on two weeks' leave – on holiday – but don't mind this intrusion into their privacy. They are happy for you to share this journey with us all.

They believe in West Australians developing our sense of place.

It's important to travel with people who have the same rhythm, and we have travelled WA's landscape and remote places together many times before. We are compatible travellers.

There are Grady and Lesley appreciating and interpreting the landscape through its plants – stopping regularly as they see the flora change. We climb a red dune, dig around for beetle carapaces, lick the nectar from flowering honey grevillea *(Grevillea eriostachya).* At one place Grady excitedly collects the botanical samples and seed of the bastard coolibah *(Eucalyptus intertexta)*, which has never before been collected for Kings Park. At another, Finke River mallee *(Eucalyptus sessilis)*, which nudges into WA from the Northern Territory in only a tiny patch near Docker River. (That night, we sit around the campfire, discussing how fortunate we are to live lives where passion rubs out the line between "work" and "holiday".)

There is Virginia appreciating and interpreting the landscape through the book she draws in as we drive the land – the red road's corrugations vibrating the tip of her pencil, adding to the darkness of her shading. (The land itself intervening in the artwork).

The road, the desert oaks, and then the beautiful Schwerin Mural Crescent Range are all there, in the notebook. And she sits in the late afternoon in the Petermann Ranges, close to the NT border, and paints wonderful strips of landscape in watercolours that merge and spread like the softening, rosy light itself.

Throughout the journey, somewhere about 4 pm, sensing the day dying and chill night coming, we edge off the road to find remote camping spots, and make ourselves comfortable. The others cook wonderful food. None of us believes in car fridges, so the camp oven works overtime with sweet potatoes, white potatoes, carrots and garlic. Lettuce rolled in damp tea towels lasts nearly a week. Avocados seem to last forever. There's a dish made from fresh mushrooms. Virginia brings her spices and makes kedgeree.

And we all interact with the country in, perhaps, rather less harmonious fashion, when we all get out our ukuleles after dinner. (*Five Foot Two, Eyes of Blue, Country Roads…*)

And so the days pass in this easy-paced, stop-and-go, fashion.

For we are not just motoring flat-out to Uluru; we are driving to the heart of Australia.

Uluru is ever-changing. The Ayers Rock you see as you drive towards it early in the morning seems to have a completely different character to the great, red body of rock that you see even a few minutes later, as you turn the bend by the Uluru-Kata Tjuta Aboriginal Cultural Centre.

Not only does it change colour – from mauve to red, from dark to light, with clouds shading it in ever-changing patterns – but it seems to change in spirit, in energy, in essence.

I have seen Uluru a number of times before, and always expected to be underwhelmed (we've all seen the photographs and postcards, haven't we) and it has always taken me by surprise. It is somewhere fundamental – somewhere for every Australian to come.

And it is completely remarkable – not only on every visit, but every day during that visit, every hour within those days.

Even after walking for three-and-a-half hours around the 10-kilometre base, when I catch a glimpse of it in the vehicle's rear view mirror as I drive away, it's like seeing something new. There is no sense of being done with it.

Geologically, Uluru is a sedimentary sandstone formation which, at 348 metres tall, is as high as a ninety-five storey building. Over millions of years the land around this harder formation has eroded, leaving it rising out of the flat central desert – what we see today started to appear about 100 million years ago. Technically speaking, Uluru is an inselberg, or island mountain, and a mix of mostly feldspar, with up to 35 per cent quartz and then some rock fragments.

Spiritually, for the Anangu traditional owners of the Uluru-Kata Tjuta National Park, it is the centre of the universe and the home of the Earth Mother. *Tjukurpa* – the ancestral period when the world was being formed – is central to Anangu life and the *tjukurpa* story at Uluru involves *mala* (the hare wallaby), *kuniya* (woma python) and *liru* (poisonous snake).

In terms of tourism, it is of course, one of Australia's three big must-do icons. More than 400,000 people a year visit Uluru, and more than 60 per cent of them from overseas – ticking off one corner of the triangle…"*the rock, the reef and the Opera House*".

Anangu people ask that visitors don't climb this World Heritage Site, out of respect as a sacred place, and also for safety reasons. At least thirty-five people have died doing so.

In 1985, the Hawke government granted the Anangu freehold title of Uluru and Kata-Tjuta – the Olgas – and the Anangu people leased the land back to the Commonwealth Government for ninety-nine years to be jointly run as Uluru–Kata Tjuta National Park.

In 1993, the agreed joint name became "Ayers Rock/Uluru", the former coming from surveyor William Gosse naming it for the then chief secretary for South Australia, Sir Henry Ayers, in 1873.

In 2002, the official name was reversed to "Uluru/Ayers Rock".

The Olgas are now more known as Kata Tjuta. Within sight of Uluru, their thirty-six domes always remind me of a pile of soft, rounded babies.

Formed perhaps 850 million years ago, these granulite forms were thrust northwards over metamorphic rocks some 550 million years ago.

Although both Uluru and Kata Tjuta are made of sediment, both have a chemical composition similar to granite. Scientists using techniques date them at 600 million years old.

I stroll up the Valley of the Winds to the Karu Lookout, staring over these baby bumps and back towards Uluru. And from here, it looks quite different again.

As you have read, even though Grady Brand is on holiday, he can't stop collecting. With his backpack loaded with plant-collecting bags and secateurs, he sets off up the rocky side of the range, in search of plants.

On the map, he has shown me a cluster of red dots out here in the Great Victoria Desert, quite close to Western Australia's border with the Northern Territory.

Up that sheer rocky side, he hopes there are a few more *Prostanthera centralis* plants, though a hot fire has been through, riding high up the shoulders of this range.

"These are very fragile places," Grady says. And fragile plant systems, too.

It's not just that Grady can't stop collecting – more that he clearly can't stop being enthralled by WA's arid landscape and excited by its flora. He can't stop interpreting and interacting with this land he lives on, and which lives with him.

Both *centralis* and the other plant he's particularly interested in here, caustic bush *(Sarcostemma viminale)*, are, he says "very unusual". Caustic bush is rare in that it is a true WA succulent.

"Particularly the caustic bush is a very unusual plant," Grady says. "So, for interpreting the landscape it's a good one to use in the botanic garden. It's how you can tell many stories because of its unusual form. It's a vehicle to describe the landscape.

"Picking out plants that are weird and unusual tells you about a remarkable place."

Prostanthera centralis falls into the other good display category – "just pretty and attractive".

He explains: "It's the opposite to what this environment is. It's a hard, a prickly, environment but among it are these jewels that are pretty and delicate flowers."

Centralis is a "category three" plant, meaning there are several known populations, but Grady says "Collecting it now broadens the collection of plants that are on display to the public."

Kings Park and Botanic Garden displays plants on a regional basis..."it celebrates the regions of WA".

"The other thing about the gathering of the plants is that the knowledge of cultivating WA's flora, on a world scale, is very underdeveloped. Seeing them in their environment gives you more understanding of their needs.

"That's why the park still has a collector and staff go too – it helps to unlock some of the mysteries."

Grady says that the science of keeping seeds and their long-term storage is so much more developed, that collecting now is as much about conserving for the future – "protecting the flora".

We are sitting in this remote and remarkable range near the border, in the arid lands we both love, by a fire of mulga wood, a good meal cooking.

We have travelled WA's remote places many times before – we know each other well.

But when I ask Grady what coming to a place like this means to him, he takes a long time to answer. With his lap full of plant books, he just looks slowly around the gorge, its trees and slopes, and thinks.

"I think coming to a new place just reinforces how diverse WA landscapes are and how they accommodate so many microclimates for a range of species. It reinforces the complexity of WA."

And what about emotionally, I prompt him? (I know it has a big emotional impact on him.) Tell me about that.

"I think it's because you become so busy doing the other stuff in your life and doing these things just re-energises you for the main task that you do all the time."

In other words, even though he has been collecting all day, and just sat filling in the books detailing those collections (the location, terrain type, and many other categories) and bagging them in a specific way to travel home in good condition, this is still a holiday.

He adds, "The basic reason that gardening is a popular pastime is because it is linked to emotion. It's about looking after yourself better and being in touch with the emotional side."

4

Rain

As I write this book, *Beautiful Witness*, my novel *As the River Runs* has been published and has a life. I perform some of the novel's story to music. While the book's plot is a secret proposal to dam a river and pipe water from remote country to the city, for me the real story is about empowerment through honesty and integrity, and about how a portrait can be influenced by the frame around it. Country can do that to us. Change the landscape around us, and we might look different, too.

At this moment, I am also fully immersed in writing another novel, set in agriculture in both the remote eastern edge of the Wheatbelt of Western Australia and the more delicate wheat fields and hop gardens of England. In both landscapes, water is crucial.

Wherever I travel, conservation and landscape issues often manifest in concerns over fresh water; while the number of humans is the underlying environmental pressure, it is in water issues that it surfaces. As I write this, around 800 million people around the world are still without good drinking water, two-thirds of the world's population faces conflict over water, and around 100 countries are involved in violent clashes because of water-related crises.

And so, perhaps, with all this in my head, it is not surprising that I have themed this chapter on rain. Soft, refreshing rain. And once again I see these thoughts rise together in the echo of a hymn from my childhood...

We plough the fields, and scatter the good seed on the land.
But it is fed and watered by God's almighty hand.
He sends the snow in winter, the warmth to swell the grain,
The breezes and the sunshine, and soft refreshing rain.

Casey begs to differ. He doesn't like getting wet but I have, on more than a couple of occasions, found him waiting listlessly where some porter's left him, in the rain, soaked through. (Is there anything worse than grumpy baggage?)

Rainforests are quite difficult places to work. Photographically, I need long lenses for wildlife, which is often high in the canopy, and it's generally dark and I'm shooting against the light. Add serious rain, a bit of mud and quite a few leeches and you have demanding circumstances. I have experienced this, for example, in the rainforests of Borneo and Madagascar, sensitive digital camera with its 400 mm lens and 2× teleconverter slung over my shoulder in a long roll-top, waterproof bag; smaller camera in another waterproof bag slung over the other shoulder; backup body in a waterproof backpack. There I am trying to keep it all dry, to keep the end of the lenses clear of fogging and rain smear, sliding around in the mud.

And back in my room at whatever-lodge, there is Casey, still morose. Oddly enough, at one lodge there is a rather elegant pair of stand-on scales, of classic design with weights, much as it dates back to perhaps more than 2,000 BC in the Indus Valley and, in the current human era, championed by Englishman Richard Salter in 1770.

And, indeed, these are vintage Salter scales.

Intrigued to see them on the verandah when I arrive, I weigh Casey, just to see them work; to hear the clunk of brass. On another whim, I weigh him again when I leave, and find he is "three pounds, three ounces" heavier; around about 1½ kilograms, or 1½ litres of water, just from the damp which permeates everything inside him.

The Kimberley in the Wet Season

Rain is hammering on the roof and the frogs are calling. It is 3 am, and I have been lying in bed listening to this symphony of the Kimberley's wet season in the north of Western Australia. The pulsing white-noise of rain on tin, now lighter, now heavier and heavier; the chainsaw and motorbike and rhythmically croaking frogs, and the violent percussion of occasional thunder.

I am warm and dry and comfortable in my bed, but it's all too enticing, and I get up and walk to the door.

Lights in the tropical gardens show palm leaves glistening, their fronds waving under the fall of rain.

And I step out into it – the gorgeous just-warm rain, not sharp as needles, but like a stiff gossamer falling in sheets, solid.

And I leave my towel on the teak table under the roof and step into the lap pool. Diluted by the exotic mixer of the freshwater deluge, it has been cooled from the tepid, blood-like temperature of the day – a temperature that seemed so equal to the body's that I felt foetal.

And I stand in the chill and then slide forward and swim, twelve strokes a lap, and then turn and see the sky from the other direction.

It is lit only occasionally by thin, shimmering lightning, for this is not a big Kimberley wet lightning night.

When you get those, the sky pulses like human organs.

You might believe there's Zeus up there in an armchair – a magnificent man with curly beard, given thunder and lightning by the Cyclopes, throwing brilliant white spears. Angry or just reminding us. Or God himself, all in white.

Or you might think it's just an atmospheric electrostatic discharge – a spark – ripping through this Kimberley sky at perhaps 20,000°C, if that's easier to imagine. Heating the air around it to a temperature about three times that of the sun.

Yet, in the morning the rain has gone and it's cooler than Perth. The Kimberley's wet season is, perhaps, my favourite time to be in the north.

There are few visitors, just the locals who have been through a build-up that starts in November – sometimes until it feels like the whole place could burst, that they could burst with the anticipation of rain.

And then it comes. A big drop the size of a twenty cent piece. Then another, and another. The rain has come.

The wet is here. And with the rain comes the release of tension. I've walked outside before now and stood in it, feeling it first like pinpricks and then like knitting needles and then moving in under a verandah and watching it fall in a heavy, solid sheet off the roof. Just being poured straight out of the sky.

And then I realise that moment was exactly 20 years ago. In 1993, I was here in a big wet season.

They called it the wet of the century. The road was closed between Broome and Derby as the Fitzroy River spilled out, red-brown over the country.

There's science and shape behind the three-act annual northern monsoon that's drawn down from India and Asia. First that steamy build-up, with a lot of lightning pulses. Then the deluge arrives, turning rivers to chocolate. And then comes the dramatic greening of the land, a wild, fluoro, high-vis green.

What comes through the Kimberley is part of the bigger Asian–Australian monsoon system that sweeps Indonesia, Malaysia and Papua New Guinea and is crucial to crops, and for refilling underground water supplies.

The Fitzroy River catchment covers 65,000 square kilometres, coming off the high plateau and funnelling into the river and through places like Geikie Gorge. There, I look up high above in the roofed interpretive centre and see a sign near its pinnacle that says, "1993 flood level 2 metres above roof." I am 10 metres above today's river level, and the roof is at least 4 metres tall.

Flooding is part of the rhythm of life here.

Rain is hammering on the roof of the Fitzroy River Lodge on the side of the river in Fitzroy Crossing.

John Rodrigues, of Leedal, which owns the lodge and historic Crossing Inn, tells me that every year there's a lot of work cleaning up after the wet. Last year there was mud this deep on the tennis courts…and he is pointing halfway up his thigh.

"But that's the way it is," he says. "You love it, you hate it."

He loves the place and the rhythm of the land. "When I'm in Perth, I can't wait to get back here," he says.

But there's the erosion and flooding to be watched, and lived with. A sandbar he saw in the river this morning was completely gone by this evening.

In the extensive 'Fitzroy Valley Indigenous Cultural Values Study', a 2001 report for the Water and Rivers Commission by Sandy Toussaint, Patrick Sullivan, Sarah Yu and Mervyn Mularty Junior from the Centre for Anthropological Research at the University of Western Australia, indigenous people unanimously described the long and solid downpour during the wet as a natural way to clean the river.

The research showed that most people were prepared to live with flooding and possible isolation because the result was so positive. "Clean water, and a hope for increase in plants and wildlife, including fish." The river flooding is generally referred to as *warramba*.

Darby Nangkiriny explained to the researchers the importance of a seasonal cycle which relies on flooding. "Big *warramba* is good for the country. When he running, he get *raparapa*, 'side of the river', gets all the dry leaves and old water in the river and some in the creek. Have all the water living in the billabong. Billabongs get their water from the *warramba. Bakarrarra* (dreamtime) story about the big flood because some bad people cause the flood to come. In the *marduwarra* (river) he (*warramba*) finish coming in the cold weather time."

It was also commonly said to the researchers that rain which contains invisible seeds enters the ground, and that it produces animal species associated with water – goannas, frogs, land crabs, freshwater eels, turtles, fish and ducks.

Depending on flood levels, fish may find the barrage on the Fitzroy River impassable for up to ten months of the year.

I sit in shade by the water of an old quarry and Dillon Andrews mentions Jandamarra – the man the whites called Pigeon.

In the 1890s, Jandamarra was caught on the line between black and white cultures. He was a Bunuba man, a talented shooter and rider, who lived in the Napier and Oscar ranges as a youngster, then worked on pastoral stations.

At that time, Aborigines charged with spearing sheep or cattle were chained around the neck and forced to walk to Derby. There, still chained, they worked off their sentences.

Jandamarra, accused of spearing a sheep, was jailed, halting his education in tribal law. When he returned home, he was censured for breaking the strict rules that banned relations between some men and women.

Disenfranchised, he became friends with a police constable named Richardson and started tracking for him, eventually helping to apprehend some of his own tribe. But while they were being held at Lillimilura Police Post over the next few days, tradition ate at him and his loyalties swung.

Jandamarra shot Richardson, set the Aborigines free and stole some guns.

With followers drawn to him, he soon attacked a group of Europeans droving cattle to a station on Bunuba land, killing two at Windjana Gorge. It is said to be the first time that firearms were used against Europeans in such an organised way.

Jandamarra and his gang hid in Windjana Gorge and the Tunnel Creek area and continued their armed rebellion against the settlers.

Late in 1894, a big posse of armed police and station people launched an offensive on Jandamarra's hideout at Windjana. The Aboriginal leader was badly wounded but, as it turned out, did not die. The police set against the camps around Fitzroy Crossing.

For three more years, Jandamarra fought for his country and people, attaining legendary status for his ability to give pursuers the slip. So much so that his own people thought he had magical powers.

Some said he could fly like a bird and disappear like a ghost. Some believed him a manifestation of a spirit that lived in a water soak at Tunnel Creek.

They said only an Aboriginal person of similar powers could end his run.

The police recruited a man in the Pilbara known as Micki, who had no fear of Jandamarra. It was Micki who tracked and eventually killed Jandamarra at Tunnel Creek in 1897.

Jandamarra is usually a focal point of Dillon Andrews' Bungoolee Tours days and the story can only really be told in its country. "When you come back," Dillon says, as we sit by the water. "I will show you the story. You will come back."

Thunder is roaring overhead, and lightning briefly but regularly illuminating the landscape with a weird sodium light. The frogs are calling. I am back at the lodge, perched by the Fitzroy River, watching lightning intermittently illuminating the big, white-bodied eucalypts.

I watch it from the deck outside, and then the rain comes again, and I move in and lie back in my four-poster bed, lights off, watching through the four, fold-back floor-to-ceiling glass doors.

The most dramatic show on Earth from the most comfortable bed on the planet.

Out of the blue, there's a clap of thunder so loud that it feels like it might push straight through the roof. And then it goes quiet.

There's just the rain hammering on the roof and the frogs and insects calling.

A Soft Shower in Bali

The first drops of rain come as we walk slowly through the enchanting village of Nyuh Kuning, just south of Ubud and edged by the Sacred Monkey Forest Sanctuary. Up here, in Bali's central highlands, rain often comes in the warm afternoons.

The quiet street, in this quiet village, with its bungalows and villas, yoga and health centres, is only a stone's throw from the bustling main thoroughfares of Ubud, but a pleasant walk-around world apart.

We stop by a little open shop, where a few wooden monkeys – each just smaller than a soccer ball – are in various stages of being carved. The carver's three mallets lie idle, as do his handmade carving tools, among chips and shavings.

In the shop, there are glass bottles of soft drink, plastic bottles of water, a few biscuits and other bits and pieces.

As we look at the carvings, the rain starts to come harder and the woman inside beckons us in. "Raining," she says. Then she looks up to the sky and smiles. "Raining."

She puts sheets of cardboard on the steps for us to sit on, as if offering the best sofa in the house. We sit and she sits with us and we all huddle in the humid air, watching the deluge thicken.

Another woman, who has a multi-coloured umbrella with a broken spoke, sidles under the shelter too, and sits near me. She has a much-repaired carrier bag, filled mostly with empty water bottles, and she digs around in it and pulls out a flute, which she may want to sell, and plays a few notes, to show it works. I smile but shake my head.

The percussion of the rain grows and another woman appears, walking down the middle of the flooding road. She comes in too, and we all greet one another with nods but she soon sets off again into the rain, and the other two women exchange shrugs and smiles.

As the rain eases we prepare to leave, and the shop woman offers us her umbrella. We thank her but we have our own.

And we step out into the gentle river of the street, and turn to wave her goodbye, and I treasure the minutes we just sat together and watched the rain.

Delhi in the Rain

It comes like a soft veil but drapes hard over the city, adding a zushing sound to the compressing traffic and muting even the chorusing horns. Delhi in real rain. What we used to call "wet rain" when I was a child. The air cools just a little and the moisture in it seems to soak everything. Everything gets wet with a capital W.

It is near the end of the monsoon but it is late this year, and heavy. It falls in great gobs, slapping on concrete polished by wear. It gives the pavements a much-needed sluicing, washing smells into the gutter. It gathers on corners and sprawls out, like the crowd itself.

The cyclists are unperturbed, wet-cottoned and fearlessly peddling their heavy Hercules steeds. The trumpet crescendo rises in this city of motor horns.

It has been a slow, steady day of eating through the traffic. I have come from Jaipur – the pink city of Rajasthan, the city of yellow and orange, where they dare to dye with the stigmas of crocus.

And for more than seven hours we have chomped our way through the crisscrossing traffic and arrived here, first in the satellite outskirts of clean, new buildings and homes set amid green. "The face of new India," the young man with me sighs.

And then into the city proper, with its ageing boulevards and the grand buildings the British Raj built for itself but ended up, just 16 years later, leaving for independent India.

A stream of police sirens is heard behind so we move over and make way for a cavalcade of cars. First a slightly lopsided khaki police Mahindra four-wheel drive, then the Prime Minister of India in a black Toyota Camry, with a gaggle of semi-official vehicles behind and then a cram of traffic urging them on.

The long, blue canopy of Bahrisons Booksellers in Khan Market calls like a siren. It's a higgledy-piggledy affair, crammed with books, and I run my thumb down the many shelves of paperbacks by unknown Indian authors, and take pot luck.

Serendipity. Ah, serendipity. Just before this I was in Arabia, meeting lots of Indians who work there, and yesterday in Jaipur I was with an Indian who told me that he recognised the stories of *Arabian Nights* as old Indian moralistic tales. I had just read some of them, intrigued by their complexity and ability to "jump around" subjects.

I have started to write a story called "India and Arabia" but so far I have only that title and my name at the top and an optimistic idea that loose ends might be tied together into something interesting. And I tilt from the shelf a book called *When Dreams Travel* by Githa Hariharan (possibly simply because the word "travel" triggers a reaction in my index finger), turn it over and read that the book "weaves around Scheherazade – or Shahrzad of the *One Thousand and One Nights* – to deliver a vibrant, inventive story about that old game that's never been played out: the quest for love and power."

And I turn to the inside pages and see Githa Hariharan grew up partially in Mumbai and now lives in New Delhi – here, where I am, in the rain.

There is a long, slow roll of thunder and staccato Hindi blurtings from a loudspeaker, oscillating as if under water.

Delhi in the rain is darkening, and I ride the lift to the seventh floor of my hotel and look out across a city designed by Europeans and inhabited by 17 million Indians, writing a new chapter in its history.

Down in the streets the motorcyclists are soaked across their chests to the top ridge of their shoulders, wet down their shins, mud is welling up along the footpaths and piles of rubbish are swelling to mulch. Black umbrellas have appeared and a police siren wails, motionless, stranded in the congealing traffic.

Rain gives the pavements a much-needed sluicing, washing smells into the gutter.

Dedication under Umbrellas in Sri Lanka

Soft but persistent rain falls on what I think is the longest queue I have ever seen. On the road between Anuradhapura and Hatton – driving from Sri Lanka's dry zone to its lush, tea-growing high country – I first notice a cluster of umbrellas.

One purple, one striped, one red with black spots. Through the coach's rainy window, it might just be a queue for a bus. But when I glance out again, a few seconds later, there are more people under umbrellas on this tepid day, all facing the same direction.

And we drive past and past and past them. The queue is kilometres long, barely moving, just shuffling forwards occasionally, many of the people clutching the same booklet.

And that booklet tells the complete story of their patience.

For not only are these Sri Lankans clearly devout Buddhists, and not only are they celebrating Sri Sambuddhathva Jayanthi, the 2,600th year since the enlightenment of the Buddha – the moment when, meditating under a tree, this actual man finally managed to let go of earthly things and elevate his mind to a higher state – but they are waiting to see the Kapilavastu Sacred Relics.

According to the Mahaparinibbana Sutta text written in the fifth century BC, when Buddha died (or entered Parinirvana, the final deathless state, abandoning his earthly body) 2,600 years ago, one of eight portions of his bodily relics was handed to the Sakya tribe of Kapilavastu.

These Kapilavastu Sacred Relics were rediscovered in 1898 at a site believed to be the ancient city of Kapilavastu, in the ancient Sakya kingdom, in Nepal, where Buddha was born a prince and grew up.

They were brought to be seen in expositions in Sri Lanka in 1978 but, because of their "inestimable value and delicate nature", the Indian authorities later decided that they should remain in the National Museum of India in Delhi and never travel outside India again.

Then, in June 2010, Sri Lankan President Mahinda Rajapaksa asked Indian Prime Minister Manmohan Singh to send them again, that Sri Lankan Buddhists might pay homage. More than 70 per cent of Sri Lankans are Buddhist.

Making an exception, the Government of India decided the relics could travel, and a series of five expositions has been held around the country in recent weeks, with yesterday being the final day.

At each exposition, the faithful have queued in their many thousands to catch a glimpse of these bone fragments, considered so sacred.

For the Kapilavastu Sacred Relics coming here is not only important for the faithful, but also has been seen in Sri Lanka as recognition of the country's new peace and stability after the end, in 2009, of a long civil war.

And so, a little rain and a long wait under umbrellas in Anuradhapura is nothing really, is it?

5

Questions of Belief

I was given a seat beside a stranger at the dinner table. We introduced ourselves, and she asked, "What do you believe in?" It is one of the more unusual and stimulating conversation openers.

What do I believe in?

I believe in belief. I believe in god, whatever your god. I believe in honesty, kindness of thought, ethical behaviour, the strength of humility, patience, family, friendship, fellowship, decision making, responsibility, accountability, loyalty, hard work and being tough. I believe in listening, self education, a sense of parity and connection. I believe in humour and fun. And I believe in both having respect for, and an interest in, the belief of others.

I believe in them and I strive for them.

I believe in you, and I believe in me. In other words, I believe what just about everyone believes, deep down. (Casey believes in all these things, plus gentle handling.)

This is what I told the stranger next to me at the dinner table, which was possibly more than she'd anticipated (but then, she started it). When I asked about her beliefs, she said she believed in Jesus Christ and the Bible, and then nodded me on, so I also told her about two virtually identical moments experienced during my travels (one in Thailand, one in India), where someone asked me "what do people in your society believe in?" Money, real estate, sport, the individual? It seems unfathomable to people of deep, recognised faiths that societies without such belief embedded can function. It seems impossible to them that, without this structure and framework, the world doesn't fall apart.

From animism to Hinduism to Islam, from Christianity to Sikhism and Buddhism, and beyond all these, belief is utterly implanted in some lives and societies. I am fascinated by this innate belief; by blind faith. And while my backdrop may be my Anglican childhood, there are perhaps elements of all of these in my thinking and my belief.

For mostly I believe in belief.

The Water of Life in Sri Lanka

The ancient kings of Sri Lanka had two particular responsibilities; to look after the temple and to bring water to the people.

In this countryside in the cultural triangle at the heart of Sri Lanka – at Kandalama, north-east of Colombo – there are several big "tanks", or reservoirs, seventy medium tanks and perhaps 15,000 village reservoirs. There are channels and old canals, one of which has been reckoned to drop just "sixty feet in sixty miles" – 18 centimetres for every kilometre is an impressively accurate engineering feat.

The network of irrigational channels and clay pipes are ancient but still working. And they are still vital, particularly in the drought that the dry zone of Sri Lanka is enduring.

Irrigation is, of course, vital for growing rice, and many reticulated areas of Sri Lanka can harvest two crops a year. Water is the lifeblood of the food supply, and rice is more than just nourishment; it is cultural and intrinsic to everyday life.

But now, 32 kilometres from Kandalama, I walk through the Pleasure Gardens of Sigiriya, built during the reign of King Kashyapa between AD 477 and AD 495, and see ancient water channels that were used for quite different purposes – those of both delight and outdoor air-conditioning.

For these fifth century pleasure gardens are among the oldest landscaped gardens in the world. And, apart from the boulder, cave and terraced gardens, the water gardens provided somewhere for King Kashyapa to cool off. He had, after all, usurped his father, murdered him by walling him up alive, and so seized what should have been his brother Mogallana's throne. Perhaps it was the fear of his brother's revenge that drove him to build the fortress high on Lion Rock which is the backdrop of these gardens.

Kashyapa is popularly cast as a young playboy king, and there is evidence to support this.

It is recorded that he had 500 concubines from all over the world – girls and young women sent to him as gifts. Girls of all races. There are the remains of four indoor swimming pools where the concubines bathed. Around those pools are platforms where they danced.

The king's swimming pool has a swim-through channel leading to a room which has only windows and no door. The king would swim through with the chosen concubine of the moment. Susantha Jolita is showing me around, and explains that this was "for further discussions".

Its water gardens are designed symmetrically, linked to an outer moat on one side and a tank the other. An underground network of pipes and channels, fed from the lake, links its pools.

There is a miniature water garden with watercourses and small pools.

The ancient city of Sigiriya is one of the most remarkable places I have ever visited. A UNESCO World Heritage site, it sits in the cultural triangle of Sri Lanka, the points of which are Polonnaruwa in the central east to Kandy further south and Anuradhapura to the north.

The government of Sri Lanka's Cultural Triangle Project turned its attention to Sigiriya in 1982 when, for the first time, archaeological work began across the site. However, some areas remain untouched, left for the archaeologists of the future, with their future techniques.

I climb steps and then a metal staircase and ladder, a pilgrim of history, and there indeed are the concubines, painted in frescoes 1,500 years ago, facing me. Beautiful, exotic princesses with their attendants. Black, Asian, perhaps one from the Americas.

It is believed there were originally 500 frescoes but today about eighteen remain.

What is remarkable is not only their figurative style but that they look almost as if they were painted yesterday. They were painted on plaster made of limestone, bee honey, eggwhite and resin, using minerals for the browns and yellows, herbs for violets and greens. And there is a bright blue – still vivid today after 1,500 years exposed on these walls. There is uncertainty about what it was painted with, after the scenes were first line-sketched on the plaster.

I have been fortunate enough to see the Ajanta Caves of India, and they are reminiscent of these.

Further up the steel stairway, the top of Lion Rock covers just over a hectare, and also has a swimming pool, which was once fragranced with herbs. Water was pumped with a hand pump.

There are remains of the gardens and palace walls. The palace had water arteries built into the walls to keep it naturally air conditioned.

Lion Rock is the larval plug from a volcano, and from high up here from the citadel on its flat top, I look back down into the Pleasure Gardens, just as Kashyapa must have done, with pride that was short-lived. For eventually he committed suicide, after loss in battle to Mogallana in AD 495. Mogallana took the throne and turned Sigiriya into a monastery palace. It served this meditative life until the late thirteenth century.

As I walk through the gardens, finding quiet and thoughtful moments even among the Sri Lankan and international visitors, it seems to me that it is more suited to this life. Today it draws modern-day pilgrims of gardens and landscaping, and those who just wonder at the use of water. It fulfils pilgrims of human history and epic story.

And the echoes of its vibrating chants will surely permeate pilgrims of atmosphere and ambience.

After driving on in a mellow mood to stay at the hotel Ulagalla Walawwa at Anuradhapura (my beautiful two-room chalet on stilts, surrounded by the hotel's own paddy fields, which make it self-sufficient in rice), I turn to my travelling dictionary to round off the thoughts of the day.

And I turn to the letter P.

Pilgrim: devotee, believer; traveller, crusader; literary wayfarer.

An extraordinary day for a pilgrim.

Temples of the Cosmic Dancer in India

It took stonemasons and carvers 190 years to complete the 20,000 statues at the temple dedicated to the Hindu god Shiva in the Indian town of Halebidu.

Shiva, the Lord of the Cosmic Dance. Destroyer, ascetic, lord of beasts and synonymous with the bull. The lingam – a representation of divine, phallic, generative energy.

And he is here, all around this temple in the central southern Indian state of Karnataka.

There is Shiva, the destroyer, having dismembered a demon, holding his head, and the blood, carved from the same stone, "pouring" from the bottom stump of it and a dog jumping up to catch the drops.

The carvings are intricate and exquisite – some tiny, some big, most three-dimensional, standing off the walls and playing with light and shadow.

The temple's designers settled on a star shape to give more walls for carvings and work began in AD 931.

A twenty-minute drive away in Belur is the temple dedicated to the god representing the other line of Hindu religious thought, Vishnu. It took three generations 103 years to build and carve and was opened in 1117. "On March 10," says temple guide S. R. Ramesh. "Saturday." He rolls his head side-to-side on his neck.

Ramesh points out the carvings of dancing girls, for which the temple is famous.

And then a strange carving of a couple – a young man and another figure, obviously of a young woman's body, but with a donkey's head. "In the great text the *Kama Sutra*, it says that when the female body is 16 years old, even with a donkey's head she is desirable."

He looks around dramatically and then grins. "Love is blind!"

Inside the temple, it is the dark that is blinding but gradually its forty-eight huge pillars, each covered in carvings and each unique, reveal themselves. One is a complete representation of the temple.

One has the alluring figure of a woman, complete with bangles, carved from the same piece of rock, which move on her wrist. Another figure of a woman has a moving rock pendant on the forehead.

And, in the deep dark near the inner shrine itself, still always attended and used, and with a lamp burning, is another figure of a woman.

This, says Ramesh, is of what might be considered a perfect woman's form.

He ignores her obvious assets and concentrates on the face. "See, it is moon-shaped. Her eyes are the shape of fish. Her nose...see, her nose is one-third, her forehead one-third, her chin one-third. Her eyebrows curved, like this." He traces her features with care. "This is the face of an intelligent and knowledgeable woman."

Ramesh pauses. "And you will notice her other most beautiful parts." The figure has hard, round, pumped-up breasts but Ramesh bends. "See here...she has a very good bridge to her foot...a good arch. Yes, very good feet."

But while Ramesh is talking, I have become rather side-tracked by my own bare feet, for they are standing on a stone floor that has that strange, waxy sheen that comes only with thousands upon thousands of bare feet over hundreds and hundreds of years.

And not just the hundreds of thousands of people who have walked through here, but those who have danced wildly, too.

"Yes, dance is a service," Ramesh explains.

Both temples were built by the Hoysalas, who ruled this part of India from the eleventh to the fourteenth century.

I feel I am levitating, just a little. Or perhaps just buzzing with the overwhelming nature of the stories, the saturation of belief, the beauty of the physical artwork and how these combine into something which both reflects, directs and invigorates the human mind and society.

The visits to Belur and Halebidu are combined in a morning coach trip from *The Golden Chariot* luxury train, which does a weeklong loop out of Bangalore (now called Bangalooru) in the central southern State of Karnataka.

With my train companions, I have already visited Shiva's big bull temple in Bangalore, where the monolithic beast carved from a single rock had just been anointed with 5,000 litres of milk, and the almost equally big bull at the Mahabaleshwarvara temple on Chamundi Hill, overlooking the historic town of Mysore and dating back to the year AD 950. We had also seen the Jain pilgrimage centre of Shravanabelagola, with its big statue of Lord Gommateshwara.

And then, on the fifth day of the eight-day train tour, I am in the sacred town of Hampi.

This UNESCO World Heritage site is where the ancient city of Vijayanagar rose in 1336 and fell in 1655.

Vijayanagar was the capital of south India's biggest, richest and most powerful kingdom.

The "City of Victory".

It is also the setting for much of the Indian epic story, the *Ramayana*.

Today, ruined temples and buildings lie woven through the striking, dishevelled, hilly granite landscape, giving the sense of the Earth re-absorbing the local stone from which they are made.

A big statue of Ganesh, the elephant-headed fourth incarnation of Vishnu, sits looking across a landscape that is reddened through mineral-rich rock and greened by irrigation. An elephant's trunk has 5,000 muscles and can tear down a tree and pick up a pin. That's the point, says S. (Sethuram) Pradeep, showing me round.

Near the sacred centre of Hampi is the royal centre – a groomed enclosure with 12-metre-tall granite-block walls, a long elephant enclosure topped by domes, and the Queen's bath, a big pool inside a square building, complete with balconies for musicians to play as the women bathed. Hampi also has a striking step tank, a square-shaped pool with steps down to the water.

Nearby is the Temple of A Thousand Ramas, with its carved dolerite pillars and the compete story of the *Ramayana* depicted around the outside.

But, says Pradeep, it is the Vitthala temple complex which is the highlight of Hampi, and he is right.

The big courtyard is dotted with temples, galleries and a wedding hall that all have columns each carved into columnettes. But it is not just this that burns this fifteenth-century temple into the memory.

As the lights fade, they turn the lights on for me. Vitthala temple complex. With this strange, false light, the characters and stories carved from the rocks seem to come to life, throwing shadows, suggesting movement. And I sit in the dark, on the steps of a temple, back to rock still resonating heat, in the soft, oily night, with this creamy illumination all around me, and these figures and characters seem to stir to tell their stories.

As I eventually walk away from the temple, the lights of a single vehicle behind me throws my loping, moving shadow over the carved ones of dancing girls and celebrations, and it seems almost that I am blended into the story.

And in a moment which one might call a small enlightenment, I realise that such rare but precious moments are one of the great touchstones of travel for me. Why do we travel? We find our own reasons – for the thrill of a fish on a line or an idea in the layout of an illustrious garden that we might replicate at home in some tiny way, to watch a grand prix and visit a motor museum or even just for the rush of different oxygen that brings whatever-novel alive – and for me, one reason is this.

I felt this buzz four years ago after visiting the temple caves of Ellora and Ajanta, near Aurangabad in Maharashtra state in north India, which date back to the fifth century. Some 2,300 years ago, the rhythmical chip of hand chisels could be heard in the valley of the Waghora River in India. Craftsmen were whittling away at these basalt mountains, first as a flat incision into them, and then downwards. They shaped rooms, columns, temples, shrines and statues of great intricacy, all from this great mountain of volcanic rock.

Ajanta Caves were forgotten for centuries, until in 1819 a British army officer named, innocuously enough, John Smith, not only discovered an entrance while on a tiger hunt, but scrambled his way in and scratched his name on pillar.

Many of these twenty-nine Buddhist caves are covered in paintings which tell stories from Buddha's life – they are recognised as artistic masterpieces.

The carving work dates back 2,200 years, but paintings were added later, around AD 500. The five main colours are yellow from ochre, blue from lapis lazuli, green from green jade, red from rubies, white from agate.

These precious stones were ground to a powder to make the pigments. After the carving was finished, walls and ceilings were coated with potters' clay, and then a fine, white lime plaster, before this precious paint was applied.

In Cave 1, every square centimetre is painted. It transfixes. The paintings in Cave 2 are darker, and Cave 10 has paintings from both the second century BC and fourth century AD.

Work on the second set started around 600 BC, says knowledgeable Rajesh Raut, who is showing me around.

The Ajanta Caves were formed and used for almost 700 years, and then, apparently quite abruptly, abandoned. They are now a UNESCO World Heritage Site.

About 100 kilometres away, the thirty-four Ellora Caves are carved into the Charanandri Hills in the same fashion, but for Buddhist, Hindu and Jain devotees. It is believed they were built between the fifth and eleventh centuries AD.

The most dramatic is Cave 16, known as the Kailasa. Some 200,000 tonnes of rock were removed over more than 100 years to leave a three-storey temple full of big statues, facing west.

As the sun drops into a hazy horizon, the temple fires golden.

Yes, I felt this buzz at Ellora and Ajanta.

I felt it too, a couple of years later after leaving Wat Po (or Pho), one of the most important Buddhist temples in Thailand. I felt it earlier this year as I stood and let my gaze wheel around Worcester Cathedral, in the West Midlands of England. Founded in AD 680, in the chancel is the tomb of King John, who ruled England from 1199 until his death in 1216 and signed the Magna Carta, the first document of human rights.

There is layering – some *charge* – to these places. Something about the belief in belief which invigorates, intrigues and animates me.

I feel it again a couple of days later at the cave temples and UNESCO World Heritage site of Pattadakal and Badami.

Pattadakal is the only place where north and south Indian architectural styles are seen together. The Virupaksha Temple is reputedly one of the best in India, unusually with three sanctums, one for each of the main deities, Brahma, Vishnu and Shiva, and three entrances. A combination of the three great streams of Hinduism.

The four cave temples of Badami are carved – decorated pillars, statues, sanctums and all – into and from the solid rock of a sandstone mountain. One is dated AD 578 and two are probably even older.

As the generations of craftsmen lay on their backs, carving the ceilings upwards, they covered their eyes with transparent leaves to protect them.

The first cave has a carved statue of Shiva, Lord of the Cosmic Dance, with, unusually, eighteen arms. "If you look at any pair of the arms, they give one of eighty-one dance positions," says guide Chandru Katageri. "This was the sixth century, I remind you." There is also a most unusual larger-than-human figure of the Hindu deities, Vishnu and Shiva, combined, with their respective consort, Lakshmi, and wife, Parvati.

Followers of Vishnu and Shiva were the two great, competitive and sometimes antagonistic, lines of Hinduism. This is a representation of combining the factions, says Chandru, who has two university degrees and is in the midst of postgraduate studies in education.

"I could be a teacher now," he says, proudly. Teachers here are revered and respected.

He adds: "These temples were not just religious – they have always been social educational centres. And I think this is teaching, too. Teaching the world."

Sikhism in the Subcontinent

He is a fearsome looking Sikh. His dark blue turban is wound tightly and precisely around his head, its elliptical lip firm, a piece over his crown. A tight, silk tulip. Where it settles in an upside down 'v' on his forehead, the red cap beneath it shows in a perfectly horizontal line.

He has a short, grey, perfectly trimmed beard and a moustache with waxed ends.

The precision of all this is quite beautiful, but he wears a stern expression.

His glasses sit on the end of his nose.

He is an immigration officer at New Delhi's international airport and it is he, and he alone, who will allow me to leave India.

I stand before him. "Good afternoon, sir." If I have learnt one thing, it is that addressing senior, proud, self-possessed Sikh men "sir" is a good and respectful thing.

Sikhs follow a monotheistic religion founded in Punjab in the fifteenth century by Guru Nanak, who lived from 1469 to 1539 and preached that spiritual liberation could be achieved through meditating on the name of God.

They are known for being religious and good cooks. Social justice and harmony are central to their belief, though Sikhs have never been shy of militant action. After two Anglo-Sikh wars between 1845 and 1849, Sikhs joined the British Indian Army in great numbers and were awarded fourteen Victoria Crosses in the Second World War.

The Sikh looks fierce but there is nothing malevolent about him.

He looks up at me, over his glasses, and fixes me with a steady scrutiny; this man standing before him, hat in hand, calling him "sir".

He looks down at my passport and reads it slowly, then my boarding pass, then my outgoing passenger card.

"Step Hen Spen Sir." The syllables of my first and middle names are read out slowly and deliberately out loud. His mouth forms a great arc, the corners pointing down as he thinks about them. Then, having considered them, his mood seems to brighten and he nods, once, to himself.

The fearsome Sikh draws breath and reads the next line. "Scour." Pause. "Field." As if the two are divorced from one another; quite separate entities. He looks up at me, to study this Scour Field who stands before him, silently requesting his approval to go home, then he looks down again.

"Writer." The Sikh doesn't look up. Perhaps he is considering which of India's fields I might have been scouring for stories to tell. "That is good," he says, his tone just perceptibly warmer.

"Thank you, sir." It sounds quite ridiculous.

"Good," he says, as if that piece of conversation is concluded.

He retraces a D and a 7 in the flight number I have written in block letters in their little boxes, as if they are not good enough – certainly not good enough for a writer.

He wobbles his head, only just perceptibly.

This varies from region to region throughout the thirty-two states of India. The people of Kerala are really quite enthusiastic head wobblers but, in my experience, Sikhs are more likely to use it conservatively.

It is the visual equivalent of the ubiquitous Hindi word *accha*, which can mean anything from "I understand" to "good".

It is most often used in the affirmative, which, despite his corrections, is a good sign in this instance. (Equally it might be used just to acknowledge someone's presence or to say "thank you". It has several times been explained to me that a slow, soft wobble is a sign of friendship.)

I am vaguely aware that, as all this has been progressing, a number of people have passed through the immigration desks either side of me, but I realise how I am delighting in this little play going on, in which we are the only two actors.

The Sikh has paused again, and then he reaches for his stamp, lifts it to check that all is correct with the digits showing and that there is enough ink, and then he deliberately and very sternly stamps my passport, my boarding pass and the outgoing passenger form. He looks at each intently, studying the marks he has made, and then he looks up at me over the top of his glasses, "You may go."

"Thank you, sir," I say to the fearsome Sikh.

I collect the documents he has put back on the shelf before me, and he looks at me, narrows his eyes and smiles warmly and intimately.

We both understand the formality and ritual that has passed between us.

"Namaste." He says the respectful Hindu greeting not in passing, but directly to me, fixing me with his blue eyes.

I have turned to go, but now stop and face him full-on again. "Namaste." And we both bow out heads a little.

My fearsome Sikh, indeed.

Indiana Jones & Cambodia's Temple of Angkor Wat

There is more than a touch of Indiana Jones to the story of French naturalist Henri Mouhot first seeing the temple of Angkor Wat in Cambodia's dense jungle.

For many centuries, Angkor Wat had been hidden from Western eyes by the thick jungle that covers the centre of Cambodia.

French colonialists heard local rumours of temples that had been built by gods or giants, and some believed there was a lost city of a Cambodian empire which had been rich and powerful.

Mouhot arrived in the Thai capital of Bangkok in 1858 and set out eastwards, following these stories about a lost city deep in the jungle. It took him two years to find the medieval temple complex, and it was completely overgrown and hidden.

Yet a year after his discovery, Mouhot was dead of malaria in Luang Prubang, in neighbouring Laos. He was thirty-five years old.

But there is clearly some romanticism to the story. Locals say the Khmer never forgot these temples – the city was "lost" in the sense that it was abandoned around 1450.

Today the temples of Angkor Wat – particularly the main temple, which has appeared on every Cambodian national flag since 1863 and is a source of great national pride – are a magnet for tourists and are certainly changing the economy.

This is a region of traditional subsistence farming, particularly in rice. There is crushing poverty and many struggle just to feed their families. With tourism has come American dollars, jobs, education and infrastructure.

Mom Vannack, who is showing me round, is a case in point. From a rice farming family, he was sent to school, learnt English, passed the exacting guiding examinations and got his licence. "I did not want to work in the rice fields," he says.

And the restoration work on the temples is another example. The bas-relief gallery which tells the traditional Hindu story of The Churning of the Sea of Milk is being restored as a World Monument Fund Conservation Project, and French and Indian organisations, in particular, have been involved in restoration work at the many temples.

Temples spread over 60 kilometres around the town, but it is the Temple of Angkor Wat that lies at their heart. Reputedly the world's biggest Hindu temple and religious construction in stone, it took King Suryavarman II more than thirty-five years to build, during his reign from 1112 to 1152 and it is dedicated to Lord Vishnu, and was later turned into a Buddhist temple.

I cross a causeway over the wide, water-filled moat that surrounds and isolates the temple complex – this crossing symbolic of the Hindu rainbow bridge between the worlds. And I am in this other place of belief and learning and art. The temple complex covers 81 hectares, with five towers believed to represent the five peaks of Mount Meru, the home of gods and centre of the Hindu universe.

It has the longest continuous bas-relief in the world, running around the outer gallery walls and telling the great stories from Hindu mythology, the *Ramayana* and *Mahabharata.*

I have just been in India again, visiting temples dating back to the fifth century, so to see the influence here puts another piece into the puzzle. But, while the galleried temple is based on early South Indian design, it is infused with Khmer architectural style.

Cambodians recognise the Indian influence. Norodom Sihanouk, king of Cambodia until his abdication in 2004, pointed out, "In fact, it was about 2,000 years ago that the first navigators, Indian merchants, and Brahmins brought to our ancestors their gods, their techniques, their organisation. Briefly India was for us what Greece was for the Latin Occident."

The Temple of Angkor Wat has a moat and three galleries encircling the five central shrines. But it is the bas-relief walls that stick most in my mind, with their shiny figures at elbow height, where countless hands have been run along them over, and particularly the western wall, with scenes from the *Mahabharata.*

When Henri Mouhot saw the temples of Angkor Wat, he wrote, "One of these temples – a rival to that of Solomon, and erected by some ancient Michelangelo – might take an honourable place beside our most beautiful buildings. It is grander than anything left to us by Greece or Rome."

In one morning, Banteay Srei and Banteay Samre, in the afternoon, Ta Som, Neak Pean and Preah Khan.

These vary from the small, jungle surrounded and beautifully carved Lady Temple to Neak Pean – "two twining snakes" – which has a round, centrepiece shrine set in a square lake. Each side, with its own shrine, is dedicated to one of the four elements: earth, fire, water and air.

"It is a hospital temple," says Mom Vannak. "People come to purify themselves with the element that the priest says they need."

On the causeway in, a band of landmine victims plays, in a country that saw the brutal Pol Pot regime conduct the genocide of perhaps 1.7 million people in the 1970s. Twenty-six per cent of the population.

I climb to the top of Bakheng Mountain, just outside Siem Reap, and the area is laid before me, as the sun sets. Temples in the jungle, not so dissimilar to what Mouhot saw, and grand indeed.

But there my comparisons with him must end. My lunches have been in excellent local restaurants, where a few dollars buys a good meal, and there are many good restaurants in Siem Reap.

I stay in a small comfortable hotel, and behind timber shutters and under a wall hanging of golden Cambodian silk, I lie in comfort and think of one of the stories Mom Vannack told us today, of the twelfth century temple dedicated to a cucumber farmer.

The king had so liked the farmer's cucumbers that he told him only to grow them for him, and gave him a sword to keep others away. When the king visited one night, the farmer killed him, not realising who it was.

People knew the cucumber farmer was a great friend of the dead regent, and in turn made him king.

Perhaps, when he died, they hid gold, diamonds and books in the sand under a temple for him, as Mom Vannak describes in one of these shrines.

Romanticised tale, maybe. But then, we are still doing that, aren't we, Indie?

The World's First Christian Country, Armenia

In AD 301, Armenia became the first country to adopt Christianity as its national religion. Indeed, many think of it as Christianity's real birthplace.

I have just walked through the Etchmiadzin Cathedral in Armenia's capital Yerevan, which is the oldest state-built church in the world, constructed between AD 301 and AD 303 by Saint Gregory the Illuminator.

I have listened to the hooded bishops of the Armenian Apostolic Church chanting and watched the faithful light candles; an old man with nineteen medals and bars of ribbons in contemplation before a painting of the last supper, a young boy kissing a *khatchkar*, a carved stone Armenian cross.

And, in a museum through a door at the back of the cathedral, I am now standing in two of the most remarkable rooms I may ever visit.

In a flat, understated voice, the nice young guide takes me around it, briefly describing items.

First she points to a relic of St Stephen the Protomartyr, the first person to be martyred for his ministry in Christianity. In this context, the word "relic" means a small piece of his actual remains.

She then moves to a relic of St Luke, and there is one of St George and one of St John the Baptist.

She moves to two separate relics of the cross of Jesus Christ – shards of wood believed to be from the actual cross on which Christ was crucified.

And then to a cabinet which contains a piece of fossilised wood from Noah's ark.

It is the last, to a greater extent, that has brought me here, and I have been teased today by glimpses of Mt Ararat, the snow-capped volcanic mountain on which, the Bible says, Noah's ark was eventually grounded after the great flood, animal cargo and all.

Today I have visited the tomb of St Hripsime, in a church built in AD 618 on the foundation of a previous pagan temple.

I have seen tombs of Catholicos, the patriarchs of the Armenian Church, and visited Vagharshapat, 18 kilometres west of Yerevan, which is the spiritual centre for Armenians.

A forty-five-minute drive out of Yerevan, I am in green mountains terraced by the hooves of animals grazed over thousands of years, small orchards in the original natural environment of the apricot, and visit Geghard Monastery, with its Christian temples carved out of the mountain and where sheep and roosters are still sacrificed and their meat prepared with blessed salt.

I visit the village of Garni, with 4,000 years of history, and dine on local fare – Armenian cheeses, herb salads, paper-thin lavash bread and a fish caught for us and cooked in spices on coals. Garni has a first-century temple set dramatically over a river gorge, and third-century baths and mosaics for its king.

You cannot think of Armenia, or Yerevan, separately from its religious history. It is intrinsic to the place.

Equally, it is impossible to grasp Armenia without considering its geography. For it has Georgia to its north, and Russia overshadowing above that, Iran to the south and Turkey and Azerbaijan flanking either side.

There are fractious borders which the Russian army guards for Armenia.

There are also disputed territories, and throughout Armenia's museums there are maps which show it as quite a different shape by including land that Armenians believe to be rightfully part of their country. Historical Armenia, as they refer to it.

And lurking behind that, and also manifesting from this political geography, is something else which pervades the Armenian consciousness.

Between 1915 and 1918, in a country of just three million people, there was a genocide conducted by the Turks which saw one-and-a-half million people killed and another 500,000 forcibly deported. Two-thirds of the population gone. Towns of 40,000 people were wiped out over a few months. The Armenian Genocide Museum in Yerevan tells this devastating story.

Every family in Armenia is touched by the genocide, says Inga Sargsyan, who is showing me around the city.

For all this, Yerevan is a winsome and rather beautiful city, with wide, tree-lined streets and a clean, elegant architecture that relies on a local volcanic stone which varies from dark grey to beige, to almost-orange and pink, put to good effect in simple but striking design.

There are coffee bars and good restaurants, and the late-night jazz scene is big. The Opera House usually has performances going on and much of the daily conversation is about the great poets, writers, artists, thinkers, scientists and intellectuals of Armenia in general and Yerevan in particular. There are statues of them throughout the city.

Mesrop Mashtots, a monk, theologian and linguist who, in AD 406, invented the Armenian alphabet, deciding on thirty-six letters (though three were added later) is a national hero. It was important for the written history and culture of a country that had been invaded by Persians and Byzantines, points out Inga.

Mashtots is as alive in the national consciousness as sports stars might be in other cultures. There are sculptures of him in many places in Yerevan.

He sits in stone outside Matenadaran, the Mesrop Mashtots Institute of Ancient Manuscripts, which is one of the world's great stores of manuscripts and books, many hand-painted on skin with pigments often derived from semi-precious jewels. Some 17,000 manuscripts are kept here.

Yerevan's excellent History Museum of Armenia continues to peel the layers off this country, with artefacts ranging from a rock carving of a deer from 5000 BC to the oldest shoe in the world, of skin and lace and dated at 3500 BC, to many clay vessels bearing the swirling symbol of eternity and dated to 2400 BC, and then leading into beautiful historic jewellery for which Armenia is also renowned. There is a model of the solar system, in bronze, from perhaps the twelfth century BC showing, significantly, the Earth as round.

Yerevan's Cafesjian Center for the Arts was founded by businessman, philanthropist and collector Gerard L. Cafesjian and is dedicated to bringing the world's best contemporary art to Armenia and showing the best of Armenian culture to the world.

It is an extraordinary collection, housed in The Cascade in Yerevan, a museum and cultural centre which is built in layers into the slope of a hill, dramatic architecture providing perhaps as much art as the exhibits.

And here the historic and the contemporary come together. For though the Cafesjian centre has been hailed as one of the most interesting and radical museums to be opened in years, The Cascade was originally designed by the architect Alexander Tamanyan, who lived from 1878 to 1936.

He aimed to join the northern residential and central cultural parts of Yerevan with a big green area of gardens and waterfalls, coming in layers down the hill.

His plan was shelved and mostly forgotten until the late 1970s, when new ideas were added such as a monumental stairway and a series of escalators inside.

Construction began in 1980, during Armenia's Soviet period, but was abandoned after a big earthquake in 1988 and the Soviet Union's break-up in 1991.

Mr Cafesjian, in league with the city council and Armenian government, revived it in 2002 and seven years of construction followed.

At the base, there's a landscaped walking area, with restaurants, cafes and bars. The place is optimistic, points out a companion. And so too is the whole feel of The Cascade. Elegant and strikingly beautiful women, for which Armenia might also rightly be famous, promenade beside men that have a stoic quality. Both by day and by night, Yerevan is safe to walk.

Today is warm, the trees green, and I pass a couple, both sitting reading outside a cafe.

She has jet-black "big hair", an elegant long cream-coloured dress and wears a gold Armenian cross on a chain.

She is engrossed in a book with Ruben Sevak's name on the front – I'd guess at some of this revered Armenian writers' lyrical poems. Sevak is considered one of Armenia's greatest poets of the twentieth century.

The woman's partner, by comparison, is short-haired, thick-set, wearing an Ajax AFC soccer shirt and engrossed in a football magazine.

Armenia has a truly extraordinary past, but Yerevan today has a healthy air of normality about it.

Spreading the Word through Turkey

Jesus Christ's disciples St Paul and St John the Evangelist both walked along this wide street in Ephesus, Turkey. They stepped on the actual stones on which I now tread.

In fact, St John had to leave the city for his own safety, exiled to the nearby Greek island of Patmos, but he wrote the New Testament's Book of Ephesians, an epistle to the Church of Ephesus, and completed the Book of Revelations in the Ephesus area.

Even Cleopatra, queen of Egypt from 47 BC to 30 BC, walked exactly here with Mark Antony, with whom she formed a romantic and political alliance after a brief liaison with Julius Caesar.

In fact, Cleopatra so loved the high-quality shops which flanked Arcadian Street, where I stroll now in this ancient city in Turkey, that when Mark Antony came here without her, she insisted he bring back gold and silver jewellery for her.

After her, Hadrian, Roman emperor from AD 117 to AD 138, came here at least three times in travels that took him to the north of England, where Hadrian's Wall was built, and to leave his mark in Athens and Rome.

Today, Ephesus, in the west of Turkey, is visited mainly by tourists who call in on cruise ships and take this as an excursion. They dock at the port town of Kusadasi and usually travel in coaches the 16 kilometres to Ephesus.

And that is the journey I have made today in the capable hands of Sertan Somnez, who has been a guide for eighteen years.

Mr Somnez explains that, in fact, there have been several phases of the city.

In the eleventh century BC the Greeks came, but from 300 BC to AD 700 it was developed and run by the Romans, and that is what the archaeological site today shows.

"It is one of the greatest Greek and Roman archaeological sites in the world," Mr Somnez says. It stands out among a remarkable 2,500 sites in Turkey, all of which are more than 1,000 years old.

Being on the cusp of East and West – of two worlds – Ephesus has been tugged this way and that. Mr Somnez himself is quick to point out that the Turks as we see them today are not indigenous, but came from Mongolia 1,000 years ago.

Turkish history starts in the eleventh century, along with the first presence of Muslims, though it is a secular, not Islamic, country and there is freedom of belief.

Today Turkey is often thought of as "part of Europe" and aims to be part of the European Union, but it is in Asia. In fact it is on the cusp of what was traditionally called Asia Minor and Europe – the port of Ephesus was regarded as the gateway to the East just as, further up the coast, the Turkish city of Troy had been in earlier times.

Indeed, Ephesus was such a busy and important hub that it was compulsory for visitors to take a bath before entering the city. The remains of those baths can still be seen.

It is all a little difficult to visualise now, as Ephesus is 5 kilometres from the Aegean Sea, but the Menderes River, on which it was built, silted up to such an extent that the standing water encouraged mosquitoes, which spread malaria and other diseases. The city was eventually abandoned in the seventh century AD and the sea's edge slowly pushed to its current line.

The city's demise was complete and over the centuries since it was covered by dirt, which has been gradually removed.

That has revealed the temple to the goddess Artemis, which was regarded as one of the Seven Wonders of the Ancient World. Some 20 metres high and with 127 columns, it was three times the size of Athens' Parthenon.

There is also a grand or great theatre, which could seat 24,000 of the city's 250,000 inhabitants.

There was also an *odeion* in Ephesus – a small concert hall. And in this word alone we start to see other histories. For in Arcadian Street, lined as it was with shops, we see origins of the word arcade. Near it, the ancient Agora was used for political and religious gatherings. It was a massive square founded in the third century BC, and in this we see origins of the word agoraphobia – the fear of open spaces.

At the public toilets – the *latrina*, built in the first century AD – people sat side by side and socialised. Four aqueducts brought spring water down from the hills, and there were terracotta pipes into houses and sewers under the main street.

Thirty million people visited Turkey last year, 10 per cent come to Ephesus. There is plenty for them to see, from Hercules' Gate to a statue of Nike, the female goddess of victory (her pose resembling the shape of a tick). The Library of Celsus was built between AD 117 and AD 120 – a massive and impressive building.

There are the remains of a statue of Emperor Trajan, who ruled from AD 98 to AD 117, with one foot on a world that is clearly spherical, at a time when it was still widely believed that the world was flat, and 300 years before it was proved otherwise.

But surely the most impressive part of the visit is seeing the terraced houses of the Roman royalty. These were built on the slopes of Mt Bulbul in the seventh to sixth centuries BC.

The houses, in rows, were two-storey, covered from 2,700 square feet (just over 820 square metres) and had bathrooms, toilets and heating similar to today's radiators. The floors had mosaics, giving the appearance of today's rugs, and walls were covered with frescoes, like wallpaper.

Restoration work by Austrian archaeologists is being concentrated on one of the houses, where up to 100 fragments of fresco are being computer matched and placed each day. Perhaps the ultimate jigsaw of 120,000 pieces.

An earthquake in AD 270 interrupted their habitation for several decades, but some of the houses were used for between 600 and 700 years.

Mr Somnez paints a word picture of a privileged lifestyle. "This was the Beverly Hills of Asia Minor," he says. "They weren't just rich, they were filthy rich." They lived a lavish lifestyle, complete with ocean views, at the time.

"Location, location, location," Mr Somnez says. He looks down the valley and across the plain and shrugs.

Peace on Patmos

For visitors who come to the small Greek island of Patmos today, it is a holiday place of back lanes and waterside restaurants with tasty food. Of white buildings and blue shutters, domed Greek Orthodox churches, and gardens planted with tomatoes and herbs. Of hill paths looking down into the cup of the harbour, timber fishing boats and a sense of creativity.

For English ceramicist Barbara Scales, it has been home for 72 years, after teaching in Athens and deciding to move away from city life. Patmos is a small island, home to about 5,000 people and, she says, she knows most of them. "It's a warm, friendly, safe place. Everyone looks out for one another."

But for Christ's disciple St John, Patmos was the place of exile where he wrote the Book of Revelation, the last book of the Holy Bible.

In 1088, for St Christodoulos, it was the place to build a monastery dedicated to St John, high on the hill and fortified against constant raids from pirates. On the site of a previous ancient temple for the Greek huntress goddess Artemis, the monastery has five water cisterns underneath, and had a bakery, so that the 250 monks could hold out against sieges. Burning oil could be poured from its high eyrie.

The Monastery of St John the Theologian, to which fifty monks are still affiliated and which still owns half the island, has what is often recognised as the most important collections of religious icons in the world. The monastery also has an important Christian library, with the fifth-century Book of Matthew written in silver on purple vellum.

In AD 95 St John, who had been to Ephesus, was exiled to Patmos, which the Romans were using as a penal colony. During his eighteen months on the island, with a scribe to write his words, he had prayed in a cave and been instructed to write down what he heard and saw and send it to the seven churches of Asia Minor. The result – the Book of Revelation – is apocalyptic, about the end of the world but with hope for the future.

John was, perhaps, the apostle with the closest ties to Jesus Christ and his mother. He was the apostle who heard Christ's last words, and to whom was entrusted the safekeeping of Mary. A widely travelled evangelist, he was also the only one of the twelve apostles to die naturally, at the age of 105.

And all these lives of this volcanic island come together as Barbara Scales leads me down narrow steps and along a passageway to meet Yanni Sotiriou. Mr Sotiriou is the head restorer of the monastery's icons and his workshop is rarely seen by the public. In fact, Mr Sotiriou says it is probably the only workshop of this kind that is ever opened to the public.

"It is responsible for the restoration of the icons and frescoes in the whole of the monastery and all the icons of the churches of Patmos and the surrounding islands."

An icon is a painting of Jesus Christ or another holy figure, in a rigid and traditional style, often on wood, which is venerated and most associated with the Byzantine and other Eastern Churches.

They are used as an educational tool, to depict biblical and moralistic moments.

"There are so many treasures that need restoring," says Mr Sotiriou. Some of them cover the table in the middle of his small studio, awaiting work. There is a wooden carved cross from the 1500s under restoration, and an icon on a stand which is complete but has taken many months of work using chemicals and a lot of medical equipment. Another that is half done – the picture revealed from under a layer of soot.

Candles burn as an important part of ceremony in the little church, and over the years soot covers the icons and frescoes. Mr Sotiriou, in this case with some help, has spent years cleaning frescoes that date back 1,000 years.

In an earth tremor in the 1950s, parts of the frescoes came off, revealing more underneath. In his studio, Mr Sotiriou, who has a degree in restoration from Athens University, uses X-ray, as often icons are painted one over the other, and it helps him access the images.

The monastery's museum is full of more treasures, the most famous being an icon painted in the sixteenth century by El Greco, who was born on the island of Crete in the 1500s. His real name was Dominikos Theotokopoulos, but when he moved to Italy, he simply became known by his nickname – "El Greco", the Greek. Barbara Scales expertly takes me through it all.

Outside again, under the blue of the Mediterranean sky and surrounded by the inky Aegean Sea, I look down into the cup of Skala harbour set in a landscape layered in human history.

Patmos was mentioned by Thucydides in the fifth century BC. Its first full-time inhabitants were the Doriens, then there was Roman occupation, the Venetians succeeded the Byzantines, the Ottoman Turks controlled the island for more than 400 years, Italians took over in 1912, it was briefly administered by the British in 1948 with author Lawrence Durrell in charge and writing about it in *Reflections on a Marine Venus*, and then became officially part of

Greece. Just over 30 years ago, the Greek government proclaimed it a sacred island.

For most visitors who come to Patmos today, it is a place of beaches and baklava, Mythos beer and sunbaking. But Patmos is, indeed, sacred.

Sunday in Kenya

I arrive in Nairobi on Saturday afternoon and someone I'm with asks Andrew King'Ori, the naturalist guide who is to show us around Nairobi, Mt Kenya and the Masai Mara game park, what people do on Sundays.

"Go to church," he answers, breathing out long vowels with his soft, polite, bass-booster voice.

And so I do.

I make a few inquiries and, early the next morning, ask the doorman to point me towards All Saints.

"Why don't you take a taxi, boss? Or do you want to walk?" He says the last with all the cultural loading one might expect in a nation born to walk and wherever you are, there are Kenyans walking. (It suddenly strikes me that this literally is "God's speed".)

"Yes," I say. "I want to walk." And he bows appreciatively.

He gives me instructions – "out to the road, follow to the left, to the roundabout and then right for, oh, 500 metres" – but I miss All Saints Anglican church (though it's almost directly opposite).

Serendipitously, thankfully, luckily and perhaps even by some divine interventions, on Haile Selassie Avenue, I find Neno Evangelism Centre. "Big Jesus Miracle Crusade" painted large.

Inside, there are thousands of plastic chairs in neat rows, all empty save a few. A woman wrapped in a fabric of distinctly Kenyan print sits rocking and sobbing. A child sits staring into space.

But, where the three big areas under a roof bigger than a soccer pitch come together, there is the huddle of people around a stage. Everyone has moved to the centre, shoulder to shoulder. Cheek by jowl. I look more closely at the chairs and see that most have a plastic bag, a book or a piece of cloth, marking them as "taken".

A preacher in a red jacket, with a microphone strapped to his chin, speaks in Swahili, and people rock and nod. In his half-hour sermon in Swahili, only three English phrases are interjected…

"Everything has its season…" I suddenly recognise amid the poetic indecipherable.

"Look after yourself and look after the children…"

And then he shifts to a more serious mode, and I guess he is talking the politics of Africa "…Never allow them to sow the seed of destruction in your heart…"

And, put together, they are a complete gospel for life, whatever your belief, and I hope you have one. More than anything else, I believe in belief.

Kenya is more Christian than the other countries in Africa. Around 60 per cent of Kenyans are Christian and the American-based Pew Research Centre, which specifically undertakes religious research, recently ranked Kenyans the sixteenth most religious in the world. Nearly nine in every ten people interviewed said that religion played an important role in their lives.

But 40 per cent of Kenya's Christians are members of the 200 independent African churches which have unusual beliefs and practices and run without foreign intervention. Ontulili Bethel Church, Christopher Church Thiba, Inter Christian Faith Church Jacaranda, Oasis of Living Waters.

Christianity here blends traditional culture of the forty-two Kenyan tribes with more usual Christian beliefs.

Polygamy is practised, and men have as many as four wives, and circumcision is important in the rites of passage from boyhood to manhood.

In Kenya, Christianity is closely related to colonial rule, but it was not just brought by European missionaries.

Further north up the Great Rift Valley which runs through Kenya, over the border, Ethiopians have, for 1,600 years, carried crosses to show their faith.

At Neno Evangelism Centre, the preacher finishes and a band strikes up. Not the fusty organs of my childhood, with too much volume, too much air through the valves and inaccurate footwork.

A guitar starts picking out a distinctly African offbeat tune, and people start to sing. The preacher straps on his own electric guitar and starts to pick out lead riffs.

People start to sing. My God how Africans can sing. It is instinctive, natural, harmonious, spiritual. Their sense of innate rhythm.

They start to sing quietly, with a politeness that I have come to realise is so much part of the national character.

But gradually, over ten minutes or so, hands start to spread and be raised, people who were swaying start to pace perhaps three or four steps to one side, and back.

There is a momentum in their communal spirits, a crescendo in their voices, and at first I think it is a giving of their hearts.

But then, as the place is swept up and lifted by this massive combination of human spirit, I think of it not as a giving but as a receiving. I really feel they are opening their arms, their hands and their hearts and receiving the holy spirit.

When I walk back towards the door of the Nairobi Serena Hotel, the doorman steps forward, beaming, to greet me.

"You got blessed," he asks.

"I got blessed," I say.

The Monasteries of Tibet

In this chill, blue-sky early morning, pilgrims walk steadily clockwise around the Potala Palace in Lhasa, Tibet. Previously the home of fourteen Dalai Lamas, it is perhaps the most dramatically recognisable face of Tibetan Buddhism.

Buddhism themes Tibet and at nearby Jokhang Temple, perhaps the most holy of places for Tibetan Buddhists, the same is happening.

For this *kora* – the morning procession – is an important part of pilgrimage to these places. The faithful walk around Potala Palace before making their way inside to the Jowo Shakyamuni Buddha statue, which is perhaps the single most revered object in Tibetan Buddhism.

And I find myself caught in the movement of it. Going along with it.

These people, moving with single purpose, seem like a massive human dynamo generating power.

They carry both short and long strands of prayer beads, clicking them off with a thumb as they walk.

On these, they count the number of times the mantra 'om mani padme hum' is recited. Mani means 'jewel', Padma 'the lotus flower', the sacred Buddhist bloom. Six syllables repeated over and over, especially by devotees of the Dalai Lama. Many have hand prayer wheels – canisters on handles that are also spun clockwise. And wrapped around the axle of these *mani* wheels is that same mantra 'om mani padme hum'. Tibetan Buddhists believe that saying this Sanskrit mantra, silently or aloud, calls the powerful blessings of Chenrezig, the embodiment of compassion.

Then there are the bigger prayer wheels – rows of them, gold and perhaps almost as big as a 44-gallon drum, suspended vertically and also spun clockwise. Each turn spinning out the mantra…'om mani padme hum'.

The more times it is said and the more times the prayer wheel is spun and the more *kora* are walked, the more the mantra is multiplied. Spiritual blessings and wellbeing are spread far and wide.

I can almost see those six syllables flying off into the air, spun out with each cycle, by centrifugal force. Disseminated like seed against the blue sky up here at an altitude of 3,600 metres.

Other pilgrims on the edges of this body of people move more slowly. These are pilgrim prostraters. While some walk here to repeatedly prostrate themselves at Potala or Jokhang's gates, these beside me now may have travelled days, weeks or even years on pilgrimages to Lhasa, covering the entire distance in prostrations.

They stand straight, raise their palms together, hands above their heads, touch crown, brow, throat and back to heart, and then bend forwards and touch the ground, kneeling and pushing forward to lie flat in a straight line, face down.

Then they quickly push back up off the floor, stand and repeat the prostration.

At Ganden Monastery, 40 kilometres outside Lhasa, I see a group of young people who have come a long distance like this, some with hide aprons, and with wooden pieces in each hand upon which to lean and slide.

Outside Tashilhunpo Monastery in Shigatse, about 300 kilometres from here and founded by the First Dalai Lama in 1447, I watched two prostraters moving slowly along a street's gutter, pads tied to their knees with rope.

Beside them was a stream of humanity, counting off beads, spinning prayer wheels, murmuring their mantra, the six syllables drifting up and away like chains of manuscript musical notes in the clear, thin air.

The show around me is beautiful. I am watching the small Tibetan boy tucked in to my left, his arm resting on my leg, pouring lemonade from the can he has been given into a glass.

He watches it carefully, lets the bubbles subside, pours again.

The little Tibetan girl to my right is eating her dinner carefully, not a grain of rice spilt. She notices something spilt by another child, takes a paper napkin from a glass, perfectly cleans it up, folds the napkin and pushes it back in the glass. She is about six years old.

It is beautiful to watch these polite, interested children looking after one another, just as they are being looked after by Dolma.

For they are orphans from the Dickey Orphanage on the outskirts of Lhasa, the capital of Tibet.

Their parents may have died or they may simply have been abandoned.

Before opening the orphanage in 2002, Dolma was a business-woman, running her own restaurant, but she could not ignore the plight of the orphaned children begging on the streets.

She took in four. Now there are seventy-three, thirty of them girls, the youngest, three months old and the oldest, eighteen.

She gives them names, and they all share a birthday in September which is the anniversary of the opening of the orphanage.

They go to public school, with lessons including three languages, and stay at the orphanage until they find jobs and can support themselves.

Before this year, the orphanage ran with no government support, simply relying on donations. But the government has now recognised the work with a stipend for each child, and three of the children have done so well with their exam results that they have received scholarships for further education.

It is a triumph for these children, but also for Dolma, who has devoted her life to them, and also to her son Rabter, who has joined her in the selfless work.

If we are fortunate, when we travel, these are the lives that we are sometimes privileged to witness. Lives that make me humble.

And now I sit in a row of tourists, with ten of the orphans interspersed between us, watching a cultural show at the Himalaya Hotel.

The children had turned up in a small car, with four of them in the boot. It is a good show – local instruments, traditional dress, dance and a lovely, humorous scene where two yaks are milked. But the children around us are as interested in the players on the side lining up for the next scene, in their food, and, gently, in one another. I had been led around the orphanage by a sweet little girl, called Rabter.

I ask Rabter to write her name in my notebook. Usually in Tibet, people have only one name, but Rabter writes "Tsering Dolma".

Animism in Toraja Land

A gallery has been carved high up out of the rock face. There are six human figures in it, seated on a low bench. As I look slowly from left to right through the camera's long lens, I see their motionless features and blank, staring eyes. These are effigies of dead people, carved from wood then dressed. Almost exact replicas.

Then one of them moves. And another.

What I thought were six carvings are, in fact, four – and the two on the right are men who have climbed the temporary bamboo ladders used during the rare grave-cleaning ceremony here in the village of Loko Mate, in Toraja Land, Sulawesi. They are sitting with their ancestors, passing the time of day. One is smoking.

The effigies are called *tau tau*, which literally means "little person" and, over four days, wrapped bodies are being taken from their high graves and carried down the bamboo ladders. They are rewrapped and replaced, and the *tau tau* repainted and redressed. There are offerings and prayers before the grave is resealed.

The oldest of these graves has been here at least 200 years.

At the village of Lemo, near the market town of Rantepao, which is very much the centre of Toraja for visitors, there are more galleries. There are thirty graves dating from the seventeenth century cut high into the rock with a small wooden door on the front.

All the deceased are linked to one powerful family and at the bottom of the rock face are the graves of slaves who were sacrificed to accompany their masters to the afterlife.

"Death is not a final moment," Michael Saunders, an academic historian based in Singapore and specialising in South-East Asian culture, later explains. "It is the start of what happens next."

Human sacrifice ceased long ago but funerals still centre around a blood sacrifice – buffalo and pigs for the rich in the top of four recognised classes right down to a chicken or even an egg – broken so that it passes back into the earth – for the much poorer.

The buffalo is revered – these are soul sacrifices to the deceased.

I find the cultural experiences in Toraja Land deep, stimulating, even challenging, certainly unforgettable. And pretty much on our doorstep.

Makassar, the capital of the big Indonesian island of Sulawesi, is an eighty-minute flight north-east of Bali and there is then about a nine-hour coach trip north from there, high in the mountains, in Toraja Land. The trip is easily split over two days.

Yet the people of Toraja have more visitors from Israel than they do from Australia. An interesting fact. By far the biggest group of international visitors are the French.

Sulawesi, one of the biggest of Indonesia's islands (some say there are 13,000 islands, some say 17,000, but it can depend on tides, as there are more on low tides) is 2,000 kilometres south to north.

The majority of people are Muslim but 30 per cent are Christian, Buddhist or animist, says Sada'Dualolo. A guide for more than 30 years, he is a Toraja man, an animist, and says that 97 per cent of animist people are Christian, combining beliefs.

Toraja is a bastion of animist belief. In this, people believe that everything has a soul and worship ancestors.

"This is a culture that has not been disturbed," Mr Saunders says. "But this culture is as much endangered as is that of the orangutan."

Traditional houses in Toraja are among the most unusual buildings I have ever seen and these *tongkonan* are loaded with symbolism.

"They are something like a parent," Sada'Dualolo says. "Some have been lived in by forty generations. If you forget the house, you forget the family."

It is said that eight ships originally arrived here, bringing the first Torajans and this is the foundation of the architecture.

The *tongkonan* are the mother houses, the smaller rice houses, of parallel design are the father houses. The roof is the space of the gods, the living rooms are the place for humans on Earth, and the underworld is symbolised by the area under the house, which is on stilts.

Tongkonan are always built north–south. Crops and livestock will be to the east, symbolising life, the cemetery to the west, in the setting sun, symbolising death. (Just as the living only sleep north–south, and the dead are laid east–west.)

I stay in the Toraja Heritage Hotel in Rantepao, its rooms based on the architecture of the *tongkonan*, and it is from here that I set out with the news that a request to attend a local animist funeral has been enthusiastically accepted.

It is the funeral of a 90-year-old woman who died two years ago. As is tradition, her body has been kept with her family in the *tongkonan* until the funeral could be paid for. Traditionally, the body would be preserved using the bark of a particular tree, betel nut, and the inside of a buffalo horn, scooped out. Today it is more likely to have been injected with a couple of litres of formalin.

Delays between a death and a funeral are largely to do with cost, as the family usually has to save for what may be an expensive business. At this Pangli village, twenty buffalo and 100 pigs will be sacrificed. A temporary village will be built from bamboo for the ceremonies and visitors.

"It is not fair," says Sada'Dualolo, giving the local view, "but it is the way it is." He means that the deceased must be given a good send-off or they might wreak havoc on the family. The cost of the funeral severely affects some families but the cost of not doing so could be greater. "This is the tradition. We are thinking about where to buy buffaloes because they are very expensive."

He says a "Toyota buffalo" might start at $100, a "Mercedes buffalo" might be $25,000. Three hundred is the biggest number of buffalo he knows of being sacrificed.

Inheritance is divided in proportion to the contribution individuals make to the funeral. (It might also be worth noting that a divorce costs twenty-four buffaloes.)

During the time before the funeral, the person is not thought of as dead but having an ailment. They will be brought three meals a day and visitors will bring them gifts of betel nut and cigarettes.

And this is the day of the funeral in Pangli.

Visitors are welcome as the more people who come to a funeral, the more auspicious it is – the higher the status, the happier the soul.

There are other Western guests now, and we file into the temporary village, women first, then men, to sit in an area specially constructed for guests. We are offered tea, coffee and cakes, clove cigarettes and a little conversation.

And then two buffalo are slaughtered, their blood lying red across the ground. The death of the first signifies that the woman is no longer sick and her soul is now free. Tomorrow, eighteen more buffalo will be sacrificed and the 100 pigs, all the meat being distributed and eaten. Sada'Dualolo says that to fulfil all of Toraja's burial rituals, 10,000 buffalo and 60,000 pigs are needed each year.

"It is expensive but, if you don't make a funeral service for your ancestors, they can't enter paradise and that is dangerous for the living," he says.

And then he brightens up. The good thing about funerals is that no-one is invited but everyone can come.

Later, as I chat with Toraja man and guide Hendrick Leppayg, who was a rafting guide in Bali for three years and often leads walking treks between the *tongkonan*, staying with local families, Sada quietly begins to sing.

"*I have a dream...*"

My goodness, is Sada really going to sing an Abba song?

"*I believe in angels...something good in everything I see...I believe in angels...and my destination makes it worthwhile...*"

Sada is singing Abba and the song takes on a whole new meaning.

The Turning of the Bones in Madagascar

The turning of the bones happens only every seven years, and it is happening today. In a village near the town of Antsirabe, in Madagascar, several bodies will be disinterred from their family tomb, hoisted on to the shoulders of the living, "danced with", rewrapped in silk and put back to rest.

Today's the day because the village witchdoctor declared it auspicious three years ago, and the family has been saving since to pay musicians and feed the people who will come to celebrate.

The turning of the bones goes deep into the cultural roots here and the 18 tribes of Madagascar share animist beliefs – supernatural power, the souls of objects, animals and plants and natural phenomena, and a complicated system of taboos and revering ancestors.

Nowadays, half the population is Christian, but their Christianity is combined with traditional ancestor worship. Witchdoctors like Ramdrrianarison Jean Baptiste (Malagasies' first names are written to follow their surnames) are crucial to everyday life in Madagascar.

And so I leave Antsirabe, in the mountainous heart of the world's oldest island, and drive down a dusty track and join the family gathering in a yard. They have already been to church and now they are ready for the turning of the bones. The Catholic Church no longer objects to the turning of the bones, known as *famadihana*, seeing it as solely cultural, not religious.

A band strikes up – five trumpets, two clarinets and two drummers – in a sharp reverie and leads us in cacophonous procession to the place of interment.

Tombs are very important to Malagasies. "Tombs are regarded as our permanent homes, while the houses we live in are temporary," explains Andrianampoina Diary, a new friend, showing me around Madagascar.

Houses are built of wood because it is associated with living; tombs are built of stone because rock correlates with death.

Tombs are usually on top of hills – above the houses, between the living people and the God Creator, explains Diary.

"Life after death is their real life and the ancestors' spirits stay with the living.

"To know when to do the turning of the bones, we have to ask a witchdoctor. He must be there to open the tomb and put the body back. When the body is taken from the tomb, we put it on our shoulders and make it dance with us."

A crowd of about 300 people clusters around the tomb and chief Rakotonjanahary Berson ensures we have pride of place. There are some initial preparations to unseal the tomb, followed by speeches, and then men open the rock door. Everyone moves closer as they shimmy into the tomb and a rush mat is passed to them.

And then the first body appears, is wrapped in the mat, and held high through the crowd, being jiggled as the music plays. It is wrapped in a white silk cloth and I see it bend and flex. I sense the weight of it, just like someone asleep.

The body is taken off through the tight-packed crowd and another rush mat is laid down near us. The body is then brought back and laid on it before us.

Already another body is being brought out of the tomb. It too is danced with before being brought over and laid next to the other. And this is repeated until there is a row of bodies, becoming ever-smaller, showing how time has taken its toll. A gaggle of stringy hair protrudes from one of the parcels. The band is frenetic. In front of them, in a cleared circle in the packed crowd, men are dancing wildly, kicking up the dust. One dancer seems almost trancelike, jumping wildly and cavorting on the floor.

When all the bodies are out, family member Rakotonjanahary Rene grabs my arm and grins at me. He tugs at me to come, speaking in Malagasy. And so I let him pull me towards the tomb, thinking he is offering a glimpse inside. But when I do this, he ducks inside and pulls harder, beaming wildly. And then I am inside the tomb, with its empty bottle of local rum and simple decorations.

Back outside, the bodies are being rewrapped in silk shrouds.

The turning of the bones and this rewrapping in silk is repeated every seven years, seven being a lucky number in Madagascar. Ancestors must be acknowledged and cared for, as it is also believed that the dead can reward or punish, led by a supreme being called Zanahary (the creator) or Andriamanitra (the fragrant one).

Anthropologists estimate that 40 per cent of Malagasy people practise traditional religion. When a person dies, the body is kept in the house for days, weeks, months. One week after the interment, Malagasies practise *sasa* – going to a fast-flowing river to wash off the association with death. Uncircumcised boys cannot be interred in family tombs, so all are circumcised between the ages of two and three. "But it is taboo to throw the foreskin away," says Diary. This is eaten by a grandfather with banana. In doing this he accepts him as a man and accepts him into the family.

In the country, often with no electricity, and by the light of the cooking fire, candles or petrol lamps, it is also grandfathers who, at meal times, tell traditional, moralistic, educational stories. "It is our culture," Diary simply says. And that word, culture, holds a strength. It is what he believes in. It is intrinsically part of him and he of it.

"Despite the poverty here," he says, "people are happy." And it is true that during nearly two weeks of travel in Madagascar, I don't see a child crying.

They are happy because they have culture and community.

And there, in a dusty field near Antsirabe, as I look down at (to me) a somewhat macabre row of corpses, I see a culture that is alive, practised, and bringing people together from far and wide. And as I drop my eyes down, trying to work all this out, I see a small girl sitting in the dirt in her best frock, sneaking a good look at the bodies.

And she looks up and beams at me.

6

The Fabric of Society

A handful of village women meet in a hut and start sewing together. Others join to spin wool. Then they all start dying their own fabric, using natural colours crushed from plants, berries and beetle carapaces.

At first it is as much social, for the strength that comes from fellowship, as for the practicality of what is produced.

But then a coach full of visitors stops and buys some of what they've been working on. This self-help project has given the women a different future. More women join and they start a creche for the small children. Soon they're making enough money to employ a teacher and they set up a school room for the older children. It is not many years until there are more than 100 at the primary school and, in an adjacent room, many then go on to secondary school.

When the first three students graduate from university, all the women celebrate.

This is the story of a group of women in Africa, but I have seen such stories many times, all over the world.

Spinning, dying, weaving and sewing are often the catalysts for change; union empowers women socially, emotionally and economically. Physical fabric has the potential to change the fabric of society.

I often seek out groups at work in these crafts; not just for the story, but for the pleasure of watching a backstrap loom in sure hands, a tiny silver needle darting along a delicate pattern, or the dramatic red splash of a cochineal-dyed rug on a floor, with the very sheep its wool came from bleating outside the window.

I like sewing. At primary school, we boys were all set to work making a pencil case, using a wide range of stitches. Blanket for the sides, hemming stitch for the bottom, back stitch for strength, cross stitch for decoration. (I like to give girls, but especially boys, a sewing kit for their eighteenth birthday.)

And for years I have been working on a private project. On one visit to India, I bought a piece of hand-dyed fabric and noticed it was about the size of the panel in the back of a denim jacket. I appliquéd it on, following the lines of the picture on the fabric.

I now have perhaps twenty such jackets, each with a panel from a different country. India, Sri Lanka, Cambodia, Tibet, South Africa and Lesotho; Nepal and New Zealand are works in progress.

Inside the Vietnam jacket, I have written the words on a panel above the women embroidering in Danang: "Embroiderer through her body to contact with the universe, to touch with energies, powers and the stream of universe. Sitting to embroider is not leaving out your senses, but the opposite, using these senses perfectly, contact with the elements of the heaven and earth, with matter."

The one souvenir that Casey doesn't mind carrying is a tablecloth. (I seem to hear him endlessly moaning about anything else I might have been tempted to buy. "No wonder the planet's going to hell in a hand basket.") On most trips, he ends up with a tablecloth folded up, completely filling his base, everything else on top. At home, our dining table is graced with the colour and art of the world, and with each cloth there is a sense of the human hands that have created it and, for me, a sense of the change to which it may have contributed.

The *Bangdians* of Tibet

There is a life in this small piece of woollen fabric, this *bangdian*. There is a place defined in its colourful stripes. A person in its oily, smoky scent. And a moment shopping has led me to discover both of these.

It is not a usual shop. I am in a small square in Tashilhunpo Monastery in Shigatse, about 350 kilometres from Lhasa, the capital of Tibet.

Founded in 1447 by the First Dalai Lama, Tashilhunpo is still very much alive and today, as every day, a stream of pilgrims circumambulate its temples, bowing before its Buddha statues, adding hot yak butter milk from vacuum flasks to its candle bowls, chanting the mantra 'om mani padme hum', calling on benevolence, spreading compassion.

And some have gathered in this square, in the sun, under an indigo sky up here more than 3,800 metres above sea level, where an impromptu shop is opened on the stone steps. There is a long pile of gifted clothing, much from people who have died and, as these faithful believe, gone on to reincarnation.

I already have an interest in these traditional aprons, and step forward to the gentle scrum of women locked around them. I pick one up, attracted by its strong but not too bright colours, and an elderly lady picks up the other end and looks at me. Blue fabric is plaited into the ends of her long hair and I have just watched her pull these up, wrap them around her head and secure the ends on top.

We hold either end, looking at one another but then I realise she is not challenging me for it. She is taking an interest in what I am interested in and I have the sense of her reading the life in this piece of fabric. The place and the person in it.

She nods at it, turns it over, as if she were conversing with not the fabric but the person who has worn it, clearly for many years. Probably from touch she can tell whether it is a *xiema* – the best kind of apron and woven from fourteen to twenty kinds of yarn – or a *pulu*, the second-best quality and most common. Then she lets the end go, looks at me and nods.

She is about to move away, when she suddenly grabs the end I am holding, turns it over and looks at the price, written in yuan in a Tibetan character. This is clearly important, too. She nods again. Thirty-five yuan (a bit over $5) is clearly right.

I hand money to the young monk standing above me in his maroon robe, his traditional red shoes at my eye level. The *bangdian* is mine but as I turn away with it, other women finger it, turn it over, consider it.

My *bangdian* was probably made very close to here and worn by a woman who came to pray and chant in Tashilhunpo's temples. For Shigatse is one of the three main areas in which they are made, along with Lhasa and Shannan. Their production can be traced back more than 500 years.

Traditionally, the aprons are worn only by married women but the young and unmarried have apparently started adopting this strong statement of traditional dress. They are tied around the waist, usually over the equally traditional long black skirt.

They are of finely woven wool, which has been spun into fine thread, dyed, brushed and woven into strips. Traditionally, the wool was thought purer if the animals had been fed on clean, uncontaminated grass.

Three strips are stitched together to make a *bangdian*, the stripes on them sitting horizontally.

The colour of these stripes is all-important. It must be both striking and tasteful, harmonious and gently exciting.

Traditionally, natural vegetable dyes were used, but a chemical pink dye is also much favoured today.

It is said that women in agricultural areas prefer a stronger contrast in the colours. These bolder and brighter aprons have a wider stripe.

Women in towns prefer a milder mix and these more graceful colour mixes have a narrower stripe.

Some have pure primary colours mixed into numerous strips with secondary colours. Some are ordered, dark to light, by groups. Some seem just random.

But there is a plan and a story in the selection. For it is said that a Tibetan woman's home village can be read from the language of her apron's stripes.

And this takes on another aspect. For after China's invasion of Tibet and the failed uprising of 1959, and countless other waves since, many Tibetans live in exile, particularly in Nepal and India – away from their lands.

But they continue to wear these aprons, connecting them to place. To their past. To Tibet.

In the old part of Lhasa, I talk a little with a weaver of *bangdians*, before buying a new one for 240 yuan. In fact, there is little word talk (his English is slight and my Tibetan non-existent) but he shows me around the shop.

The various mixes of colour; the little timber pit loom which, from my later reading, is unchanged in hundreds of years.

Tightly combining a warp usually woven from wool or cotton, and a weft from wool, it is simple and portable, and nomadic Tibetans carried their unfinished work with them as they drifted from place to place with their flocks.

Back outside Tashilhunpo Monastery, I walk down the wide street and stop at a little cafe to sit in the sun on raffia-style chairs, most of their seats fallen through, and order jasmine tea. A tall glass is brought with a few dried jasmine leaves in the bottom and a vacuum flask of hot water left on the floor by the table.

Someone else has bought two aprons at the square in Tashilhunpo Monastery. His are on the table now and an elderly woman stops to examine them. Again, there is an intimacy; a sense of her feeling she has the right to pick them up; to consider and greet the former owner. It is as if she is reading the *bangdians*. As if she is reconnected to the village they came from. As if she is touching the people who once wore them.

Lotus Weaving in Burma

A youngster in a red baseball cap and purple tracksuit pants slogs along with a single blade in his laden teak canoe. He is paddling along Inle Lake in the late afternoon, making little way. And then he suddenly stands at the stern on the narrow little boat on one leg, curls the other around the long, wooden paddle, his foot giving it the final twisting grip, and starts to leg row.

And in the actions of this young man, I see that the Intha people of this high freshwater lake in northern Burma have another generation of leg rowers.

It is an extraordinary motion. The whole torso and arms are used for power and leverage – the body swung and twisted. The hip is thrown out and to take the blade through a wide arc, the foot used to create a particular sculling action.

I am in a high-powered "long tail" boat with an inboard diesel but, as we move into a narrower channel, the engine is cut and I watch leg-rower Min Tun as he stands at the bow and propels the big craft. I paddle canoes and kayaks and can see the full gambit of these leg rowers' strokes – different for forward propulsion and to steer the boat one way or the other. As many other men on the lake demonstrate, it leaves the hands free for fishing nets hauling in mainly Inle carp and, as the youngster in purple pants is displaying, can give a lot of forward power.

Such leg rowing is not known anywhere else. It is a big lake of more than 110 square kilometres but, on average, is only two metres deep and it is thought that this unique style of leg rowing originally developed as parts of the lake have a lot of floating plants and reeds, making it difficult to see a way through while sitting. Standing gives the rower a clear view. But then, it is only used by men. If alone, women usually sit cross-legged at the stern and paddle conventionally. So, maybe it's just a "guy thing", after all.

There are some 70,000 people at Inle Lake, predominantly of Intha descent and most devout Buddhists, living around the shores and many in floating villages on the lake itself. Their wood and bamboo houses are often two storey, standing on stilts in the water. They have extensive floating gardens and are renowned growers, particularly of tomatoes. They bring up weeds from the bottom and turn them into floating and fertile growing beds, tethered by bamboo poles, which rise and fall with the water level and make good perches for the black drongos and other birds.

I pass a pig in an over-water sty with a slatted bamboo floor; a boy playing with a puppy used to a watery life; caught fish kept in netted pens under the houses; women doing washing; men doing renovations, to the steady chew of handsaws. There is little electricity, and what there is passes along wires that look precariously propped over the water. Neat children are on their way home from school, paddling their own canoes in line, like the twisty tail of an old-fashioned kite, with an adept skill. Younger children are around their mothers at the lotus- and silk-weaving workshop in the village of In Paw Khon. As our skipper cuts the engine a little way out and rows us to the jetty, I can hear the familiar clacketty-clack of hand looms. Here the women weave silk, but, more interestingly, also lotus threads. The lotus plant has to be at least four years old and Ma Tho, clearly an experienced hand (Ma is the name given to someone over forty), shows me how she snicks the lotus stems and pulls the fibrous threads out of the inside, rolling them to make a thin twine.

A small scarf or shawl will take thousands of lotus threads. The people here are largely self-sufficient farmers but we stop at a cigarette-making factory at the village of Nam Pan where women, mostly very young and all with children, earn less than $2 a day packing wood chips into tobacco leaves to make big, green cigarettes. Just one packet of ten cheroots costs half what a woman will earn in a whole day, and they make cigarette after cigarette fast and with dexterity.

Another short boat ride away, the market at Ywa Ma village has just about everything you can name – fabrics and flowers, fanbelts and fruit.

The lake is not without its problems. Timber removal is allowing silt to wash down from the surrounding Shan Hills, introduced water hyacinth has a hold and there are algae blooms. The problems that come with human population, which we are familiar with ourselves. But this is a spectacular place and particularly on this afternoon as we speed across the smooth, steel-blue water, leaving a rooster-tail of spray behind. There is no wonder that it has become much visited by tourists who are arriving back in Burma, riding the tide of political change.

I'd like to be back at Inle Lake in September and October, when there are a series of festivals. During the Hpaung Daw U festival, leg-rowers turn out in force in traditional dress to compete. Traditional dress, presumably, which doesn't include red baseball caps and purple trackie pants.

Making a Difference in Africa

I arrive under a darkening sky, with thunder rolling round. The Nanyuki Spinners and Weavers group has known many such days.

This women's self-help project near Mt Kenya, 240 kilometres from Nairobi, was started by Annah Warutere in 1977. There were just six women to begin with, desperate for income and to educate their children.

"The men keep on drinking and drinking so the women are the founders of home," Lucy Wanjiru explains. There have been difficult days, but those first women, with the wise guidance of Mrs Warutere, have weathered the worst.

The fine wool of highland Kenya is excellent for hand-spun yarn, and there was an abundance of plants for natural dyes. Mrs Wanjiru, a Kikuyu woman showing me around, says they use many weeds, grass, marigold, the mould off cactus, and the cochineal beetle for a strong scarlet-brown.

They make rugs, sweaters, shawls and scarves, weave baskets and make "other appealing items".

It is all handcrafted, from spinning to dying to weaving.

When I visit, there are 137 women involved and 330 children are at the primary school Nanyuki Spinners and Weavers funds, with 212 applicants for the ninety places at the new secondary school it is just starting.

"I like my job because it helps me to educate my kids and to feed my family. I say 'thank you' to God," Mrs Wanjiru said. "Mrs Warutere is a good woman."

Destruction & Creation in KwaZulu-Natal

The artists working in Rorke's Drift in South Africa like to think of it as a place of both destruction and creation. Today, the ELC Art and Craft Centre is becoming known internationally for its weaving, textile and ceramic studios.

And all in this place in KwaZulu-Natal province, in eastern South Africa, which is one of the most famous sites of the Anglo-Zulo wars. For it was here, in 1879, that first King Cetswayo's mighty army massacred the British at Isandlwana and then, over that night, 100 mainly Welsh soldiers withstood the might of 4,500 Zulu warriors here at Rorke's Drift, nearby.

Events, some say, which set the scene for many things that followed in South Africa prior to its political shift in 1994.

But artist Thami Jali isn't particularly thinking about any of that. He was trained at the arts centre and has now come back to teach others in this small and somewhat remote South African town.

By doing that, he says, he multiplies the opportunities given to him.

"He has come back to teach the children and I am so very proud of him," says the centre's coordinator, Mthembeni Zulu, also a minister in Rorke's Drift.

Celamusa Nxumalo, behind the counter today, also takes pride in the artist's original work. "All from their imaginations," she says.

Rorke's Drift is popular with tourists exploring the history of the battlefields of both the Anglo-Zulu and Boer wars. But visiting the arts and crafts centre allows them to connect with the South Africa of today.

And they can be assured that the money for original printed cloth, beadwork, pottery and weavings is going to the local community. Weaving wool is carded, spun and dyed at Rorke's Drift under the guidance of master weavers Philda Majozi and Emma Dammann. The ceramic workshop has been producing indigenous craft for thirty years.

The centre was originally established by the Church of Sweden Mission during the 1960s. Though the mission is no longer financially involved, the centre has increasingly provided income and opportunity, and a fine art course was introduced.

"The certificate of fine art introduced in 1968 was significant in a country whose apartheid institutions denied formal fine art education to black people," says information from the centre.

The Natural Colours of India

The Indian state of Rajasthan's city of Jaipur is famous for its pink buildings and Amber Fort, but it is not these that have me mesmerised. It is a small, personal moment.

I am on the back of Lakshmi, a big elephant named for the goddess of prosperity and patterned with yellow, orange and pink dye, after being driven through Jaipur's teeming, intriguing streets to the bottom of the hill leading up to the fort. And there I joined a short queue and was quickly on Lakshmi's back for the ride to the main gate of the fort; an entrance in 18 kilometres of defensive walls. The remarkable Maharaja Jai Singh II, who ruled from 1699 to 1744, first established Amber then built India's first planned city, Jaipur. Being a student of mathematics, astrophysics and astronomy, and a man who thought both broadly and sensitively, the city was planned according to Indian Vastu Shastra. This Vedic planning would bring comfort, success and abundance to the citizens.

One might recognise in this an earlier form of the Chinese discipline of feng shui.

This stone-paved, zig zag road up the hill, which Lakshmi is now softly treading, was useful in slowing antagonistic approaches. Hot oil poured down the slope undoubtedly helped.

And, as Lakshmi settles into her big, loping gait and sways through t-shirt hawkers and the odd straining motorcycle, the mahout unfurls a long length of thin cloth of identical but even brighter Rajasthani colours to those adorning Lakshmi and begins to wind it around his head. In tying his *safa*, he is both participating in and perpetuating ritual. It is a particular motion. The mahout holds the cloth firm with his left hand, pulls it tight across the top of his head, twists the fabric, takes a turn around his head, twists the fabric, takes another turn across his head, twists the fabric, and continues this until all the fabric is used. From my position, high on Lakshmi's back above him, it looks very like a bicycle helmet, and probably nearly as firm. He turns to me and smiles and holds his hands together and up in the familiar greeting. Namaste. And I interpret his poised smile as pride in himself and in his heritage.

And the Pink City, Jaipur, is famous too for cotton, hand-block printed with natural plant dyes that have ancient roots and react with particular minerals in the groundwater to transform colours. Among them the brilliant Indian saffron, the most expensive of all, dragged orange-yellow from the stigmas of crocus.

Wooden blocks are cut and then the rolls of cotton printed over and over – first the outline and then the various colours. It builds up and up into a floral pattern.

I have watched it being made, the wooden blocks carefully lined up on the cotton, then thumped, then reloaded with dye, then moved to the next position, then thumped, and I am now looking at rolls of it in a textile shop.

"What is your name?" the assistant asks, and I tell him. "Ah, this is not your first time in India," the young assistant says, perceptively. "I'm lucky," he says. "Lucky you keep coming back to my country."

And so, to me, Lucky he becomes, and when I call him such, he is clearly pleased.

With Lucky perspicaciously hooking into my taste, we find two hand block-printed Jaipur fabrics ideal for shirts. He then arranges for me to be measured, the man doing this quickly taking eighteen measurements and calling them out to Lucky, who jots them in a sequence on a sheet of paper. "Like this?" the Indian tailor asks, frowning at the fit of the frighteningly expensive Versace Classic shirt I am wearing. "Or you leave to me?"

I see the look on his face, his manners almost masking his disapproval at this clearly shoddy fit.

"I'll leave to you."

The shirts, which are delivered to me within hours, are the most perfect fit of any I have.

From Lucky, then, there were sheets and other items, and he produces a free, handmade backpack and throws in another piece of fabric.

He may be Lucky, but lucky I am, indeed, too.

The jewellery for which Jaipur is also famous is part of this story of organic colour, beautiful design and craftsmanship. And the gems used in the jewellery are also encrusted into the story behind the Ganesh Gate of Jaipur's Amber Fort, before which I now stand.

The gate has both a strength and delicacy about it. A tough guy in a floral shirt.

For the gate, at the heart of the royal fort set on a hill in this dry part of Rajasthan, is epic and designed to foil invaders, but the paint used to decorate it was made from precious stones.

Lapis lazuli, sapphires, emeralds and rubies, all crushed, painted on to a very fine plaster called *arash* and made from eggshells, seashells and white lime plaster, which is fine like marble. For when soft gems like these are cut, water is used to stop them overheating. That water was reclaimed and the residue dust mixed with gum arabic to make a paste to paint on the plaster.

Jaipur, the capital of Rajasthan, which is the biggest of the twenty-eight Indian states, is surrounded by gem-laden mountains but some stones are brought here down long-followed trading routes, like the lapis lazuli of Afghanistan.

This gate, dedicated to the great Hindu god of learning and the remover of obstacles, Ganesh, is a focal point of the Amber Fort, which can be traced back to the twelfth century and Raja Man Singh, a respected Rajput general in Mogul ruler Akbar the Great's army. He began building the fort palace but it was the Maharaja Jai Singh II's vision that brought it to life. He founded Jaipur in 1727.

Part of the secret to the Amber Fort's presence and success is that its defence wall, which is seven metres tall at its lowest, includes lakes. Being in Rajasthan's dry zone, controlling the water not only encouraged passing caravans to stop and trade but also to behave nicely, for they would surely need to call again. The Thar Desert comprises 60 per cent of Rajasthan, which is more than twice the size of England.

But we are talking a longer human history even than that. The fourteen generations of the ruling royal family of which Jai Singh II was part, brought hundreds of years of peace. Jai Singh II, who built this city, was a man inclusive of all ideas.

And so we are back with the Ganesh Gate, which is distinctly Rajput, but with a clear Islamic influence. He had learnt to live with the Muslim Moguls who had come into the north with armies of up to a quarter of a million soldiers and ended up controlling from Kabul to Tibet and three-quarters of the way down the subcontinental peninsula.

There are water tanks under the palace, and every drop was collected and stored. It ran in channels through the buildings, cooling rooms through evaporation. Its final use was to water gardens.

Amber Fort has the biggest mirror hall in the world, its walls sparkling with convex mirrors. Colourful rugs and dress would have reflected in the thousands of mirrors. Lit by candles on the evening, flames would have had flickering reflections.

It is all worth reflecting upon.

But while the Amber Fort and the planning of Jaipur (for which Jai Singh II turned to Bengal and the Brahmin scholar Vidyadhar Bhattacharya for advice) are the most obvious highlights in Jaipur, it isn't these that have always left the most lasting impression on me.

For he also built the Jantar Mantar observatory, a collection of astronomical instruments, between 1727 and 1734. This was Jai Singh II's interest in mathematics, astrophysics and astronomy brought to a grand scale.

The Jai Prakash may well be Jai Singh's most elaborate and complex instrument. Based on concepts dating to as early as 300 BC, it is partly above and partly below ground, and when the shadow of a wire across it falls into its bowl, it reveals the coordinates of the sun.

The biggest instrument is Samrat Yantra, a twenty-seven metre high sundial which plots the time of day to within two seconds.

And this astronomy backed into astrology. By knowing where on the planet someone was born, and now precisely the time, they could use the heavenly bodies and explore the mysticism of prediction.

That's what these instruments were for.

Even today, most Indians believe in good astrology.

Even great maharajas returning from victories in battle might camp for days outside their own fort, waiting for an auspicious moment to re-enter the great gates of a wondrous fort, decorated, as it is, with paints made from precious gems.

The roads of Mysore, in the south of India, are lined with mulberry bushes – the food of the mulberry silkworm, *Bombyx mori*, and its fruit also used for dramatic and distinctive dye.

It is estimated that some 9,000 tonnes of mulberry silk is produced in the state of Karnataka (two-thirds of India's total output), and most of it around the city of Mysore.

The silk's cultivation was heavily promoted during the reign of Tipu Sultan, in the old and great days of the Kingdom of Mysore. A thinker, scholar, poet and soldier, Tipu Sultan, who was known as the Tiger of Mysore, ruled this kingdom from 1782 to 1799 (and indeed, near the Tiffin Room in the old palace, there is a stuffed tiger).

But it is not silk that I am shopping for in Mysore. It's a pashmina – and it has to be of the highest quality.

I ask in a shop. "I want the best quality."

The man gets down a sample and shows me, and I get out of my camera bag a small fragment of a now deceased pashmina. I have brought this from home and been instructed to buy nothing below this fine quality. It is so thin, so delicate, that when I hold it up,

I can see quite clearly through it. And my friend Natalie Angliss taught me the ultimate test: a good quality pashmina should be able to pass through a wedding ring.

"This is the best quality," pronounces the man, but when I compare it to my sample, it is clearly not as fine.

"It's not like this," I say.

"Ah," he says, then pauses dramatically. "You want the *best* quality? We need to go to my other shop."

And he leads me off through arcades and alleyways to a small, crammed shop, much like the first. He shimmies up a wooden ladder and gets down packets containing pashminas. Then he gets one out with a flourish. "This is the best quality."

After all this palaver, it's difficult to stick to my guns, but when I compare it with my sample, his pashmina is clearly inferior. "It's still not as fine as this," I venture.

"Ah," he says, unperturbed. "Then we need to go to my other shop."

And off we go again, down more alleyways, to the third shop. And there, shelf upon shelf, are pashminas as thin as tissue. The best quality.

Delicacies & Thai Silk

The first traces of Thai silk were found in Ban Chiang, Udon Thani. They are three thousand years old.

And at Jolie Femme, in Sankampaeng Road in Chiang Mai, I see the virtually unchanged silk making process, from silk worm to a cocoon the size of a quail's egg which yields up to 500 metres of silk, through weaving to a shop which contains the most wonderful garments.

I watch a woman study the pattern for one intricate design and then start to label the dozens of bamboo runners. In a mirror underneath the work, she checks what she has done, studies the pattern again. For such an intricate design, it may be possible to complete only perhaps ten centimetres a day.

Local markets in Phuket, Bangkok and Chiang Mai, for example, are full of cloth labelled "Thai silk". And how do you tell it from synthetics? Singe the edge of a hem, if they'll let you. If it's synthetic, it will smell like plastic, if it's silk, it will smell like hair.

Maimanee, a silk seller at the Suanlum Night Bazaar says, "The sheen of woven silk cloth is its most admirable quality. This comes from the structure of the silk fibres, which are triangular in cross section and so reflect light like a prism. It also has layers of protein that adds lustre and smoothness to its natural sheen. At the same time, this fibre is immensely strong for its light weight, and both elastic and supple. The cloth made from Thai silk has relatively coarse texture with uneven, slightly knotty threads. This imperfection gives it a special beauty and makes it extremely suitable for hand weaving.

"Today, silk is still an integral part of life in the rural areas. Women work in the rice fields during the plantation and harvesting, and turn to silkworm reeling, spinning, weaving and dyeing during the rest of the year."

They float in gracefully with long, gold fingernails, to the distinctive music of northern Thailand. A deep drum, a two-stringed violin called a *salor*, a local bamboo flute.

And then, circling, in their traditional pastel-coloured silks, the eight dancers give an intimate insight into the true potential of feminine delicacy and strength, through their hand movements and poised, drifting bodies alone.

The women are as stunningly beautiful as the delicate actions of this traditional and intricate dance, which is performed on special occasions such as greeting state visitors.

But tonight, as every night at the Old Chiang Mai Cultural Centre, there are just several hundred tourists, being treated like royalty, as has occurred continuously since April 1971.

A good proportion of them are Thais from other parts of the country, but mixed in are French, Americans, Germans, Japanese. And even the odd Australian.

The cultural centre brings to life the creativity, culture and traditions for which Chiang Mai, an hour's flight north of Bangkok, is known.

It has long considered itself a cultural capital, and its history as capital of the individualist Chiang Mai province, with its own royal family, dialect and culture, supports this. For it was the northern capital when eight provinces were joined in an earlier kingdom, Longan.

So does its modern face, for with the arrival of Starbucks and McDonalds, Chiang Mai lost none of its individuality and charm. While quietly accepting the present, this old walled city backed up to the mountainous country is still the home of hill tribes and elephant camps, and has not over-compromised.

It's hard to precisely put your finger on what gives a place character, but there is something in the attitudes and demeanour of Chiang Mai, and its surrounding area, that resonates peacefully, thoughtfully, memorably.

Certainly there is a beauty.

The Thais themselves recognise it in the people here. In its description of Chiang Mai, one Thai tour company says this of the women, "The local people always smile, and the girls are graceful and soft spoken. They are also stunningly beautiful and well known for their attractive features."

Which saves me saying it.

The same booklet says, "The most important asset Chiang Mai can claim is its people. Their beauty, hospitality and good manners are legendary throughout Thailand, and more than one city slicker from Bangkok has gone north on a holiday and never returned to the bright lights of the capital."

The same can be said, and perhaps even more so, for the hill tribes performing tonight, and "all the hill tribe people presented here are genuine and are not city people dressed up as hill tribe people," the cultural centre reassures.

For example the Mein, who have been writing their language since the thirteenth century, and for whom dignified manners and decorum are particularly highly valued.

The poise and creative spirit of Chiang Mai also comes through its artisans and craft workers. There are silver craftsmen, carvers, cabinet makers, lacquered-goods factories, handmade umbrella makers and, of course, many silk-weaving factories. At Jolie Femme Thai Silk, I watch the silk-making process, from silk worm to cocoon to weaving and finished item. I sense three thousand years of human history.

The Fabric of Death in the Indian Ocean

As you read in chapter five, every seven years, the animist believers of Madagascar bring the bodies of relatives from tombs and rewrap them in silk.

"Their spirit stays with the living," explains Diary Andrianampoina the new friend showing me round. "This is why silk is so important to Malagasy people. The butterfly can have the spirit of the dead, then there is the cocoon, and then we get this and make the silk. The spirit is in the silk."

Each body in turn is lifted into an additional sheet of silk and tied in with silk strips in a particular way, around in bands but up the centre of the body also, to allow life to continue to flow.

Embroidery in Vietnam

The flat plains between the city of Hanoi and Halong Bay, in the north of Vietnam, are a crossword grid of too-green paddy fields. Up to their calves in mud, barefoot farmers guide beasts towing ploughs made from a hand-beaten blade lashed to natural timber, and women wearing traditional, conical *non la* hats bend double, planting rice. The road is straight and wide, through these flat fields and brings with it the sensation of déjà vu.

Nick Ut's photograph of a young girl, Kim Phuc, naked, her arms out, screaming from the effects of a syrupy, sort of jellied gasoline on her skin, on a road like this. It is widely thought that his image of a young victim of napalm dropped in the Vietnam War so horrified Americans that it was a catalyst for the eventual halt of the conflict.

I am lost in all this when Nevyen Van Hao, the new young friend showing me around in Vietnam, announces that he has something to say and, without changing his amiable demeanour, takes a handful of papers from his briefcase. "During the war, the United States sprayed 28 million litres of Agent Orange; that nearly eight million tonnes of bombs were dropped (compared with two million in World War II); the US spent more than US$350 billion dollars on the war, and in the process destroyed nearly 2,000 hospitals and 500 churches; there were more than half a million US soldiers here – 58,000 of them died, compared with three million Vietnamese killed, and four million injured." He says it without anger or, particularly, emotion; just a straight delivery of fact. And they are hard facts for a Westerner. I feel implicated. But Hao just tucks the papers back into his case, smiles mildly, with understanding, and turns away. It was just something that had to be said; had to be cleared up.

At the Hong Ngoc Humanity Centre, the human face of some of the conflict's effects can be seen. Many people working here have suffered birth defects resulting from Agent Orange. There are disfigured faces, limbs, and more. They sit at tables – long rows in a workshop, each bent over a tapestry. Women and men, girls and boys, stitch intricately. I feel awkward watching them at their tasks. I have no inclination to take out a camera.

And then a party of American tourists disgorges from a coach. How will this work? But a few minutes later, I hear a girl laugh.

Two middle-aged men and a woman from the American party and some of the youngsters at sewing frames are engaged in what is clearly a totally understandable and hilarious sign-language conversation. The men's hands fly and the children sign back, laughing at the silent words flying between them. The group from America is a deaf club and many of the children here were born deaf, one of the 796 illnesses that the Children of Vietnam Veterans Health Alliance claims are connected to the use of Agent Orange.

Signing has beaten any language barrier.

The origins of embroidery in Vietnam date back at least until the first century when, it is recorded, the armies of the Hai Ba Trung district had shown the invading Chinese hand-stitched flags and slogans. They would have been novel to the Chinese, whose own embroidery was sophisticated, complicated and bright, often telling stories or showing epic palaces, while the Vietnamese works were focused on nature – trees and gardens, and rather like the simple embroidery I have bought.

By the fifteenth century, there is evidence of the continuance and development of Vietnamese embroidery in the often-stitched story of Tran Quoc Toan. In 1282, this 15-year-old put together an army of more than 1,000 men to resist Mongolian invasion. It fought under a famous embroidered flag: "Pha cuong dich, bao hoang an." Destroy the enemy's strength, repay the king's favour.

During the 1960s to 1980s, under Communism's collectivisation, which Josef Stalin had originally instituted, villages worked to export tablecloths, bedspreads, sheets and pillowcases to other socialist states.

Vietnamese teach the art of embroidery within the family. As the famous embroiderers of Quat Dong tell me, it takes a sharp eye, steady hand, commitment, concentration and patience.

It commonly takes three months and often up to a year, to complete a complex embroidery.

The fabric is stretched and checked for imperfections, then detailed sketches are made of it. Perfect thread colours are chosen – once silk, now mostly cotton. Then the needlework begins. The focus is on the moment – the moment on the fabric, and the moment contained in the image. A lily on water. The petals of a flower. The expression of a human in a portrait. Tiny needles follow gentle curves, and delicately shade. Total concentration; total commitment.

XQ Vietnam's needleworkers have previously been voted the best embroiderers in Vietnam. No mean feat. The women sit in rows, their tiny needles darting through the cotton. They produce portraits the like of which I have never seen. There might be twelve colours of cotton in a face, to give the subtle, incredibly realistic shading. The work is intricate, the concentration intense.

At the Agent Orange workshop, I buy an embroidery – the alphabet according to one youngster. V is Volcano. F is for Forest. Each letter stitched in a box in the grid, along with an often slightly oblique image of the definition. The embroidery is a perfect size for my denim jacket project. Later, back in Hanoi, I scour the markets for a denim jacket big enough for me, and when I get home, I appliqué the embroidery to the back panel.

In my novel *As the River Runs*, Dylan Ward is ethical, honest, and has earned respect in the north of Australia, from miners and conservationists, cattle men and indigenous locals such as young-buck Henny Breeze, lawman Airplane Cuttover and community elder Uncle Vincent Yimi. The Kimberley permeates and percolates through him. The country is not just geography or geology, but an amalgamation of understanding and sentiment.

The novel begins in the city, when Dylan is recruited to lead a government research trip north, and he first meets Kate Kennedy, chief of staff of Michael Mooney, the government minister behind a plan to dam a river and pipe water 2,000 kilometres south to the city.

This is her first meeting with him, as told in the novel:

He is tall and his black linen pants are pulled tight by a belt that shows a slim waist. There's a tight grey t-shirt with a v-neck under his denim jacket. It is only when he turns away to speak to the waitress that she sees a kangaroo embroidery on the back, the animal at full stretch.

After they greet, he takes the jacket off and slips it over the back of the chair, and she can see it has been sown on by hand – the delicate look of handwork.

'It's an unusual jacket.'

'A friend of mine in a community out near Laverley did the embroidery as a gift. I stitched it on.'

7

Natural World

I grew up in the countryside; in the intricate, gently undulating English landscape. A rabbit warren under the brambles, a nuthatch working its way up the old pear tree, donkeys in the field and our old hen, Flo, laying an egg a day on a straw bale. I walked the green hills and went out early to settle in for the birds' dawn chorus along the old Roman road.

I have spent most of my adult life in country; in the wide Australian landscape, often so flat and open that I have seen the curve of the earth. A mob of grey kangaroos takes off over the scrub, wedge-tailed eagles pick at roadkill, an angsty tiger snake flies like a ribbon, and I watch a thorny devil auger its spiny body into a yellow sand plain. I walk salt lakes hoping for tektites and settle to listen to the "meep-meep" of zebra finches in the desert.

Landscape and people. For me it is the crucial interplay. We affect and mould the landscape; the landscape affects and moulds us.

And all of this affects the weight of Casey's photographic department. Landscape photography gives me time to stand, to look and to think; to meditate upon the scene before and the landscape around me. I like to work with a tripod, and it has to be substantial. I can hand hold a big digital single lens reflex camera stiller than most small, lightweight tripods. My tripods have four-part legs, with their joint virtually at my eye height (the height gained from the legs is crucial to stability). Although being classed as a "traveller", my favourite, a Gitzo, won't readily fit into Casey. It used to travel separately in its bag in "oversized luggage", but often missed the plane and followed Casey and me around the world, eventually arriving home the day after us. So now, rather to Casey's consternation, I disassemble it and pack its parts in him. (Casey doesn't like mess. If you too can imagine hearing Casey grumble, ignore it.) Some of the most pleasurable travelling moments are spent with my tripod. I potter. I lock it together very firmly, set the camera on it, watch the light before me, above me and behind me. I see it shifting by the minute, and continually reset the camera and gently press the button. The light grows, changing hue. "Gorgeous. *Gorgeous.*" I can hear myself murmuring these words; I can feel the excitement in me.

On a one-night stop in the north-east of Western Australia's Pilbara region, I wander off in the dark morning and I'm surprised to find a still, blue river with a sharp range of hills beyond it. The dawn comes and fragile sunlight touches the tip of the range, turning it muted maroon. As the sun rises higher, strengthening light creeps down the rock face, firing it an ever-brighter red, until it is carmine. I take pictures, stroking the camera's button, hearing the shutter clunk, charting the change. I love the progression of these photographs, just as I love such intimate, charismatic moments. (Definition of charismatic: A compelling charm that inspires devotion.)

Being in the moment. Being in landscape. Being in the natural world, under the wide canopy of sky, surrounded by birds in the morning.

From Hunters to Guides in Madagascar

As a village boy, Theodore Farafidison used to slaughter the precious birds of Madagascar's rainforest with a slingshot. "I was a bird killer when I was a child," he admits. "Now I have become a bird nerd."

He not only now understands the value of Madagascar's biodiversity, but is sharing it with others.

Which is just what Theodore has done today in Ranomafana National Park, as a knowledgeable guide leading me into the rainforest to see plants and animals, and especially lemurs.

Madagascar – the world's fourth biggest island, lying in the Indian Ocean between Western Australia and Africa – has been isolated for 65 million years, resulting in the evolution of unique animal and plant life. There are more than 200,000 species on the island, the vast majority of which are found only here, including lemurs, an endemic primate which lives only in Madagascar.

When the island was cast adrift and isolated, primates evolved into lemurs, while in Africa and elsewhere they evolved into monkeys and apes. Lemurs are arboreal primates that typically have a pointed nose and long tail. Twelve of the species are found within the 43,000 hectares of Ranomafana National Park.

But Theodore isn't just sharing his enthusiasm with the visitors who trickle through this still largely undiscovered place. Just as importantly he's doing it with other villagers of the Tanala tribe – the people of the forest. "They were killing the lemurs because they didn't know how important this forest is," he says. "They were just hunting for food. I am trying to tell them how important it is. We are able to give them some education – some knowledge about this biodiversity."

Theo works with international researchers based here, sharing his local knowledge, and learning more about the natural science of the rainforest.

He says that when the national park was created, a lot of Tanala people were forced to move, but now half of the park fees goes to these local people. "A thousand people used to live in this area but we needed to tell them to go out of the forest because we needed to protect this area. But they get half of the entrance fee and now they are happy. If we have to do something round here, we have to use these local people."

Every guide, like Theodore, has a lemur spotter, and Theodore has already sent his ahead to look for lemurs before we enter the rainforest. He'll call on the mobile phone. There are twenty-seven local guides and the same number of lemur spotters. Theo also gives instructions to trainee guides who accompany us.

"They progress from lemur spotter to trainee guide to qualified guide," says Theo in the beautiful English he has taught himself by being with visitors, and with an elegant Malagasy accent.

Yesterday, during the first evening spotting session, within forty-five minutes I had seen a blue legged chameleon and, far more difficult for it is infinitely faster moving, a brown mouse lemur, the smallest of the lemurs.

After dinner and sleeping snugly at Setam Lodge with rain on the roof, the morning comes misty. Theo and Diamondra Ravakiniaina, another local climbing through the guiding ranks, show me down a flagstone path into the rainforest.

Ranomafana National Park, the fourth biggest protected area in Madagascar, has 350 species of spiders, 115 bird species, 75 species of frogs, 42 of chameleons and 1,000 of plants. But it is lemurs that visitors most want to see.

Of those, says Theodore, the critically endangered golden bamboo lemur is the most prized, as there are very few. Or, as he puts it, "the holy grail species."

And there's one now.

The lemur spotter has called Theo on the mobile and we have trekked into the rainforest and here we are, in the rain, looking up at a blob.

That blob, high up in the fork of a tree, I am told, is a golden bamboo lemur. In fact, it breaks up into four, two parents and two youngsters, giving a good view.

"It is different to the other kind of lemurs as it has a round face," says Diamondra. "It eats a special bamboo, waking early and eating, then resting, and being active later in the afternoon. There is cyanide in the bamboo, which it needs to digest. After eating the cyanide it needs soil, which stabilises the cyanide.

"When a female gives birth, she puts the baby in a fork in a tree and only she knows where it is." A father would kill a newborn. "She introduces it to the family after three weeks." Lemurs live for up to thirty years.

But Theo has received another call, and we are off again, through thickening rain and narrowing paths. It's worth it to see first a *sifaka*, a large lemur which is feeding and which then leaps from tree to tree, upright, and then two red-fronted brown lemurs.

Four lemur species since we arrived, and it isn't even lunchtime. After a warm shower and dry clothes, lunch, it turns out, is at a restaurant overlooking Ranomafana's Namorona River, and is jolly good local fare of salad, brown rice, a bean dish, zebu (a breed of cattle which produces a stronger taste of beef), chicken and pork dishes, a splash of Malagasy wine and a fruit dessert.

Knowing that Madagascar is self-sufficient in food somehow makes eating even more pleasant here.

At the lodge, night falls with the sound of constant and heavy rain on the roof, and I tuck myself up in bed, under warm blankets.

Who would think that, after leaving Ranomafana in the damp early the next morning, I would be in Anja National Park, near Ihosy and on the way to Isalo, in a warm, sunny valley? Who would have thought that I would be looking up into the amber eyes of another of Madagascar's seventy-two species of lemur – Madagascar's national animal, the ring-tailed lemur – and that they would be looking back at me?

Here at Anja National Park, local guide Razafimandimby Adrian explains that ring-tailed lemurs live in family groups, but when the group becomes too big, a young female will fight with the dominant female and then move out and set up her own group.

Later in the trip, when I am in my room writing at Andasibe Hotel, there is a tap at the door. Outside is the lady from the room next door, with one towel wrapped round her and one around her head.

I think she must be locked out of her room, but she signals me to silence and turns to point to a lemur on the rail outside my room. And then I spend ten minutes alone with a lemur, looking out over the damp valley.

His tail is wrapped up over his body – a fur stole against the cool afternoon air.

And to my surprise and, I think, his, he bows gently and allows me to stroke his head.

Baobabs & Boabs & a Tale in Common

If lemurs are one of the iconic species in Madagascar, baobab trees are another. And their cousin boab trees are important to Australian Aboriginal creation stories. The tale is told of a boab being so proud and arrogant that creator spirits punished it by tearing it out and replanting it upside down, and making it fat and grotesque.

In Madagascar, locals tell a strikingly similar story, says Diary Andrianampoina.

"When the baobab saw the palm tree," he begins, "it cried out and wanted to be taller. When it saw the flowers of the flame tree it was jealous. When it was envious of the fruit trees, the creator god became angry and pulled it out by the roots. He put it back in upside down for being prideful."

In both stories, pride came before the fall.

In Madagascar baobab trees are taller, mostly slightly more carrot-like than Australian boabs, and with a mop of branches on top.

There are eight species of baobab trees – one in Western Australia's north which we call boab (*adansonia gibbosa* or *gregorii*), one in Africa (*adansonia digitati*), and six endemic to Madagascar.

They are such personable, individual trees that it's not difficult to feel an emotional attachment. Western Australians experienced it in July 2007, when a thirty-seven tonne boab tree, thought to be more than 700 years old, was driven the 3,200 kilometres to Perth under police escort, after needing to be moved because of road works on the Great Northern Highway in the East Kimberley. It was farewelled with a ceremony by the Gija people of Warmun and welcomed with a smoking ceremony by the Nyoongar people when it was planted in Kings Park and Botanic Gardens, where it has pride of place.

How boabs came to be on two islands separated by a vast stretch of ocean is a puzzle. It has been suggested that if people managed to sail across the Indian Ocean from Madagascar, the boab seed, full of vitamin C and also known as "sour gourd", may have been easily transportable food.

It has also been suggested that the connection between boabs here and there goes back to the time when Australia was joined to southern Africa as part of the Gondwana super continent, but the connection was severed 65 million years ago.

Another theory stems from the discovery of the enormous egg of an elephant bird on the Western Australian coast nearly twenty years ago. This three metre tall flightless species of bird weighed nearly half a tonne and is thought to have become extinct in Madagascar some 800 years ago. The *Aepyornis maximus* egg found here was dated at about 2,000 years old (and had a volume of seven litres). Importantly, it was suggested that the egg's voyage showed that travelling from Madagascar to Western Australia could have been possible with a simple craft, as long as it could float long enough.

Borneo & a Close Encounter with an Orangutan

Paul Dimus, a guide in the million-year-old Borneo rainforest and an eloquent, mildly mannered young man from a local tribe, turns to me. "Run," he says urgently, and I am quick to obey. We soon stop but the big male orangutan that has shimmied down from the jungle canopy is still coming fast towards us, clearly annoyed.

"Run again," Paul urges and I do.

We eventually stop behind a fallen tree. The noise behind us has stopped too. The orangutan, Paul assures, would never actually attack – just run at us to scare us.

Do orangutans laugh? I can imagine it. This dominant male has sorted out two scrawny upstarts, whom he might just recognise as some distant and unimpressive relatives.

And with that, he climbs another tree and sits eating.

"We haven't seen an orangutan for a month," says Paul, breathing hard and clearly pleased that we have shared this moment.

We had followed the male's booming, guttural, more stomach than lung call until we saw him twenty metres up a tree, the early morning sun firing his orange-red hair. I glimpsed the face of a wide-eyed child pushed into a grey rubber plate. This most human of primate faces.

We had settled to watch and, in a couple of swings, the orangutan moved lower. He broke off a branch and threw it down. "I think he's in a bad mood," Paul had whispered; this mild man of Borneo watching a wild male in Borneo.

The orangutan then started to come down fast, hand-over-hand down a vine, showing his magnificent arm-span. I heard the significant weight of him hit the ground fifteen metres from us, and instantly he came crashing forwards.

I was both thrilled and puzzled, and perhaps a little stupid. Why, in this more-than 43,000 hectares of Sabah's Danum Valley Conservation Area, would an orangutan want to come down out of the canopy towards two humans, even if they did share 97 per cent of his DNA?

Oh, that's right, he's a dominant male.

While others come to this Borneo jungle from all over the world in the hope of even the slightest sighting of this endangered species, which is found only here and in Sumatra, this chap apparently wants a word, and a big male orangutan like this is seven times stronger than a human.

Danum Valley has eight primate species and we have seen this one right on one of Borneo Rainforest Lodge's fifteen jungle trails.

After arriving in this rainforest, I am soon being led through softwood dipterocarp and mengaris trees, past big ebony and iron-wood. A few hours later I am watching Borneo pygmy elephants as the light drops and the jungle chimes insect noise. There are seven in the group; one a week-old baby.

I have seen the world's smallest deer, the mouse deer and, before that, the tiger or giant orchid – the world's biggest species of orchid, with one being weighed at two tonnes. The plant was twenty metres up a tree, in flower, which it does only every three years.

I'm not a "list person" but, as you can see, one just gets led into it in Danum Valley. It has 328 bird species, 110 mammal, 72 reptile, 56 amphibian and 57 fish species.

A pygmy squirrel (the world's smallest squirrel) joins the list, spotted at the end of a 300-metre-long canopy walkway which is mostly twenty-seven metres above the ground. The walkway has five "swings" and seven platforms around tree trunks, and is stable and not scary.

And there are still more for that list, including three types of civet, a slender nocturnal carnivorous mammal. On a night drive, Paul's spotlight picks out one ground-dwelling civet, very like a tabby cat; another that lives in low branches and looks, perhaps, more like a possum; and two very high up in big trees, which is where they live.

I follow Paul to the jacuzzi pool – a waterfall into a pool where fish nibble the dead skin from your feet (or, presumably, any other part of your anatomy). He stops again and points out an endemic Bornean gibbon. "The gibbon is the best swinger of all," he says. And she sets off on long arms, describing graceful, easy arcs, a tiny baby clinging to her.

Not far ahead there is a maroon langur in the trees – a long-tailed arboreal Asian monkey.

A helmeted hornbill cries above and a chestnut-winged babbler lets out a series of descending "doop" notes. Another time it's the occasionally goose-like whoop-whoop-whoop of the rhinoceros hornbill, which speeds up as it prepares to fly, as if it is winding itself.

The number of bird species in the area is rising. Last year a new bird species, the spectacled flowerpecker, was identified. Paul's ear picks out the white-crowned shama, rufous-crowned babbler and a moustached babbler alights on a tree near us. One of the six species of local woodpecker hammers into a tree high up. A bushy-crested hornbill – one of the area's eight hornbills – flies high and fast, all feather-noise and beak.

I have been lucky, with memorable encounters. But a big, matte black butterfly passes in erratic gossamer flight and puts this virgin forest and ecosystem back into perspective. Never forget the 200 species of fungus, I tell myself. Never forget the wild ginger and yams.

Danum Valley Conservation Area is less than an hour's flight from Kota Kinabalu and then three hours' drive, from the town of Lahad Datu. Its Borneo Rainforest Lodge was originally set up in 1994 by the Sabah government, as part of a commitment to better the lives of people in the state. As the operation has matured, it has been left to be run by the people who care for it like home, and adeptly mix professionalism with a personal connection.

This whole area is the land of the river people, and they divide into more than ten tribes. Danum is named after a great chief of the tribe, Anum, who vanished one day in the forest. Paul's father, Dimus, and grandfather, Antim, are from this tribe (traditionally they have only one name, so when Westerners ask Paul's surname, he gives his father's name).

"People like me are the new generation of these tribes, on this land," he says. "I want to protect this area for the animals and plants here." It strikes an interesting chord – not a determination to protect it for future generations of humans but for the life living here now.

When this became a conservation area, people moved and Paul now lives with wife Marina in a village called Silabukan Pkt 1, near Taliwas, which is four hours' drive away. He says he works a month straight, so he can take four days off and go home to his wife and village. Returning to the kampong is important.

When Paul and I climb up to a Sugpan burial site, it is as if Dimus and Antim are with us. Local people say it's good for visitors to come here so that they know about the tribes.

The ironwood coffin, with a turtle's head carved at one end, is more than 250 years old, and in the burial site of the family of the village chief, Bunlagai. It is thought to be that of a great chief who was the leader at the time a village was set up where the lodge is now. The chief's ironwood blowpipe was put in the coffin with him and is still there. "My father has an ironwood blowpipe that was passed on from his great grandfather," Paul suddenly says. "I tried it." He thought the dart would go a long way but it just flopped out of the end.

Then his grandfather took the two-metre-long pipe, saying he was an old man but would show him. Paul was amazed by the distance the dart flew. The darts, six centimetres long and pin sharp at one end, had a bung of a cork like substance from the fruit of the nebung palm tree on the other to seal the pipe. Two types of poison were used, Dimus told Paul. One, made from the mixed sap of five trees, was highly poisonous and would kill. But tribal people mostly hunted monkeys and another sap brew was used, to briefly paralyse them but not fill them with poison.

Paul tells me about another very big ironwood coffin near here, with an ironwood flute in it. "My grandfather tells the story..."

Antim says it was the coffin of a great warrior who was with his girlfriend one day, using his blowpipe. She was standing a long way from him and said the dart couldn't reach her. But he blew the pipe and the dart hit her and she died. He was racked with grief and had the coffin made, big enough for both of them. He told the people to put the coffin in a cave and was put in the coffin with his girlfriend and the ironwood flute. "He told them that when they could no longer hear the flute music, he had died."

The tribe heard the flute music continually for a week and then it fell silent. Some people say they sometimes still hear it.

"I don't know," says Paul. "It is a story. My grandfather tells it."

And Paul Dimus retells it with pride.

"I am proud to be Malaysian," he says, "but I am very proud to be a Bornean man."

Falcons & Ships of the Desert in the Middle East

The Bedouin tribes called them their ships of the desert, but the camels I am watching in Qatar sit long lashed and soft snouted in a sandy pen in the heart of the fast developing, modern city of Doha.

The camels belong to the Emir of this Middle Eastern country, which points 130 kilometres out into the Arabian Gulf, like a thumb on the hand of the Saudi Arabian peninsula.

Sheikh Hamad bin Khalifa Al Thani is said to like having his camels on patrol in the city, connecting the culture of his desert people to their present and future. The Al Thani family has ruled Qatar in an absolute monarchy since the mid-nineteenth century.

The day suddenly becomes themed with animals. I'm then taken to the falcon market at Souk Waqif, and specifically to Mandoob Al Arab, a shop which deals not only in falcons but their paraphernalia. Traditionally in the Middle East, falcons were trapped in pits, used to hunt for all-important protein, and then released again after hunting season. But today they are popularly kept as a hobby to train and fly for the owner's interest. The shop is full of jesses (the short leather straps fastened around each leg), hoods to quieten the bird, leashes, lures and the all-important falconer's glove.

There were five falcons on display for sale in Mandoob Al Arab on Monday, sitting on their perches, and the shop sells more than 400 a year, from its breeding centre, for perhaps anywhere between US$5,000 and US$100,000 each.

Not surprising, then, that modern falconry has entered the technological age and birds now have a GPS transmitter in their body, in case they don't come back.

Not surprising, perhaps, either that looking after the bird's health is very important. Directly opposite the shop is the Souk Waqif Falcon Hospital where, in peak season, 75 to 100 falcons a day might be treated. Today, the patient list is sparse, but I do watch one falcon having what Dr Mohammed Ali first describes as cosmetic surgery on its face.

"Was it injured?" I ask.

"No, its beak is just being honed."

The immaculate, four-storey falcon hospital only opened six months ago, after being converted from its previous role as a hospital for humans. It has an intensive care unit, and departments of radiography, toxicology, orthopaedics, endoscopy and the rather more giveaway "feather imping", to repair a damaged wing or tail feather by attaching part of another feather.

But the six or seven species of falcons in the Middle East are most susceptible to respiratory diseases, not to mention worms and parasites, says the amiable Dr Ali, who, like his colleagues, is specifically trained and qualified in falcon medicine.

I then visit the massive Qatar Racing and Equestrian Club complex. Surely, alongside the camel and falcon, nothing quite conjures up the magic of this country more than a nostril-flared, long-maned and head-tossing Arab pony.

At this moment, they are rather more docile. In fact, while some are hanging out in yards near the swimming pool used for their training, others are inside in comfortable air-conditioned stables, standing on pine flakes imported from the United States of America. The stables also have shower and drying rooms. But then, many of the horses are worth a small fortune.

And then one snouts forward, pricks its ears and shakes its head. Its mane ripples and it gives me that wild, flarey Arab pony stare.

In just a few hours, the camel, the falcon and the Arab horse have taken me straight to the heart of Arabia.

A Lion Roars in the Masai Mara

Outside my comfortable tented room, a lion roars repeatedly in the cool, still African morning. But this is not the threatening sound of a lion ready to attack or kill. It pants out its roars as if simply a morning exercise that must be counted off. Roar, roar, roar. Five, six, seven.

Then there are the surprisingly delicate steps of a hippo tiptoeing through mud and an almighty splash. One of the twenty or so that wallow around in the Talek River, just below my tent here in the heart of Kenya's Masai Mara, plunges back into water, rejoining the gang making funny grunting noises and blowing up mighty, gassy volcanoes.

Then the bloat of them submerge, with only their backs showing like small islands.

The bed is so comfortable, the morning so perfect, the moment so precious, that for once I just lie in for a few minutes, and let it all seep into me. One great, osmotic memory to be saved forever.

And then James comes with tea and four delicious bite-sized biscuits.

I hear him approach and then the distinctive intonation of the Kenyan, and particularly Masai, accent. He starts five full musical notes higher than might be expected, somewhere in the high baritone, and descends through a full octave.

"Goo-t moorning Stee-phen. And how did you slip laast night?" The Kenyan way is to speak slowly, politely, softly and with grace; with an emphasis on almost every word, as if all are precious and meant.

He asks how I am feeling about Kenya. "I'm entranced," I tell him with complete honesty. "This is veeery pleasing to me," he says. He seems to breathe it more than say it, exhaling with it his own love and pride for the country.

Kenya has taken me a little by surprise. I had expected it to be interesting and I was looking forward to the wildlife and villages but I hadn't expected to feel so caught up in it so quickly. To feel the pulse of Africa beating so palpably, echoing back to the start of human history and engaged with the challenges and politics of its future.

I hadn't expected to so easily connect with so many kind, polite, inspiring people.

I hadn't even expected the climate to be so perfect. Pretty much throughout the year, Kenya has cool nights, fresh, still mornings and warm sunny days. (When the temperature is in the high twenties, the Kenyans complain it is too hot.)

I hadn't expected to feel quite so excited. For every day to be better than the last. To feel my hand on Africa's beating heart.

And I hadn't expected to feel so spoilt. The tented camps of the Masai Mara are luxurious and the majority of the people working in this one are from local villages but speak beautiful English and are both kind and polished. The service is professional and personal. My tent is big, with a proper bed and bathroom. Yes, this morning I feel spoilt, but not as spoilt as I was yesterday.

I had landed on the bush airstrip after two hops with Air Kenya, coming from Mt Kenya.

Andrew King'Ori, a wonderful, gentle, knowledgeable naturalist guide, suggested a short game drive on the way to the camp. Within minutes of him pushing up the pop-top roof of the purpose-designed safari vehicle, I was looking at the big, gnarled, curved horns of an old buffalo – one of the "big five" that game watchers crave.

And then there is a giraffe, standing proud at the top of the bank, grazing on a high vine. And then two more giraffe, and I "bag one" with a long photographic lens in a perfect shot against grasslands and sky.

But Andrew has more to come, and soon I am standing, head out the top of the vehicle, looking down at a slumbering male lion one side, and a "honeymoon couple" of young lions the other side. I never knew that lions "spoon". But, during days of mating, they sleep soundly together, him behind her, undisturbed by us. They eventually wake, amble a few metres and then flop down into the grass and fall into another deep sleep.

Not far away, there's another couple, spooning too, until they wake and he starts to gently lick her ears.

And so it goes, with gazelles, hyenas, vultures and the lilac-breasted roller. An eland with a row of oxpecker birds, like musical notes along his back, picking insects from him.

It truly is a dazzle of zebras, just as the dictionary says. I watch them drinking at a waterhole, old and young, stripes reflecting in the water.

The Masai Mara is most famous for its animal migration, when perhaps two million wildebeest and zebra flood across the plains. It's black and white, black and white, with zebra and wildebeest, I am told.

Here on my bed, in my tent, where this story began, I have just sat, propped up on pillows and written this, in one great download of the moment and these memories. It started in the dark, with lion, and dawn has been coming and coming, with first the odd bird chirping, then more and more (spiralling vibratos, piping calls) until it is the most beautiful, complex dawn chorus, with just the sound of the hippos honking and splashing beyond.

And the odyssey continues. Andrew finds a leopard, seven metres up an acacia tree, sleeping on the reed buck that it has killed and hauled up there. "A leopard can lift twice its weight up a tree." He seems to have eaten well during the night and is drowsy with it.

He raises his head, adjusts himself more comfortably along the branch, and then sleeps again.

I stop to watch seven lion cubs walking warily, yet playfully, in a line through green vegetation. This is a "nursery", says Andrew. There will be two, or three, mothers hunting nearby, and they will bring the cubs to the kill.

And then I see a cheetah that not only steps out confidently into the morning sun and golden grass for all the world as if I wasn't there, but then climbs up and "poses" on a mound, surveying the plain.

But for all this, there are three more parts to the day that I must mention.

First, I stop under a desert acacia for a picnic lunch, in a true *Out of Africa* moment, and later in the afternoon visit Kolong, a Masai village just outside the Masai Mara National Reserve. Eight families live in low, dark, stick, leaf and cow dung homes, facing a dirt square into which the combined families' 250 cattle, goats and sheep, are herded at night, all surrounded by a thornbush fence.

Masai are less nomadic than they once were, but their dietary staples are still milk, blood and meat, says Dan Silantoi, who lives in one of the mud houses and whose first language is Swahili. He has never been to school, but has mastered elegant English through a friend who did, and through tourists. And back at the camp that evening, I am led through a walkway of candles to a fireplace, where a table is laid and the chef has prepared dinner. As I chat, Masai men and women from Kolong come in from the dark, to dance for us, the men pogo-ing high on the spot (the price of a wife is fifteen cows, but less if you can jump high) and sing their throaty, rhythmical chants. It adds up to yet another extraordinary day.

I look back through my photographs; the Masai, the leopard, cheetah, elephants and giraffe, and all the birds and the savannah.

I can't believe I have been here, in the Masai Mara, on this part of the trip, for only a day and a half. And again I sleep with the night-noises of Kenya. With the occasional sound of hippo, like someone banging an empty dustbin and yawning at the same time. Of lions roaring. Eight, nine, ten. Of the Masai Mara. Of Africa calling.

An Intimate Moment with Tigers in India

Saturday morning, 8.15. She lies relaxing in the warm morning, snoozes a little, then yawns, stands and takes silky steps towards him.

He has been lying near, his eyes mostly locked on her, and when he sees her move, he goes towards her, and they are quickly together.

In this most private of moments, I rather feel I should turn away – but then, there is the need for me to photograph this extraordinary moment.

It is just eleven weeks until the start of north India's monsoon so, with plenty of fresh water and food sources ahead, a good time for these tigers to mate. There is a gestation period of sixteen weeks before a litter, usually of three to four cubs, is born.

Hopefully, this will happen and they will healthily join the thirty tigers living in the 400 square kilometres of Ranthambore National Park, these young adults among them.

Ranthambore is in the south-east of the Indian state of Rajasthan and about 180 kilometres east of Jaipur. It is one of the country's biggest national parks.

Once the hunting grounds for Jaipur's maharajas, today the tigers live protected rather than persecuted, shot digitally rather than literally.

It was declared one of India's Project Tiger reserves in 1973, made a national park in 1980 and enlarged in 1991.

And at the centre of that story is Fateh Singh Rathore, a member of the princely family of Jodhpur, who is credited with almost single-handedly mapping the park and negotiating with the people of twelve villages to move out voluntarily, having built new homes elsewhere and arranged financial compensation.

But he paid a personal price. With nearly 90,000 people within a five kilometre radius of the park, other disgruntled villagers eventually attacked him in a mob, fracturing his skull and shattering his kneecaps, angry at being banned from their ancestral lands. It is reported that, when he had recovered enough to leave hospital, Rathore just went to them and challenged them to do it again.

He was awarded the WWF International Valour Award.

Today, there are still a million livestock living within that radius, and they are more likely to be the ones straying into the park uninvited. In fact, 10,000 cattle which wandered in recently were escorted back out by police.

But a mark of the success of India's tiger project is that the Rajasthan Government has announced a new, third reserve within its state, the Mukundra Hill Tiger Reserve near Ranthambore.

And so it is that the two tigers before me now are not only watched over but a source of steady income for locals turned wildlife guides. They point out birds, peacocks, monkeys, wild boar, spotted deer and sambar deer, which is the tigers' preferred food. A tiger can eat as much as 33 kilograms of meat in one course and to dine on a big sambar can take five days.

Good food, good home, good company and, one hopes, a good future.

And, in the still, warming morning, these rather comfortable cats both stand, blink, look up the rise, and walk off.

Fishing & Paddling in Canada's Yukon

The fish wheel spins into action, its two giant, woven scoops dipping into the water, the river's current driving its paddles. The wheel itself is birch, and it sits on floats of spruce. The wheel turns, scooping up the salmon which are passing along the Yukon River – this massive, glacier-fed body of cold, fast-moving water that snakes across the Yukon, in north-west Canada, on the border with Alaska, and out to the Bering Sea.

From the scoops, the fish pour down a wooden channel and into a holding trough. For generations, Han people have built fish wheels that vary from the size of a compact car to the size of a house. This is a traditional fishing method for the First Nation Han tribes near Dawson City, a boardwalk and permafrost frontier town with a bar that serves a Sourtoe Cocktail – a real human toe is added, albeit a petrified one. *(Scary.)*

Fishing with the wheel was the way of Tommy Taylor's father, David, and his grandfather before that; of these men of the Tr'ondëk Hwëch'in First Nation tribe. Tommy points at a photograph of his father on a pin-board at his summer camp. Then his mother, Martha. There were sixteen children. He says his father retired from the fish when he was ninety-two. He lived until he was ninety-five. His mother lived until she was 108. Tommy puts this longevity down to "healthy living, healthy food and hard work." Their staples were moose, caribou, berries, and the salmon. And mostly the salmon.

The fast-flowing Yukon, drops twenty centimetres every kilometre and is a plentiful food source, when king salmon and chum salmon are running, a fish wheel can catch up to 1,000 fish every twenty-four hours. The biggest ever caught was more than 30 kilograms.

I travel on up the Yukon River with Tommy in a fast aluminium boat, past Moosehide, traditional territory of the Tr'ondëk Hwëch'in people, where artefacts dating back 8,000 years have been found, and on to Dog Island, where huskies yap on the end of their chains as we drink iced tea and eat bannock, a traditional cake.

This is summer. Winter's a different kettle of fish. Tommy has felt temperatures as low as −72°C, and he knows he must catch and air-dry up to 1,800 pieces of fish to get the dogs through that. They are his vital sled pullers from when the river freezes in October and November until the break-up early in May. Tommy in his homemade moosehide mittens with beaver fur trim on the hard, white highway that was and is the river.

The Yukon Code: "He travels fastest who travels alone, but not after the frost has dropped below zero fifty degrees or more."

The telling and retelling of tales warms the winters, when there's only brief daylight but the green dazzle of the northern lights above. It binds people to this place. The people of the Yukon love storytellers.

Robert Service, "the Bard of the Yukon", "the Canadian Kipling", is said to have been the most commercially successful poet of the twentieth century. He wrote on rolls of wallpaper, pinning them to the wall, printing his verses in big charcoal letters, pacing up and down before them, repeating them, making them perfect.

And probably no-one in the Western world is more famous for stories from this place than Jack London. *The Call of the Wild* and *White Fang*, published between 1903 and 1908. They found his hut, out there in the white wasteland, with his name carved in ("Jack

London, miner, author, 1898") and stripped it down and brought it to Dawson City and rebuilt it.

Right now, the 3,000-kilometre-long river is running, a wide, milky, turquoise, squirt of toothpaste, colder than you could probably imagine.

One of its tributaries, the Tatshenshini, pours from a glacier, and cuts through a mountain range, that has an annual average temperature of –3°C. (How does that work?)

And now I am on it, sitting *in* it, paddling. And with the first wall of water that hits me I think my heart might stop – it is so cold, so very, very cold. When my head goes under, it's like putting it in a vice.

At one point a big, red-spotted salmon, as long as a child's arm and as thick as a thigh, tracks alongside, its dorsal fin flopping up through the surface as it fights the current. Four bald eagles play overhead, then one swoops down and flies along the top of the water towards me, peeling away to give me a horizontal view straight into the eye of an eagle.

I round a bend to find a mother brown bear on the bank with her two, chocolatey cubs.

She pauses, raises herself on hind legs, and watches me pass just ten metres away as the cubs duck behind her, pop out through her legs, and begin to play again.

Such sights bring tourists now, but just over 100 years ago, the Klondike gold rush brought 30,000 hopefuls over the Chilkoot and White Passes from the Alaskan port of Skagway, heading for Dawson City and Whitehorse.

And it is in Whitehorse that I make a couple of new friends.

The first is a woman from a First Nation tribe who is a luthier (a maker of stringed instruments) and a moose tufter, making rugs out of their hair. I am pleased to spend time with her as I have such an interest in stringed instruments and particularly in the sitka spruce which grows in this landscape. It is used for the fronts of some top-quality guitars. It's better than anything else. Irreplaceable for its purpose.

The second is a chap I just get talking to in a coffee shop. He's a massive, check-jacketed Yukoner – a hunter, a trapper, writer and humourist. And he drives an equally massive Ford Yukon ute, parked outside and which seems almost the size of a house.

"What do you drive in Australia?" he asks.

I tell him I've got a Toyota Landcruiser.

He nods, thinking about it, hand to chin.

"Yeah," he says. "Some of our women drive them."

Swimming with Whale Sharks on Ningaloo Reef

It is suddenly there. I have been staring down through my face mask into the silky, warm waters of Ningaloo Reef, with the sunlit surface above, gently inky depths below, and Ellece Nicholls beneath me, like a mermaid, pointing, at first seeing nothing but the swishing, coral-spawn-speckled sea, and then, there it is.

The whale shark appears out of the blue, quite close, spotted, sharp tailed, oval mouth vacuuming plankton. *Rhincodon typus* is the oceans' biggest fish. The largest so far recorded is 12.65 metres. A slow-moving filter-feeder and a threatened species, it remains mysterious. What are their other most important feeding grounds? Where do they breed? Where do they give birth?

I have long wanted to see this and here I am, and here it is.

Many of us have seen the big, blue photographs and the "swim with a whale shark" slogans in what has become one of the iconic symbols of the Western Australian environment, wildness and ecotourism. Here one is, in the flesh before me, gills pumping, eye clearly visible, a small flotilla of hanger-on fish under its soft, white belly, and it's personal.

I hadn't expected that. For just this moment, it feels like it's me, alone with this elusive and mysterious whale shark. Me with nature – a human feeling simply part of that nature.

I didn't say this to Ellece, who is in her second full season with whale sharks, but I know it will delight her when she reads this. For this young woman, who started on a dolphin swim boat when she was sixteen and has tackled a double degree in commerce and science, says, "I want everyone to have their own little experience – just to feel they are on their own with the shark."

And I do, despite the other seventeen people on the boat out of Exmouth, split into two swim groups to conform with the strict code of practice the industry and environmental science experts have devised for Western Australia. At this moment, I do.

The day had begun at 7.20 am in Exmouth when I was picked up from my accommodation and driven by coach half an hour to the boat, then ferried out to the boat by inflatable dinghy. There are five crew on board, and a spotter plane up in the air, looking for whale sharks.

Once on board the boat, we are briefed on the rules of swimming near whale sharks – certainly not in front, and not within 3 metres either side of the body.

Then there is a morning swim just to get the confidence up and for the crew to see everyone snorkelling. It is followed by a comprehensive morning tea.

But it isn't long after that that the boat veers.

"We are about ten minutes from a whale shark. Everyone get ready." Having been supplied with masks, snorkels and fins, we get them ready, group one first near the marlin board.

Then we are in the water, following instructions, leaving a clear passage for the whale shark. And there it is, appearing out of the blue.

This first whale shark is about 4 metres long; a fine male. (It is one of Ningaloo's mysteries that the whale sharks feeding annually here after coral spawning are male.)

One group is in the water, then the next, then the first group again – thus restricting the number of swimmers near the whale shark. Ellece swims ahead, pointing to the shark, keeping swimmers in the correct position.

The boat steams off to another sighting, and there we are treated to a 7½ metre whale shark. It looks like a submarine. It swims slowly and we track alongside it, comfortably keeping pace.

When my group gets back on board, the whale shark follows us, right up to the duckboard – clearly unaware of the 3 metre rule. "It's quite unusual," says Brad Norman, with understatement. Mr Norman is a guest on board, and the world authority on whale sharks.

The final whale shark of the day is 4½ metres long.

Three whale sharks – one of which dives and comes back up and we swim with it again – four big swim sessions. I have lost count of how many times we were in the water.

The last word must go to Ellece. "Wasn't he just beautiful? Did you see the markings behind his gill and that big tail?" She jabbers on and on excitedly, eyes wide. You'd think it was the first time she'd seen a whale shark, she's so thrilled. And I can understand that.

Budgerigars & Zebra Finches in the Australian Desert

I walk up the Valley of the Winds in Kata Tjuta (the Olgas near Uluru, or Ayers Rock), and then on down a track into the valley. It is flanked either side by huge red shoulders of conglomerate; big, round boulders glued into other mud-turned-rock. And at the end of the valley is a small pool in an almost dry creek bed.

Budgerigars and zebra finches.

I can hear them both – that distinctive, grating budgie chatter of one of the world's most-kept pets, a stunning little parrot, and the 'meep-meep' of the bulletproof little finch that can be found in Western Australia from Kununurra to Meekatharra and beyond, and way out through the Great Victoria Desert to this, the Central Desert.

I sit quietly out of the warm sun on cold rock and the zebra finches quickly get used to me being there, and come in flitty, flighty threes and fours to dip in, whirr their feathers madly, bathe and zoom off again. *Taeniopygia guttata* in its element.

The budgerigars are more cautious. A brilliant natural green and yellow, with intricate feather detail, one comes in from a branch, tilting and rotating its lion-like head to check around with its tiny eye, before ducking in for a quick, wary splash too.

And then he's off in a fast, looping flight to his mate above, on a branch.

The River Red Gum trees in this part of the valley make good homes for the budgerigars, which in fact are small parrots and range across Australia's arid and semi-arid zones. The ends of branches often die, and there are holes where these dead ends meet the live branch. I have just been standing by one, watching a proud-heading, chirruping male, when a smaller, duller female hopped out of the hole. They moved together in a small and intimate choreograph.

Up on another tree, another pair mates, *for ages,* him with his right wing around her as they do so. Afterwards they seem to kiss beaks, nibbling at one another before snuggling together on the branch. Budgies are good bonders; the rather romantic *Melopsittacus undulatus.*

Budgerigars are generally heard before they are seen, and I hear a cascading flock now, and manage to pick it out, high up against the blue sky, madly fast, spread out, wheeling. Green-yellow-green-yellow. I look up further but can't spot a bird of prey above them, as I did yesterday. Commonly around here, it might be a brown falcon. Raptors above and snakes below are their main natural predators. Human beings were the others, particularly between the 1860s and 1880s.

The English ornithologist John Gould, had seen budgerigars on an expedition to the great southern land in 1839. He later wrote that he had seen flocks numbering in the thousands. When he returned to London the following year, only two of the nineteen "animated cheerful little creatures" with which he had set out survived.

Soon Queen Victoria had a pair (as Queen Elizabeth II does today) and it is reported that up to 100,000 birds were exported to Europe within one six-month period alone. Big breeding operations were then turning out consignments of up to 15,000 birds at a time.

When a blue mutation was shown in London in 1910, it caused a real commotion.

The blue budgerigar. I have long considered this a measure of our own species and, indeed, the budgerigar makes an appearance in two of the stories in my book *Unaccountable Hours: Three Novellas.* The first is in 'Like Water', which follows the romantic friendship between elderly Beatrice Hansard (*dear Bea*) and young Matthew Rossi. Here, Matthew remembers Old Tom, a next door neighbour from his childhood, and his garden aviary:

> *To Tom, the aviary was exotic. You could see the normal world through the mesh, but it was very far away and quite irrelevant. Inside the aviary there was the whirr and buzz of wings, flashed colours, the smell of bird dust, and magic. Tom would sit in there for hours, among the branches and white-specked bushes. It was like being Abroad. He only ever had budgerigars in their native green and yellow colours, reminding him of the bush. They flew together, coherent as a storm. A flash of green and gold. A flag. 'Matthew,' he would say. 'Matthew, you must love the simplicities of such things.'*

It is all rather reminiscent of an uncle's aviary in my own childhood; a place I loved.

The budgerigar's second appearance in that book is in the novella 'Ethical Man', the story of Dr Bartholomew Milner, a scientist whose reputation is discredited and who returns to country; to the Little Sandy Desert of Western Australia to do a bird count.

> *The day planned, some mission in mind, he might fill a small water bottle from the jerries, hang his binoculars over his neck,*

> *sling his canvas satchel over his shoulder, and set off walking, noting landscape and birdsong in detail. Even the agitated mobs of budgerigars, flying like a flickering flag – now gold, now green – got him excited. And the meep-meep of zebra finches, sparkling in the small bushes like Christmas decorations, drew him to settle into the dirt, part hidden in a nook of rock, and watch for hours, feeling each one remarkable, unique, personal.*

As a Masters student, Bartholomew had turned to his cherished *Melopisittacus undulates,* but before that, at a young age,

> *It amused him to think of white explorers finding these extraordinary types of parrot in the desert, resplendent in their green and yellow, and wondering whether they could be 'made' in blue. Blue budgerigars. Why would you? 'What kind of species are we, to think like that?' he had thought to himself; the seed, perhaps, of his grander themes, and the ideas that have followed him and grown in him.*

Around thirty primary-colour mutations are now recognised in the budgerigar fancying world. Hundreds of variations. But the birds rising before me now, from the red earth and spinifex, are natural green-yellow-green-yellow.

These desert budgerigars and zebra finches are a joy, and just two of some 170 species counted in this part of the Northern Territory.

Grey honeyeaters. A flock of slaty-backed thornbills flying up like wild, wind-driven grey confetti from the desert grass. Crested pigeons with squeaky wings. A crimson chat or the spectacularly red painted firetails in small bushes near a waterhole.

But it is the combination of zebra finches and budgerigars that thrills me most. These most common of cage birds in this, their most uncommon, uncaged natural environment. Here in their desert.

8

Sustenance

I am about to leave a tea plantation bungalow in the highlands of Sri Lanka. Another traveller is departing, too, and a porter has left my big blue Casey and her little red Carrie on the front step together. They look rather guilty but completely fulfilled.

Ah, sustenance.

In every way, body and soul have been sustained here in the Bogawantalawa Valley. Wonderful cuisine; a real sense of relaxation. I feel nourished and strengthened. I have the feeling that Casey doesn't want to go.

The broadest definitions of the word "sustenance" permeate my travel thoughts. It is travel's sustenance that fuels my sustained effort and delight as a travelling writer, for sustenance is intellectual and spiritual as much as it is culinary and physical.

But, of course, in a chapter so-titled, I must start with food. Local food not only gives the flavour of a place, but also the landscape. The minerals of the earth are served with history and culture. Buffalo curd in Sri Lanka, the cheeses of Georgia, the many courses of a Roman lunch. Not to mention, of course, the true delight of a good breakfast buffet.

And then, moving on from food, I know travellers who find a form of sustenance in shopping (like my dear companions B1 and B2, with whom we will shop presently).

But the final word comes from close to home – from an Indian gentleman behind the counter of a service station in urban Western Australia. I am buying milk. "Ah," he says. "Milk. The cow gives sustenance for our whole life. But you cannot eat the cow and drink its milk." Food and philosophy. And in this, the broadest themes of sustenance are brought succinctly together, in one carton.

Tea in Sri Lanka

I am sitting in the warm early morning, facing palm trees, golden sand and the ocean, sailing canoes passing with big, seemingly tea-stained cotton sails, surrounded by sarongs and saris, eating my first beautifully spicy breakfast of the trip.

Where to start with Sri Lanka? Well, at the beginning. For the island's flavour will both gently and strikingly unfold day by day but I simply must start with this scene – this breakfast – because spiciness permeates this Indian Ocean island off the southern tip of India.

And so I enjoy my first *hopper* of the trip. A *hopper* is a Sri Lankan food specialty. Similar to a bowl-shaped pancake, it is swirled around the deep lip of a small pan while cooking, giving crisp vertical sides and a thicker, soft yet spongy, bottom.

With it, usually, comes *sambol* or *mallum* – leafy vegetables blanched and chopped finely, often with grated coconut, to make a dry dish. And with that the moistness of lentil dhal, and vegetable, chicken or fish curry.

Curry for breakfast?

It is a quite wonderful and appropriate start to the day; the unsuspecting Western stomach's delight.

And tea, of course. This is, after all, the land of quality high-country tea, and there is nothing quite like a pot of deep-biscuit-coloured Ceylon English Breakfast to start the day.

I am in Colombo and after breakfast, without further ado, on the road with Susantha Jolita, a knowledgeable, gentle-mannered and humorous guide, and with Donald at the wheel, the amiable Rasanga as his offsider. "It's a little bit complicated, our way of traffic," explains Susantha, as Donald weaves calmly through it. We are in safe hands through the melee of three-wheel auto rickshaws and motorcycles, past fish drying by the ocean. We head east, to the interior, past bungalows and rice paddies, coconut plantations and brick-makers, teak trees and clay-tile factories, white mourning decorations and washing drying on bushes.

At the hotel Heritance Kandalama, I get a taste of the depth of Sri Lanka's human history. For while the outstanding architecture of the hotel, built into the rock and jungle surrounding it, makes it a contemporary artwork in its own right, it looks down upon a reservoir, or tank, built in the third century.

But at Cinnamon Lodge Habarana, the cuisine stakes are raised. At its buffet, lotus root tempered (which clearly means "blanched"), *kekiri* red curry, cabbage leaves *mallum*, beans dry curry and curry leaves *sambol*, with mango chutney, lime pickle, ladies finger *sambol* and coconut *mallum*.

And, of course, the ubiquitous rice (both white and the more textural local red rice) and a golden-glow dhal. Throughout my travels in Sri Lanka, the texture and flavour of dhal and "standard" Sri Lankan curries varies from place to place, maker to maker.

But surely Cinnamon Lodge Habarana's showpiece this evening is its chilled dessert room. Mango cheesecake, passionfruit mousse, cashew nut blondies, homemade avocado ice-cream and marshmallows, and even dishes of jujubes sweeties.

Breakfast is a *hopper* and curd. This divine dish is a kind of thick yoghurt produced from the milk of buffalo in the hotel's own farm, which also includes six cows. I can almost see you squirming, so you will just have to trust me on this. It is one of the most incredible dishes we've ever eaten.

I sleep in a room that is a little cottage with low, arched windows that throw a chapel-like light into the room in the early morning.

The hotel Ulagalla Walawwa, based on an eighteenth-century manor house at Anuradhapura, is set on 23 hectares and has its own farm. Resort manager Roshan Dylan explains, "We grow our own rice. We have about thirty varieties of vegetables – we are trying a lot of things to see what grows well and will get it down to ten or fifteen." Yam and beetroot, chillies and watercress, pomegranate and lemongrass. The hotel also generates 60 per cent of the energy it uses and 60 per cent of irrigation water that goes on the land has been recycled.

And from there, on to the antiquities of Polonnaruwa, with Buddhas carved into a rock face and the remains of its twelfth-century garden city. And then, with Donald at the wheel, up into the high tea country.

From the dry zone behind me, which has been enduring drought, I am suddenly in the cool, and the soft, soaking rain of the Bogawantalawa Valley. At 1,400 metres above sea level, Bogawantalawa is known as the Golden Valley of Tea – a land of rolling green, tea-bush hills, mist and tea pluckers.

Me & 'Bed Tea'

I have ordered my "bed tea" for 6.30 am, at which time there is a polite tap on the heavy wooden door. "Morning tea," is breathed, singsong, on the other side. A Sri Lankan man, barefoot on the wide old wooden floorboards and wrapped in a black-and-white sarong, brings in a tray with a big pot of best high-country tea, steeping nicely inside its orange tea-cosy.

Some readers of my weekly writing in Travel find it amusing, apparently, that I not infrequently mention stopping somewhere-or-other for "a nice cup of tea". Too often that comprises a tea bag dunked too hastily in an uninspiring mug filled with lukewarm water.

But God forbid that I should even mention any of those things here.

For I am in the tea-growing hills of central Sri Lanka, in the northern Indian Ocean, an island itself steeped in the history of powerful indigenous kingdoms, Dutch and Portuguese eras and, of course, the British, who brought tea here.

They had started with coffee but a leaf disease quickly destroyed that industry in the late 1860s, and the resilient planters who didn't turn tail turned to tea.

Planter James Taylor had introduced tea to these slopes in 1867, after taking the only holiday of his life, to Assam in north-east India, and bringing back tea seeds. And it is his descendant Andrew Taylor who is laying the story out before me, as we stand surrounded by the grassy smell of this morning's tea pluck, being processed in the Norwood Estate tea factory near Hatton. Mr Taylor's great-grandfather was James Taylor's first cousin – he represents the fourth generation of his family involved in tea. His grandfather and father were planters, too.

Mr Taylor now explains the many intricacies of tea – the plant, the industry, the drink – to the guests who stay in any of Ceylon Tea Trails' four bungalows in the Bogawantalawa Valley.

Built in 1939 but with a settler history dating back to 1888, Tientsin Bungalow has six beautiful rooms and suites and is set in English gardens created by the colonial planters' wives. There are rose terraces, a tucked-away arbour, the surprise of a pond, and half-hidden paths. There's also a swimming pool and croquet lawn. It's all rather wonderfully British. (Casey is beside himself.)

The bungalow has polished wooden floors and high ceilings, a library, sitting room, long-table dining room, and wicker furniture out on the verandah.

I have slept in a four-poster bed adrift behind draped white nets, with the window open on a lukewarm night and soft rain falling. With the dawn, the window fills with viridescent light. Green is the colour of the soft hills of Hatton. Every tone and every shade of it. Grass green, leaf green, emerald and lime. Pea green, sea green, olive and jade.

My "bed tea" is served in my room, after being selected from a tea menu. And in the pot this morning is a tea grown higher than 1,000 metres above sea level, dark gold brown with a biscuity taste, described on that menu as "a handsome and impeccable tea" and just the thing for a strong start to the day.

This is tea on a higher plane.

Sri Lanka is the world's second-biggest exporter of tea, and Ceylon tea considered the "cleanest" tea in the world.

At the factory, Mr Taylor explains that tea bushes are of the camellia family and would grow to more than 7½ metres tall if they weren't kept pruned to bushes on these slopes. They are plucked four times a month, the best tea coming from the bud and top two leaves. About 5,500 bushes are planted for every 510 hectares, every four years the bushes tire and are pruned to about forty-five centimetres, reinvigorating them. "I could show you some bushes over 135 years old on the estate that are still producing good tea," Mr Taylor says.

There are about 1,200 workers on this estate alone, living in provided accommodation (even after they have retired), with free water and power and earning a minimum wage of just over $4 a day for women plucking 16 kilograms of leaves, though they can easily pluck more than 30 kilograms.

Over the factory door are three signs: 'No Child Labour', 'No Betel Chewing' and 'No Smoking'. The estate produces certified Fairtrade tea. Education through school and university is free in Sri Lanka and some pluckers' children have become doctors, teachers and lawyers, Mr Taylor says.

The pluckers start at 7.45 am, the harvest brought to the factory and the leaves first spread to wither before being rolled in machines almost identical to the first made by James Taylor. The leaves are chopped small in mincers, left to complete their precise oxidisation, dried at 120°C, sifted, graded and bagged in sacks.

"A shoot is plucked at 7.45 am, and by 7.45 am the next day it has been turned into black tea, and within three weeks it has been sold and turned into cash," Mr Taylor says. The 20,000 kilograms of green leaf handled here every day produces 5,000 kilograms of black tea.

It's a precise, twenty-four-hour-a-day process that, quite frankly, is enough to make you need a cup of tea and a lie-down.

And on this second morning, I have again ordered my "bed tea" for 6.30 am, at which time there is an equally polite tap on the heavy wooden door, and a tray is once again brought in.

But I am now aware that the biscuity brown tea might, just a few weeks ago, have been the delicate green tips of bushes on the slopes around me, plucked at just this time of morning and tossed gently into the baskets on the backs of women.

Zen & the Sustenance of Shopping

These girls are good. This is not going to be a random shopping day. This is going to be a planned and sustained assault, or, more specifically, a precise, surgical incision into the economic heart of Colombo. This is the last day of a week in Sri Lanka and I have joined two ladies for one big shopping day. It has been much thought about, long-discussed, and is to be a precise and paced exercise.

There's a frisson of both excitement and fear in the air. Will there be bargains?

I fully realise that I'm a junior partner in this. A tag along. A bag-carrier. A stretcher-bearer. I fear that, if it gets rough and there are crowds, these modern-day shopping warriors may instruct me to throw myself on the barbed wire while they run in over me. I comprehend my rank and drop into step behind them, armed with patience and not much more than an interest in local fabrics.

Our shopping army has decided to split in two: a classic pincer movement, with two wings coming in to pillage the hapless vanquished. Recognised as one of the most effective manoeuvres in warfare, there is no reason to think that it won't work just as effectively today as it did when first deployed by the Athenians at the Battle of Marathon in 490 BC.

Team A breaks off to stay in another hotel and attack from the Colombo 7 suburb of the city. They have set their sights on fabrics, tableware, and "stuff you just couldn't find anywhere else".

Team B (my two gals and me, their batman) are coming up from the south, initially by taxi, then taking to auto rickshaws, weaving through the traffic and confusing the enemy.

In our B-team, shopper B1 is clearly set on napery and wants to graze through the men's shirts.

B2 claims to be most focused on a big hardback book about the work of Sri Lankan architect Geoffrey Bawa (we have just stayed in one of his fine and interesting hotels).

But she has an "all's fair in war" glint in her eye and mentions she'd like to call in at that place where cricketer-cum-commentator Tony Greig always goes for a pedicure when he's in Colombo. (This seems to me way outside the shopping mission but, fearing charges of insubordination, and bearing in mind that commitment to "sustenance in every sense," I keep my own counsel.)

And then we are out of the taxi and in the thick of it, straight into a shop with cloth and clothes in brilliant colours and of high quality. Bags and books. Brilliant. But apparently this is just a reconnoitre. B1 and B2 explain that we need to size it up and then come back later for "a serious shop".

We arrange to split up and meet back at the door in thirty minutes. There's a lovely cafe outside under the trees and I think I might get coffee there, but then get stuck into books by Sri Lankan authors (including several pages of *The Cat's Table* by Michael Ondaatje) and turn up late.

On to another shop with clothing, footwear and accessories for women, men and children. I am struck by the good quality as much as the good prices, from home wares from bed linen to cutlery. B2 emerges with a slightly bulging carrier bag and unsheaves a pretty "shimmery, barbecue-y thing" that she wafts around seductively. "Nice buying," I encourage, getting into the swing of it.

But then B1 and B2 decide it is to our strategic advantage to take victuals often. Regroup and re-energise for the next assault. So, we set off to eat.

On the way, we stick our heads into the Galle Face Hotel, in Galle Road, built in 1864 and the oldest hotel in Colombo. The foyer has busts of the first man in space, Yuri Gagarin (seemingly with bad false teeth), and author Arthur C. Clarke, both of whom stayed here.

A carved granite noticeboard celebrates an odd collection of others who have stayed – Lord Mountbatten, Queen Ingrid of Denmark, Emperor Hirohito of Japan, John D. Rockefeller, Richard Nixon, Gregory Peck, Cole Porter and one Athol Thomas of *The West Australian*, who must have been here in the late 1970s or early '80s.

The hotel was built in 1864, and another granite board puts that into perspective – "before the first Australian cricket team visited England in 1882", which seems to me an odd landmark for Sri Lankans. At the bottom of that piece of granite, the hotel announces that it is "dedicated to yesterday's charm", a commitment to which I can relate.

We wander further in and there's a wedding going on, with Kandyan drummers from Sri Lanka's cultural triangle and an interesting collection of guests. Another wedding party tumbles through the foyer, kaleidoscopic.

On the way back out I pass again the bust of Mr Clarke who, in fact, wrote the last chapters of *3001: The Final Odyssey* here. It strikes me as appropriate, particularly as I notice actor Carrie "Princess Leia" Fisher's name up on the granite, as I actually feel I'm stepping out of the bar scene in *Star Wars*.

And then we taxi off to the old Cargill's store in the Colombo 1 district. David Sime Cargill and William Miller opened a general warehouse, import and wholesale business in this building in 1844, and it seems very little has changed. Curving glass cabinets are mostly empty, except for somewhat bizarre displays, and a supermarket, liquor store and KFC have moved in. But there's still the old grilled cashier's stand and the overpowering scent of the past.

Then the final stop with the taxi we have taken for the morning is to Dutch Hospital Shopping Precinct. Built around 1681, the Dutch Hospital is one of the oldest buildings in the Colombo Fort area. It has been converted into shops, eateries and a brewery but retained the seventeenth-century Dutch-colonial architecture.

We know that A1 and A2 will be heading to a particular restaurant at some stage and try to cut them off at the pass, but it's still closed. We mosey along to a cafe for fine cups of one-estate tea (not a mix done by wholesalers). B1 and B2 decide it's a good ploy to share the baguette – to not overfill and slow ourselves down; keep stopping for little top-ups to keep us going.

And so, renewed for the fight, we *tuk tuk* on to the Colombo 7 district and finally it comes – the tablecloth I have been waiting for. It's a long rectangle in creamy, undyed cotton with characters from Sri Lanka's native Sinhala language, mother tongue of the 15 million Sinhalese people of Sri Lanka. The oldest Sinhala inscriptions have been found on pottery of the sixth century BC.

I'm happy. It's useful. It's appropriate. I came, I saw, I consumed.

B1 and B2 seem happy enough, too, but they're not doing the celebratory war dance that I am.

"You're a good shopper," B1 says, in a moment of supreme recognition that I find quite emotional.

We are closing on the final assault but, in keeping with our policy of "a little and often", we head for "another little something" at a cafe in the Colombo 3 district. Culinary paths diverge. B1 goes cake and coffee. B2 goes cocktail and something (I forget). I settle on savoury, and what turns out to be one of the "dishes of the trip" – fried tofu in chilli.

We have one final shopping stop and set off back to the first shop. You may remember at the beginning of this story that I mentioned our recce. Well, having sized up everywhere else, B1 and B2 are ready for the kill. "Would you like to take a *tuk tuk* back to the hotel?" B1 asks me.

No, I say, I'm fine. I'll watch.

A little later B2 asks: "Are you sure you wouldn't like to take a *tuk tuk* back to the hotel?"

Why, is something ghastly going to happen? Will there be blood? Will it scar me for life?

No, I say, I'm fine, and happily fossick through the fabrics for a while.

B1 has her spoils of war. She approaches the counter with an item and a man asks if that will be all. "No. That's mine, too," she says, pointing to the pile of goods behind him.

But B2 has suddenly shown what truly great emporium warriors are made of. She has filled a basket to overflowing with cloth, tableware, place settings, goodness knows what. It has all been totted up and she is just about to pay when a look of horror comes over her face. She is aghast.

"What?" I say.

"The book. The Geoffrey Bawa book. I've forgotten it." And she runs off back into the bowels of the stores.

She looks fleetingly back. She looks happy.

Yak & Hotpots in Tibet

There are 30 million yaks in Tibet. Correction. Make that 29,999,999, because they have just served one for lunch.

And what a yak steak it is – tender, succulent and with mashed potatoes, vegetables and a thick and delicious gravy. I am not much of a carnivore, but at Ai Khyu restaurant in Lhasa, the capital of Tibet, yak steak is the thing to have. It is clearly a meat that has to be cooked with care, and this is.

For the evening meal I head off to Namaste restaurant, just a stone's throw from the Jokhang Temple at the heart of old Lhasa, and my companions immediately settle on yak burger, which is promptly nicknamed "a Hungry Yaks". It comes with chips, of course – and wherever I travel in Tibet, chunky fried potato is the go, even cold, which is interesting as Tibetans serve hot water with meals which, I must say, is very soothing to the digestion.

Namaste caters for many tastes. There's yak chow mein and chilli yak on the Chinese menu, yak steamed *momo* (a dumpling) on the Tibetan menu, and on the Indian and Nepali menu, yak *chhoela* (the meat is grilled and spiced) or yak *masala* with rice or naan. On the continental, yak steak and that now-famous 'Hungry Yaks' burger.

But there's plenty for those who don't want yak, of course, and for vegetarians. I go Indian, thankfully veg, and enjoy a splendid meal. The locals love this place.

But if you really want to go local in Lhasa, Chong Qing is the place. Full of locals, there's a big restaurant at street level and private rooms upstairs. No signs in English; probably you won't be understood or manage to navigate it alone – and it really is somewhere you would need to be taken by locals.

It is a hotpot meal, with a big heated bowl in the centre. There is an outer rim with a hot stock, and new friend Mingma ("Tibetans only have one name"), shows the high alpine spices in it. In the centre is a mild chicken stock.

Then guests make up their own accompanying sauce, out of oil, parsley, spring onion, garlic, salt and spices.

The cooking begins in the hotpot – thinly sliced yak meat and stomach, sausage, seafood, meatballs, tender bamboo shoots, tofu and many types of Tibetan mushrooms, which have been used as remedies for thousands of years.

The ingredients are gradually added to the hotpot and diners help themselves with chopsticks, dipping the cooked food in their sauce.

I must admit I avoided the stomach – but I could happily dine on Tibetan mushrooms for ever.

Ouzerias on an Old Greek Island

The old Greek islands, the way we imagine them, are still there. The harbour with small timber fishing boats and olive-complexioned men repairing their nets in the morning sun.

Small coves where you can find a piece of the Aegean Sea to yourself. Roads where there is little traffic and you may have to slow to pass an old woman side-saddle on a donkey. Where you buy a map, but there is really only one road, from top to toe of an island, with another coming sideways off its waistband into its biggest town.

A village set in a bay where there is an *ouzeria* with just a few painted chairs, and you can dine on tzatziki, in which the yoghurt is local and fresh and the garlic comes in crunchy pea-sized pieces, and the tomatoes and cucumber in the Greek salad burst with flavour.

The mountains themselves are covered with horizontal terraces, built by hand, rock by rock over hundreds of years for intimate agriculture. The high crests topped with a line of windmills that once had canvas sails.

And, either tucked into valleys or the backyards of houses, or even higher on the mountain tops, domed Greek Orthodox churches with chunky crosses on top. The doleful ringing of a bell carries and mingles with that of the goats.

This is Amorgos island, a pretty, interesting, quiet island in the Cyclades. It is still largely off the tourist trail, though the Luc Besson film *The Big Blue* was filmed here and has drawn attention to it.

Even in landing at Katapola, in the south-west, I know I am somewhere special. Authentic. The quayside is quiet and I stop to chat with a young man who has a couple of loosely restored BMW motorcycles. He is preparing his waterside cafe for the day. "I'll be back for lunch," I say. "If you want," he says, and smiles.

The hardware store is crammed full. There are goat and donkey bells on heavy leather collars.

Opposite is Xilokeratidhi, the northern end of Katapola Bay, which has more restaurants overlooking the clear Aegean water, and through which shoals of fish as long and wide as my forearm cruise.

What surprises me is that there are so many car hire firms. Motorcycles and Greek islands go together like ouzo and water, and there are quad bikes too, but there is also a choice of car hires, and I pick the nearest and ask for a car for the day. He tells me how much the car is and, in doing so, is clearly asking to be paid up-front, so I hand him the cash, but he doesn't ask for a credit card imprint. I just sign his form and he hands me the keys to a small Hyundai. "Back by 9 pm, please."

When I go to the car, I point out a dent in the front wing (I have good reason to be nervous about car hirers). "You know about this," I ask. "Yes," he says, laying a palm flat upon his chest and bowing slightly. "It is all mine."

And that is it. I buy one of the good "hikers" maps that I have found on just about all the islands I have visited. This small island of just over 120,000 square kilometres is covered in walking paths and its main fifteen trails are popular with walkers.

The only main bitumen road – that one from top to toe – on the island was only built in 1955. And I am off on it, ostensibly heading towards the seven-storey monastery of Panagia of Hozoviotissa, founded in 1088 and which "hangs" from a cliff face overlooking the Aegean Sea on the east coast of Amorgos, near Chora, and where a few monks still live.

But first there is the zigzag road up, giving a spectacular view of Katapola and the bay, and the terraces all around. Chora is an interesting high town of white buildings and a nearby string of windmills.

After the monastery and swim, the route is north to Agios Pavlos, with its offshore island and the quiet town of Ormos Eghialis, on the north-west coast.

Here and there are signs for "studio rooms" and pensions, and there is a bigger hotel at Ormos Eghialis.

It is easy to sit and watch the men repairing their nets. To see a slower life going on. Just to be footloose and fancy free, off the tourist trail, in the old Greece I had hoped to find.

Food & Family in Italy

I spent a couple of weeks in Rome with my Italian friend Carmelo. He was filming. I was writing. We were both enjoying Italy… stylish clothes, women with jet black hair on scooters, and eating, of course. Eating consumes Italians. What they eat, and how they prepare it, is fundamental to the cultural identity of the country.

From the back seat of the Lancia, someone is harmonising to the rendition of "O Sole Mio" which is belting with gusto from the car stereo. Carmelo's boisterous, arm-waving embellishment (especially the high parts, volume atoning for lack of accuracy) rips up through the open sunroof, out the windows and rattles the shutters of Rome.

I can't remember who said it, but someone broke off from the in-car concert…"Write *this*. This is Rome."

And, indeed, this *is* the spirit of Rome, and, indeed, way down the hillside, bathed in the sunlight of spring, sits the spirited city itself. A city of passion; cobble and concrete, pillars and panache. A city of human history in intriguing layers.

Maurizio is at the wheel, slicing through the thick wedges of Rome's traffic, slamming on the brakes, flamboyantly raising, in threat or exasperation, a cupped hand in the air, playing the car horn.

Maurizio, with his slicked black hair, sharp moustache and tiny beard, his immaculately cut clothes and a suave smile that leaks from one side of his face.

Aah, Maurizio. A young chef with a passion for food, which he and his extended family has just shared with us. *"You maast come to lunch. You maast eat with us."*

Delivered like this, there is really no question about it. Indeed we *maast*.

It is a typically Roman lunch, with a procession of courses (somewhere along the line, I lost the number). There is coffee, its bite belying its size, more talk, more sign language and the afternoon wears on as we sit talking with Maurizio, Bettina and Andrea. Then Maurizio's brother Roberto joins us, and Andrea's mother, Fiorella, and his father, Aldo. This long, languid, day passing in companionship and community. In family. In connection. In the finest traditions of Italian family hospitality.

"*Here.* Here she is. *Aaah, look at her talking.* She's *faaaantastic. Ehhh,* just look at her."

Carmelo is glued to the screen of his video camera, playing back footage shot a few days earlier. People close in. By now, just about everyone he has met wants to see his Nonna – his grandmother – in the flesh, so to speak. We've all heard so much about her.

And there she is on the screen, the woman he has been expansively describing and praising in that passionate way, where conversation is performance.

And now I, too, am transfixed by this little old, cottage-loaf Italian woman in black, with her neat, tied-back white hair, staring straight into the lens, telling her anecdotes, laughing at her own stories, reliving memories, passing on her wisdom and the family's history to her grandson. And all with such unaffected confidence. Waving her arms – it must be genetic – and communicating so clearly, so entertainingly, although I can't understand a word she's saying.

"Ah, my Nonna. Isn't she *wonderful?* She has such wisdom."

Carmelo has just spent two days with her, in the village where he was born, and come back overwhelmed. A powerful insight into the strength of family, the bond of blood, the gifts that our elders have for us.

"You walk in and there she is in the kitchen, welcoming her lost grandson..."

She had made up a bed for him so they could sleep in the same room. And there they were, talking in the dark, with just a slice of light coming in through the window, exchanging parts of their lives. There was a fire in the room, which had frescoes on the ceiling. It was furnished sparsely. With no curtains – just shutters – there is a kind of echo.

Carmelo says, "So, what did she tell me? She told me '*love without strength, without backbone, without force, has no validity*'. Isn't that *FAAANTASTIC*. She's 87 years old and she's telling me that.

"'Why are you telling me that?' I ask.

"And she says 'I thought you'd like to know'."

Carmelo was born at 3am. His father had gone down to the village with a donkey – he was the only one of six brothers to own a donkey, he was quite progressive – and he brought the midwife up on the donkey and it was November, and very cold. Carmelo was born on soft sheets all handmade on a loom.

Carmelo got up early one morning and drove with his uncle to that house where he was born – a tiny stone cottage which is now dilapidated. Outside, there's a pool made out of rocks where they used to wash the clothes by hand. Half a kilometre away is the tap where he used to get water in earthenware pots, his mother with them on her head. The tap is still there, with water coming out.

Carmelo's family left for Australia when he was six. His father left the feudal system of having to give eggs and olives to the baron. They came to Australia for a better way of life. Life moved on, but the mixture of food and culture is intrinsic.

Carmelo bought a goat. In a suburb. Twenty minutes from the centre of Perth. "When I tell people I've got a goat, they say '*what?*' And I say, hey, other people have dogs which bark and dig holes and are revolting. I tie my goat up on the lawn. It fertilises the garden, we get milk, I make my own yoghurt."

Italian culture lives in its cuisine. Local food makes you see the heart of people. Local food is the soul of culture and the tradition of a country. Messages in simple and healthy eating.

To walk away at the end of a good meal is to have walked away from a table as from a symphony.

Life moved on, even for Nonna. She used to have no running water, no electricity.

But last time Carmelo saw her, she took him outside to listen to the water meter – *tick, tick, tick* – with the tap on.

She'd got a self-lighting gas oven, but there in the corner of the kitchen was this welded drum, cut in half, that the blacksmith made for her, with embers she roasts tomatoes and capsicums on, then peels them.

Carmelo inhales the air, as if to smell the sweet scent again…

"She starts cooking on it and the whole house smells so beautiful. When I got close, I could smell dinner cooking even before I got there."

He could smell food, culture, family, and every scent of his own, deep, comfortable past.

Of his connections. Of all our connections.

Sustained to 121 years old in Madagascar

Ravao Razaisoa is extraordinary not only because she is 121 years old, but because she's still a livewire. She rocks back and forth, laughs, shows us the tooth she has just had trouble with, and then rocks again. She's animated and funny. I have settled on the floor of her home in the village of Andasibe in Madagascar to try and photograph her with the little light that is coming in from the window. It's almost impossible. Ravao won't (can't) sit still.

Her family says documentation proves Ravao's birth date, and she still lives at home, at the heart of her family, and is much loved. She had eleven children, only one of whom is still alive. Andasibe village, where Ravao lives, is home of the Betsimisaraka tribe, who farm, but still live mainly off the forest.

And Ravao puts her long and healthy life down to being with family – such an important factor for her – and that she has never eaten meat, though she does eat fish.

The World's First Wine in Georgia

Nunu Kardenakhlishvili is tired because she had many visitors here yesterday, but even so, within minutes she brings to the big wooden table cheese made from the milk of her cow, bread baked in her clay oven and wine made underground in the ancient way.

This is hospitality in Georgia, this country sitting under the great brow of the Caucasus Mountains where western Asia and eastern Europe meet, and it is an authentic welcome.

Georgia is the birthplace of wine making, or "wine culture", as Georgians tend to put it. Scientists have dated cultivated grape seeds back 7,000 years, which is now explained in the Signagi Museum, in the wine-growing region of Kakheti. The word "wine" itself is derived from the Georgian "g'vino", which has been in use for longer than most languages have existed, and ceramic wine jars have been dated to 6000 BC.

Through gene mapping, the heritage of more than 100 modern grape types has been traced to Georgia. It is home to some 525 endemic species of grape, says Shergil Pirtskhelani at the Pheasant's Tears winery in the medieval town of Signagi.

At Pheasant's Tears, as at Nunu Kardenakhlishvili's Khareba winery and museum in nearby Kvareli, wine is made in the traditional way, in terracotta pots called *kvevri* (also spelt *qveri*) that are buried underground, up to their necks and sealed with a round stone placed on top.

Kvevri may be just a metre or so tall for family use, or big enough to hold up to five tonnes of crushed grapes, says Shergil. After being cleaned, they are heated and lined with beeswax to waterproof them, and Iliu Datunashoili adds that it also removes bacteria.

"The *kvevri* are the magic of Georgian wine production," Shergil says. Nothing is added. "It uses the grapes' own natural yeast and resources to ferment itself. We don't add anything. Because it ferments on its own sugars, it uses itself to age itself."

While European winemaking separates the grape's flesh and juice from the skins and stalks, with the *kvevri* technique only the stalks are separated, and the complete mash is placed in the underground terracotta pot. It both ferments and then ages there. The *kvevri* are sealed and left to ferment for three or four months, resulting in a vitamin- and tannin-rich wine which is completely organic. It is ladled out and into bottles, with the clear wine at the top and mash dropping to the bottom.

From the residue *chacha* is made, a clear, strong liquor sometimes known as vine vodka and which many Georgians use as medicine as much as for pleasure.

Shergil adds that making wine in the *kvevri* is not as easy as it sounds, but the result is unique flavours, and he explains that even their white wines aren't chilled, so the flavour "cannot hide behind temperature".

The Pheasant's Tears name reflects this old style's rarity, and also followed a visit to an old man still making it the traditional way.

After buying the old building they are based in in Signagi, they found the cellar beneath it, filled with dirt to hide it during the period in the country's history when it became part of the Soviet Union, because the Soviets didn't want families producing wine for themselves. When they remarked upon its extraordinary taste, the old man said: "Ah, isn't it just like pheasant's tears."

Shergil says, "In the old times wine was so rare, so special, so hard to find, it was as rare as pheasant's tears."

And now there are new times, and a new era for the world's oldest wines.

"When the Russians closed their doors to Georgian wine, it was the start of Georgia's rediscovery," says Shergil. In 2006, when Georgia strengthened its links with the Economic Union, Russia banned wine imports, but now Pheasant's Tears exports to seventeen countries.

The story is borne out by Iliu Datunashoili, at Schuchmann Winery. "Interest in this wine is increasing rapidly." Schuchmann's biggest export client last year was Sweden and the winery is building a third room for an additional forty *kvevris*. Many of theirs hold three tonnes of crushed grapes.

Dark red *saperavi* is among Pheasant's Tear's most unusual. Shergil says it has twenty times more antioxidants than most other red wines. In the old days it was said that people "ate it" for health, rather than drinking it. "They would eat the mash like a soup, with bread."

And Shergil expands: "What I like most about this wine is that it is full of energy and it is produced in the same way that it was 7,000 years ago."

Cleanly, intensely, handmade food and drink from local produce was full of life – of energy – all coming from a deep culture of agriculture in a land where the green mountains are criss-crossed with terraced paths made by thousands of years of passing hooves.

He puts his two index fingers a fist's width apart on the table. "We used to have to eat this much to get a lot of energy" (he moves his index fingers a shoulder's width apart) "and now we have to eat this much to get the same energy". Freezing halves its energy, cooking by microwave just about kills it, he says.

Then his jaw moves and he seems to chew on the wine in his mouth. "This is like a dark, dark room. Maybe a library. Maybe a winery.

"What I like about wines is that they have a personality. They say, 'this is myself'."

In the background is the many-voiced polyphonic singing for which Georgia is also famous – many voices (Shergil's among them) singing traditional Georgian songs.

He has also just shown us through rare Georgian rugs which Pheasant's Tears owner John Henry Wurdeman V (an American married to a Georgian) has collected and now sells.

Pheasant's Tears collects and maintains Georgian culture, and allows it to live on. It is reviving old Georgian traditions, including those of music and dancing.

And wine culture is also integrated into its devout faith. The energy from wine and spiritual and cultural life are intertwined.

Khatia Rekhviashvili, who is showing me around, says, "When I smell wine it releases my good emotions. I want to realise my emotions."

And yet, Iliu points out that using the *kvevri* method means high tannins and thus less alcohol.

The female Saint Nino, who brought Christianity to Georgia, held up a cross of grape stems when she arrived in Georgia. In AD 327, as a result of her presence, Georgia became the second country to declare itself Christian, after it neighbour Armenia in AD 301. St Nino is known as the Enlightener of Georgia.

"Christ said 'I am the vine and you are the branches'," points out Shergil.

Among others, I visit Ikalto Monastery, which has medieval *kvevris*, and wine presses from the eighth century.

The Christianity is no surprise to me, neither is the hospitality for which Georgians are famous. It runs deeply through this country, right down to the way it has opened its doors and accommodated refugees from Azerbaijan and Turkey. "They had nothing," says Khatia. And, asked about her feelings for the recently aggressive Russians, she says, "We are Christian people. How could we hate?"

But I ignorantly hadn't expected the sheer quality and variety, history and unique flavours of Georgian food and wine.

For one early dinner at Signagi, I sit outside with friends for *khachapuri* and the best cup of Turkish-style coffee I have ever drunk...smooth, not bitter, more like drinking chocolate. *Khachapuri* is a delicious meal of Georgian bread, cottage cheese and egg – an extravagant, early form of pizza.

With it I have local Nabeghlavi sparkling mineral water which, every local I meet assures me, comes out of the ground effervescent. Khatia insists that in her village in northern Georgia, at the foot of the Greater Caucasus mountains, there is water naturally much fizzier than this.

Water does bubble out of the ground here – people stop to fill their water bottles at these spouts. Georgia has more than 2,000 mineral water springs and it is unusual for me to be in hotels where there is no supply of two bottles of complimentary water. The water out of the taps here is sweet and pure.

On the roadside and in local markets, Khatia stops to buy *churchkhela*, which is a delicious, smoothly chewy roll made from boiled grape must, with walnuts on a string through the centre. It originated here in the Caucasus region and they are hung in "sausages". Two mouthfuls of this and you feel you have had a meal – they are so natural, so full of energy and vitamins, you literally feel full and invigorated.

And finding fresh food is as simple as, again stopping by the roadside, buying an 8-kilogram bucket of fresh, juicy cherries, translucent red and straight off the trees, for $6. Or the same amount in strawberries that taste like strawberries used to, just picked, for $10.

Cheeses are served in big triangles, such as the light, salty and non-fatty *sulguni*, *imereti* and *imeretian*, almost squeaky and full of fine holes.

Georgians love mushrooms, and Khatia has fond memories of collecting them in her village, a favourite family day out. *Soko ketsze* is mushrooms and cheese served in a sizzling pan. Delicious.

For breakfast we have Georgian *shoti*, or *shota*, bread, named for twelfth century poet Shota Rustaveli and cooked stuck to the sides of a clay oven, local cheeses and breakfast olives in a thick, sweet syrup.

And then there is *supra* – the big, traditional meal for friends and family. The head of the table (the *tamada*) in charge of proceedings and offering philosophical toasts.

Which is what happened here at Nunu's place yesterday, with 150 guests. It is no wonder that she says she feels tired.

But she brings wine and bread and cheese and says that though she gets weary, God gives you power if you are doing something good, something you love, and something for your country.

There is a strong energy when produce, food, wine and faith are intertwined.

Ramsay & Onsen in Japan

In a world dunked in spin, marinated in hype and drizzled in political correctness, Gordon Ramsay is an interesting kettle of fish. The whole brand of him has been built on honesty. Blunt, mostly. Rude, often. But the main ingredient of that famous Ramsay serve is just telling the truth.

I'm not interested in Gordon Ramsay's swearing and I wasn't even that interested in his food, until I tried it at his first restaurant in Asia, Gordon Ramsay at Conrad Tokyo. But the Gordon Ramsay phenomenon is fascinating. Ramsay has made his mark in this slick city of more than 13 million people, which has 200,000 bars and restaurants.

Tokyo has more restaurants listed in the Michelin food guide than any other Asian city and Conrad Tokyo is among them, having just been awarded a Michelin star for one of its three restaurants, China Blue. Appointing Ramsay as consultant chef is fundamental to Conrad Tokyo's success; he brings internationalism and innovation to their menus.

But you'd have wondered how the Ramsay rudeness and foul language that we have seen on TV might go down with the polite, formal and generally conservative Japanese, who have elevated manners to an art form.

(Just think of the judges on the TV show *Iron Chef...*"*the texture of this dessert is so...nice...*")

The answer is that it is cardinal to Japanese to respect experience and achievement, and the Ramsay TV persona isn't necessarily the everyday Gordon Ramsay.

Gordon Ramsay was born in Scotland, brought up in Stratford-on-Avon, was a young professional soccer player for the Glasgow club Rangers, and then set about his kitchen career, first working for legendary chefs Marco Pierre White and Albert Roux before eventually becoming chef of Aubergine, where he won two Michelin stars within three years of opening.

In 1998, he opened the self-named Gordon Ramsay restaurant in Chelsea, London, and gained his third Michelin star in 2001. More Gordon Ramsay restaurants and even pubs followed and, of course, the TV shows such as *Ramsay's Kitchen Nightmares*, *Hell's Kitchen* and *The F Word*. He has also published best-selling cookery books and an autobiography.

And apart from a commitment to hard work, he shares something else that is fundamental to the Japanese psyche – an obsession with striving for perfection. Attention to detail lifted to an art form.

The Japanese themselves at Conrad Tokyo tell me it is a national trait to want to make things consummate, exemplary, flawless.

Ramsay says it is one of the easiest places he has opened a restaurant, as the Japanese pay such close attention to detail and replicate each dish exactly, time after time. Precisely the same temperature, texture and presentation as the first. Every time.

Pan-fried scallops with mille-feuille of potato, parmesan velouté and black olive smarties.

Ballottine of tuna carpaccio with marinated *mooli*, spiced pineapple, cardamom and mint yoghurt.

Roasted best end of lamb with confit shoulder, lentils, Provencale vegetables, and thyme lamb jus.

Pan-roasted fillet of sea bass with braised fennel, baby artichoke, kohlrabi, candied lemon and vanilla velouté.

Evening meal highlights? Open ravioli of crab and mango in chilled melon, mint and champagne soup. Peach soup with basil jelly. Hot chocolate fondant, cardamom and bitter chocolate, Arabica ice-cream, citrus *tuiles*. The crust of chocolate cake, when broken, exudes warm chocolate sauce.

It's sheer performance.

Shall I go on?

Have you had enough?

Well, just let me just finish by telling you about breakfast at Gordon Ramsay Conrad Tokyo, as it is quite simply one of the best breakfasts I've ever had. One can easily understand that making fine-dining courses from exotic ingredients and exceptional menus will leave its mark, but to elevate scrambled eggs, crispy bacon (prosciutto-thin), mushrooms, sausage and tomato to an art form – well, that really is something.

Japanese Sustenance Gets Physical

We sit on little plastic seats, facing the wall, naked, washing ourselves. There is a mirror, and in it I can see the backs of the men behind me, thoroughly sudded. They sluice themselves off with a hand shower, then lather up again.

I do likewise, knowing the basic etiquette of *onsen* bathing in Japan but keen not make a faux pas. I know that one must thoroughly wash before heading into the natural hot pools, and that it is part of the purification process of *onsen*, but I'm not sure how long is long enough.

"There's only so much washing you can do, you know," says my new companion, a comical Sydneysider who still has a broad English accent belying his heritage. (Coming here with him was always going to be risky.)

The "naked communion" of *onsen* is a part of Japanese people's physical and spiritual sustenance and I am being brave. I know, I know. We are all born naked, but wandering around starkers among men who may be taken for sumo wrestlers, and dads with their young sons, leans on all sorts of cultural barriers for me. Call me old-fashioned.

I should let you know that Kuttari Onsen in Sahoro is segregated into men's and women's sections, but this is not always the case elsewhere.

I had been warned that although we are given a small towel, it is against etiquette to carry it into the *onsen*. So it's hard to explain how relieved I am when I see a Japanese man take his in, carrying it modestly in front of him, and then another. With relief, I do likewise.

The volcanic landscape of Japan means there are many hot springs and these have long been developed into *onsen*. By definition, *onsen* use water heated naturally underground and produced from geothermal springs. There is a legal definition, in Japan, that the water of an *onsen* must contain at least one of nineteen designated chemical elements, including radon and metabolic acid and be 25°C or warmer. The most common are sulphur *onsen*, sodium chloride *onsen*, hydrogen carbonate *onsen* and iron *onsen*. The water in Kuttari Onsen, which is next to East Taisetsu National Park and looks down on Kuttari Lake, contains alkaline sodium.

While there are the obvious therapeutic effects of a mineral soak for general aches and pains, some Japanese believe *onsen* can also help constipation, menstrual disorders, diabetes and other conditions.

None of this is on my mind.

I am not concerned about any of these things, but more about a small tattoo. I'd forgotten about the moon and star on my shoulder. Some spas in Japan will not massage people with tattoos and many *onsen* ban bathers with them, even if they are small and inoffensive, as they are traditionally associated with Yakuza gang culture and seen as a badge of criminality.

The rule is often strictly applied, even for foreigners. But nothing is said. Men either ignore me, or nod as they pass.

I sit outside in the cold winter air for which Hokkaido, Japan's most northern island, is famous, and watch the sun set red over the silver trunks of birch trees.

My body is poaching, my head and shoulders freezing. The man near me has folded his tiny towel and put it on top of his head, which is quite usual practice.

I notice this, but try not to look directly at him. It's a good policy.

The Poppies of Thailand's Golden Triangle

There are 250 species of poppy but only one yields the white sap that is opium and can be made into heroin. And those poppies, *Papaver somniferum*, once covered the hillsides of the Golden Triangle. This mountainous northern tip of Thailand was renowned for its opium growers, heroin factories, drug lords, opium wars, for its porous border with Burma, for smuggling and death. The Golden Triangle, straddling the Mekong River between Thailand, Burma and Laos, produced more than half of the world's illegal heroin, which spread its tentacles through Asia, Africa, Europe and America.

But in 1988, Princess Sangwal drew a line in the sand. She initiated a project to restore and reforest the land in the Doi Tung area, and to offer the hill tribes here who were just trying to eke out a living (the growers rather than the drug lords), new industries and incomes.

The King's Mother didn't stop there. She then initiated a project to build the Hall of Opium just north of Chiang Saen, at the spot which is physically the centre of the Golden Triangle, and where I now stand on the bank of the Mekong River and look across to Laos on the opposite bank and Burma to the north-west.

The Hall of Opium, in Golden Triangle Park – one of more than 3,000 royal projects in Thailand – is there to bring to life the opium history of the Golden Triangle. The hall, jointly prepared by the Tourism Authority of Thailand and the Mae Fae Luang Foundation, shows its physical, social and economic toll. The scene is set by walking through the long dark entrance tunnel, walls sculpted with contorted figures depicting addiction.

Opium has a 5,000-year history. It was used by Egyptians, early Greeks and Romans, and for 300 years as laudanum. Laudanum is opium dissolved in alcohol and the word means "to praise" in Latin.

The exhibition also details the Opium Wars between Britain and China and how, by the mid-eighteenth century, 13 million of the 40 million people in China were addicted to opium.

At one stage during the reign of King Chulalongkorn between 1868 and 1910, the opium tax on its legal production represented 25 per cent of government income in Thailand.

An opium department was established in 1906 to process the poppy's produce and in 1943, the government was buying opium from hill tribes. Now, opium poppies can only legally be grown in India, Turkey and Tasmania.

It was only sixty years ago that opium became a big illegal trade. Hall of Opium displays warnings of the personal and social effects of addiction. Those who have admitted heroin use include Diego Maradona, Eric Clapton, Robert Downey Jr, Charlie Parker and Kurt Cobain.

It tells the story of a beautiful, dangerous plant that brought vital pain relief for hundreds of years, and misery to millions.

Eating in India Where All Are Equal

Men and women here pray to their own god. "They bring their god with them," the young devotee gently smiles.

I am shoeless, head covered, at the Sikh temple in Hanuman Road, Delhi. There are gold panels, a central dais with a book, but no images inside the temple – nothing like statues of the thousands of Hindu gods, no Jesus Christ hanging on the cross, no big Buddha with auspiciously drooping ear lobes.

"No. Each man and woman can pray to their own god. Freedom of expression." This young devotee, who has offered to show me around, gently smiles. A smile he is used to wearing, for Sikhism does not accept the ideology of pessimism, but advocates optimism and hope.

Three musicians fill the temple with rhythm and spiralling sound. Two are singing, one of them is playing a small harmonium, and the third man is playing a tabla drum.

They will make music for an hour, and then the reading of the book will continue. The Sikh holy book, Guru Granth Sahib, teaches of brotherhood.

For the Sikh religion was founded by Guru Nanak, who was born in 1469 and followed by nine other gurus, who added to and developed the belief. But the tenth and last, Guru Gobind Singh, who died in 1708, ordained that the Guru Granth Sahib, this holy book, would take over as the ultimate and permanent guru. And so it is here, in the centre of the temple, and central to these lives.

Sikhs are baptised (and anyone accepting the beliefs and lifestyle can be baptised into Sikhism), do not cut their hair, do not drink alcohol or smoke, are vegetarian, regard another's wife as his sister, another man's daughter as his own daughter, and women as of equal soul to men. Women do not wear a veil, but are expected to dress politely. Marriage is regarded as a holy union, not a contract.

Any person can visit the temple, regardless of creed, culture or nationality and, indeed, my new Sikh companion emphasises, Sikhs do not recognise caste.

"Everyone here is equal. It is a brotherhood," says the young Sikh who is now with me.

Part of me wishes I could tell you his name and show you a photograph of him, but the bigger part of me is happy that it seemed inappropriate to ask him for either. He just appeared, offered advice on removing shoes and head covering, and then asked, "Would you like me to show you around my temple? It would be my pleasure." He emphasises the words *my*.

Indeed, he refused the money I later offered him – it was a service and a pleasure for this young man, who had spent his childhood running around the temple.

The visit to the Sikh temple is one of the most interesting and insightful things I do in Delhi – just head into the door that says "Information Centre", look confused and slightly lost, and someone is sure to help. Like, in my case, this young Sikh. As we step into the temple, devotees kiss the ground – "the top of my being is going to the bottom of my being, in utmost respect".

"Do you have time to sit? Perhaps for ten or twenty minutes?" And I do, listening to the music, letting it spiral inside.

"Some people come and sit, others don't have time," says the young Sikh. "If you don't have time, it's OK. If you have work to do, go and do your work. It's no use sitting here thinking of horse selling in Bagh. You should go and sell horses in Bagh."

It is a Monday and the place is busy. But then, it is every day.

For one important aspect of Sikhism is food and dining together, and every day perhaps 10,000 to 12,000 people will be fed here by volunteers. The food is free.

From all walks of life, locals and visitors from all countries, all religions, sit cross-legged, waiting in an organised queue, until a dining area that can seat up to 800 people in rows on mats on the floor empties, and the next wave is let in. It happens about every twenty-five minutes.

Stainless steel trays, with compartments for different foods, are brought to each person. A man walks the rows dropping a spoon into hands held up together as if in prayer. Then *chipati*, dhal, vegetables, rice.

In the kitchen behind, pots holding perhaps 100 litres are boiling away over gas cookers, and a *chipati* machine is turning out the flatbreads like a tennis ball serving machine, before they are put on big, hot plates and flipped like fish. It takes two hours for 25 kilograms of lentil dhal to cook.

Food is served for eight hours a day – four hours at lunchtime and four in the evening.

And then, about 9 or 9.30pm every day, the book starts to be gradually moved to another place, where it will spend the night, away from the centre of the temple.

As if, as the people sleep, the guru rests, too.

"Inside the temple, men and women pray to their god, listen to their god and to music," says the young Sikh. "Inside, there is only the word. All untouchability is abolished. Everyone is equal."

They are the last words I hear the young Sikh say. He has shown me back to the entrance, and he is there with me, but when I turn to thank him the room is empty.

Silver Scales in Oman

In the Sultanate of Oman's capital, Muscat, fish traders sit on low stools and spread their knees so that their ankle-length cotton *dishdasha* gowns spread to form a big cotton bowl in their lap. And in there, they sort their *rial* – winnowing the grubby money notes to the top and coins to the bottom in a motion that has been practised here for generations.

And then, with everything in order, they slip the neat little embroidered *muzzar* hat off their head, put the notes flat inside and slip it quickly back on, with not a sign of its contents.

The motion is repeated over and over – to add new notes after shoppers have wrangled gently over price, then paid; to reassure themselves of the financial progress of the day.

The fish souk in this capital of Oman sits on the end of Muttrah Bay in Old Muscat. Anchovies are scooped and weighed by an old man who implores passers-by to consider these, his only fish for sale. Another sits next to two game fish, their sail fins spread, bodies almost as long as himself. There are small tuna like those I have seen caught off the beach in Kovalam, in south-west India – the other side of this big rim of the world and the place where, one day, I sat on a beach and thought I would like to come to Oman one day. To complete some connections.

Indeed, the people shopping at the fish souk seem an equal mix of Omanis and Indians. I chat with one man about the quality of what is warming on the marble slabs, and he tells me he is from Kerala in India ("where the tuna are finer") and after we have shaken hands in parting, I notice delicate fish scales twinkling in my palm.

9

The Music of Life

Stringed instruments hang, sculptural, on the walls of my secret writing study. There are four handmade by luthiers – a classical guitar, a steel stringed guitar of Australian timbers and a wandoo hardwood mandolin all by Scott Wise in Margaret River, and a vintage electric guitar by Queensland luthier Peter Morrison. There's a modern version of what, in 1951, became the world's first electric bass guitar, a Fender Precision (the legendary *FPB*), and an acoustic bass guitar. There's a ukulele from Hawaii, made from the island's koa wood; a *baglamas* from Greece; a monochord from Vietnam; an Appalachian picking stick from the United States; a *lesiba* from Lesotho.

When I go to write in this hidden studio (not at an airport, not on a plane, not sitting on a rather begrudging Casey *elsewhere*), I pluck them off the wall and play them. I most often have the mandolin on my lap ("my weapon of choice") and play a little between thoughts. Its high, sharp notes give a sweet punctuation.

There is also a violin, which my mother bought me when I was a child and on which I had years of lessons. Violin is so important to me (as an instrument, as an object, philosophically) that I now rarely play it, because my playing can't do it justice.

My feelings for violin are manifested in one of the three stories in *Unaccountable Hours: Three Novellas*, my book of fiction. 'The Luthier' is the story of Alton Freeman, an Australian maker of stringed instruments who benefits from being first generation and innovative, rather than confined by the strictures which may bind long-established violin-making dynasties. His story develops many themes which I see as the essence of this book, *Beautiful Witness*.

Authentic local music connects me to culture. I dig around online and buy regional rarities. When I travel, I scour backstreet shops for recordings of traditional music. It's all I play while I'm there. I seek out recitals; I can talk a language with local musicians that is away from tourism. And when I'm writing (in an airport gate lounge, in a train in England; wherever it is), I can plug in my ear phones and listen to Amjad Ali Khan playing sarod; to Naseer Shamma on Baghdad lute; Munir Bashir playing traditional *oud* music; to Yehudi Menuhin and Ravi Shankar combining in Shankar's Concerto No 1 (or Shankar with Professor T. N. Krishnan on violin); or to J. S. Bach's partitas and sonatas, and be elsewhere.

But I suspect that some musical instruments may be like food and fashion. The local coffee that tastes so gorgeous in its native land seems like herby mud when I get it back home. The batik shirt that looked quite snazzy in a factory shop in Malaysia probably should have stayed there. Was I really ever going to wear a *dishdasha*?

Once home, I wonder just what I was thinking.

My *baglamas* sounded well enough on the balcony overlooking the Plaka district of Athens, but I make it sound rather shockingly bad in my study. I've never managed to get a note from the *lesiba* and the monochord, unfortunately, has become a decoration. (I'd still like a sarod and an *oud*, but have resisted as I suspect they'd fall into the same category.)

A Sitar Lesson in India

Ram slouches back against the crumbly wall, right foot under, left foot out, the big bowl of the sitar resting on the turquoise cushion beside him. He strums a cacophony of drone notes and his fingers climb up the arched frets, sending out a quavering top line.

This is Ram's emporium in Agra, India, a city with 3,000 years of history known firstly for the Taj Mahal, secondly for the Red Fort and not at all for Shiva Music Shop in Fatehabad Road.

Ram's music shop is not much more than 2 metres square – the classic size of rooms that families of six or so in Agra have traditionally lived in. It is dark, damp and swelteringly hot. It feels like the heat has sucked all the oxygen out of it.

Three full-sized sitars and one smaller child's one hang on walls that are tattooed by mould. There are posters pinned up of Hindu gods – a handful from the religion's 330 million. Shiva, naturally, seeing as the shop is named for him. Destroyer, ascetic, lord of the cosmic dance. His wife Parvati and their elephant-headed son Ganesh.

There is a small stool, and Ram pulls it forward for me. I have tracked this place down, furthering an interest in stringed instruments and a particular interest in Indian music. Sarod's the first love, sitar not far behind.

It is a small quest.

"What instruments do you play?" asks Ram. I name stringed instruments and tell him I'm not very good.

He politely rolls his head on his shoulders as if to say "surely this cannot be true".

He asks if I'd like him to play for me, to prove he is a musician and not just a shopkeeper.

I say I would think it a privilege.

And with his left fingers, he turns the hefty wooden pegs to turn the drone strings, then the strings for note playing. Other strings will just vibrate, he says. "You only need three strings for the tune."

And then he starts to play, with a finger pick giving the notes a sharp edge, bending them by pushing the string. Sitar is one of the most popular stringed instruments of north India, and part of the Persian connection established by Mughal rulers which also left the Islamic architectural precision of the Taj Mahal. The word sitar comes from the Persian *sehtar*, meaning "three strings".

"I am a musician," Ram suddenly announces again. He specialises in raga, ghazal, bhajan and vocal and gives free musical concerts every evening.

He says he makes some money as a musician and in selling the instruments but it is very hard to make a living in India.

"I sell marijuana too," he announces brightly, as if the thought has cheered him. He rubs his fingers and seems to imply it is more lucrative than music.

"You want to smoke a little?" He raises his eyebrows furtively, though marijuana is legal here.

Not me, I say.

He makes other suggestions and I shake my head emphatically.

"OK then," says Ram. "Sitar."

Sitar it is.

Ram tells me Ravi Shankar was his teacher but I am not sure about this. I was listening to Ravi's Concerto No 1 on my digital music player most of yesterday as I sat in a minibus on the Grand Trunk Road coming here from New Delhi, revelling in the fact that Ravi's friendship with violinist Yehudi Menuhin, who plays the concerto with him, is one of the best things I know about.

When I don't react to Ram's announcement, he starts picking out a song, and to sing out of tune, "*I...once had a girl...or should I say...she once had me...*"

He looks up and smiles and rolls his head from side to side, "See, you can even play Beatles songs. You know Beatles songs?" Of course, Liverpool's Fab Four had a famous dalliance with Indian culture, religion and music, and with sitar and sitar players, but they never sounded quite like Ram's slightly faltering version, in which the words are lost in a sea of quivering notes.

He shows me a little of the technique.

The instrument's body is a spherical gourd and the hollow and deeply concave fretboard is 3 feet (or 90 centimetres) long and 3 inches wide (just over 7½ centimetres). The sitar originally had only three strings but modern instruments have seven, including side strings for drone and rhythmic accompaniment. There are between sixteen and twenty-two slightly-curved brass or silver frets.

Then I ask him about sarod – if there might be any around that I could at least see?

That is more difficult, he says.

But the next thing I know I am in a sandwich between Ram and the rider of a small motorcycle heading through Agra's traffic – this city of one-and-a-half million people's weaving, heaving mix of auto rickshaws and trucks, motorcycles and hand carts, donkeys hauling dirt in hessian side-sacks, horses hauling cart loads of tourists, bicycles with steel rod brakes, all punctuated by Brahman cattle strolling in random directions.

And horns. Always horns.

And here I am, between the young chap riding the bike and Ram behind, setting off helmet-less around Agra. "We are friends now," Ram says, and wants to shake my hand.

But I don't get to see a sarod.

And it doesn't matter. I have added to my experience of stringed instruments.

I have met Ram and heard him play in a suffocatingly airless little room, and it was a moment.

Kabosy, Valiha, Djembe in the Indian Ocean

When the Malagasy music and dancing ends, Diary Andrianampoina introduces the performers.

"This is Mihata, my wife." A diminutive woman from among the six dancers steps forward, eyes down, quickly bows and steps back again.

"This is Fetra, my sister," Diary says. Another step, another bow.

"This is Fany, my brother.

"And this is Tanjona, my…" Diary thinks about the title to be given…"neighbour".

Several more neighbours and a cousin are then introduced in quick succession.

"We are not professional musicians, just people together," Diary says, stating his regret for the quality of the performance. "We have only rehearsed twice. Some things were not…"

Diary has no need to apologise, for what I have just been treated to is not just the traditional music and dance of Madagascar, naturally harmonious and complex in timescales and shifts, but a personal gift from these people of Antananarivo, the steep-sided capital of two million.

Madagascar is 400 kilometres off the coast of Mozambique (I have just flown here from Johannesburg in South Africa), and it was not unreasonable to expect it to feel more African.

But it doesn't feel like that at all. Geographically isolated for more than 65 million years, the world's fourth biggest and oldest island has been inhabited by humans for only about 1,300 years, with those migrants thought to have come first from Indonesia (locals say specifically from Kalimantan) and Malaysia, but with Arab, Indian and African waves. Then the British, before the French arrived in 1896 and a revolution led to independence in 1960.

There are glimpses of these other influences, but Malagasy culture is its own.

The *afindrafindrao* that the six dancers have performed (the three ladies in long printed skirts and white t-shirts and with long scarves, the men in baggy black pants, long shirts tied at the waist with scarves and brimmed hats) might have echoes of the French quadrille seen in the Malagasy court in the nineteenth century, but it is now quintessentially part of Malagasy culture. And so it is with the Malagasy music. For more than a decade, I have been hoping to see and hear a Malagasy *kabosa*, *valiha* and *djembe* – but so often when you actually get to a place, traditional music is hard, or impossible, to find. Everyone's downloading Britney Spears and still doing cover versions of 1970s hits.

And yet, on my first night in Antananarivo, Diary has just played traditional songs on *kabosa* and harmonised with his friends, as his family and neighbours danced.

The *kabosa* (or *kabosy*) is a four- or six-stringed guitar played mostly by Betsimisaraka and Betsileo tribes – two of Madagascar's eighteen ethnic groups. Today the soundbox, or "body", is usually square or rectangular, but was originally made from a tortoise's shell (as were early Greek stringed instruments I have recently seen).

Kabosa probably evolved from guitars brought here by Arab or European sailors, the goblet-shaped *djembe* drum came from Africa and the *valiha*, which is a bamboo tube with strings along its side, rather like a cylindrical zither, evolved from instruments brought by the first Austronesians who arrived in outrigger canoes.

Not only is the *valiha* considered the national instrument of Madagascar but I am to hear Jean-Baptiste Andrianarimanana, one of its leading exponents, play one for me.

The next day I see Jean-Baptiste's band Zamba perform. Beside Jean-Baptiste on *valiha*, is Jean Hubert Andriafaraiahy playing a *kabosa* combined with a guitar in a double-neck (his invention). On the other side, Jean Donnee Ramananerisoa is playing a *djembe*.

Many of the songs are instrumental, but when they sing it is with the innate polyharmonic ability of Africa.

Music is intrinsic to Malagasy culture, playing a vital part in spiritual and cultural ceremonies. The people of Madagascar are still strong in their animist beliefs, worshipping the ancestors and combining this with other religions such as Christianity.

Diary is Protestant Christian but still practices animist rituals. He describes the *tromba* ceremony in which a witch doctor talks to the spirit of an ancestor in front of everybody. "Only he can talk to the soul of the dead. You can tell the witch doctor to transmit a message to the dead," he explains.

"And people must play Malagasy instruments...*kabosy*, *valiha*, *djembe* drum, *sodina* flute...to make the ancestors happy. To make them come quickly." With the help of the music, the witch doctor will lose control, entering a trance-like state.

The line between music and ancestors is so strong on the east coast that some musicians put rum or valued objects inside an instrument – even stuffing it through the tone hole – as an offering to the spirits.

The musicians in the band Zamba have proudly taken their culture overseas, playing in the United States of America, Europe, Africa and Japan.

Jean-Baptiste has spent fifteen years developing the *valiha* from a diatonic to a chromatic instrument and just to show its diversity, he announces that they will play a little Mozart. (To emphasise that diversity, perhaps, they manage to make it sound rather like a country and western song.)

At one stage, at their beckoning, Diary is also invited to pick up a guitar and join in with them. "I was blown away to be able to play with them," he later confides.

Diary was born and grew up in the Antananarivo area and, before studying tourism for four years, for a bachelor degree, he was a singer in a cabaret band.

"I like talking to people," he says but, while he likes learning from the guests he travels with, he adds, "my first and big reason is to protect nature – that is my first reason to get into tourism.

"I would like to take part in the protection of our animals – mainly lemurs which are only found in Madagascar. So I would like to be among the guides who preserve our nature. I communicate with people not to cut down the trees – to set up sustainable tourism." As part of that sustainability, he wants to see local culture stay strong. In this mainly French-speaking country, he has mastered beautiful English (part of his studies), but Malagasy remains the national language.

He says Madagascar is still "untapped" as a tourist destination. "Malagasy people are interested in tourism but they don't know much about it because it is a new industry here. I talk to my friends and neighbours about how important Madagascar is. That is part of my responsibility."

Diary sees the global picture, but thinks and acts locally. And Madagascar's living culture inevitably comes back to friends and family. His father, Ndriana, has twenty-two brothers and sisters. "Madagascar's greatest richness," Diary says, "is babies." He has met a man who has forty-eight children from four wives.

And then, at the end of Zamba's performance, I chat with Jean-Baptiste.

He turns to introduce Jean Hubert.

"He is my brother," he announces.

But, of course.

The Ancient Music of Greece

The Central Square markets in Athens have led me to this squat, 150-year-old building and music beckons me down marble steps to its basement that have been worn to shiny scallops. A bouzouki, accordion and guitar, and young voices singing. In Diporto, one of the oldest taverns in this ancient city, intellectuals and students are often joined by market workers for music and warmly boisterous conversation.

Fifteen young Greeks sit around tables pushed together, arms around one another's shoulders, snuggled like birds, smoking by the 'No Smoking' sign, and singing songs from the 1940s and '50s. They all know the words, and pass the instruments around, so that with the three new players the music takes on a different timbre.

An old man, who has been sitting alone, stands to dance in a slow and considered whirl, arms spread wide, eyes closed. An elegant, unassuming performance. *Zeibekiko* is danced alone and of free choreographic structure. In eras past, if someone got up to join in, it was more than bad form, and possibly caused conflict. Today, it is just a matter of etiquette, and other men will wait for a turn. Traditionally, applause is not sought nor given, out of respect in a country where I am continually startled by the sort of manners, gentleness and kindnesses I have generally, and sadly, come not to expect.

The young people acknowledge the man with polite, complimentary nods. It is like something from a classic movie and, indeed, Diporto is the right setting. Its furnishings haven't changed since the 1950s.

At a table covered by a sheet of paper and flanked by fourteen big barrels full of retsina, or resinated white wine, owner and cook Dimitris Mitsos, better known as "Barba Mitsos" (old man Mitsos), charming to me but renowned for being somewhat gruff on occasions, automatically brings big bowls of food, a tin jug of wine and stumpy glasses. A basket with six kinds of bread. Everyone is served the same meal, in waves. Another dish, another dish. Chickpea and bean stews, feta cheese and olives, all from fresh market produce. This is old, political, hospitable, mature Greece. This is real Greece, where antiquity and modernity meet and are often one.

In Diporto, the young people are still snuggled, singing. A young man beautifully plays a bouzouki which has six strings, not the more common eight. Later, in Pegasus Art Store in the Plaka, which has its own workshop for stringed instruments, I am told that this was the style of bouzouki played before the 1950s, along with the smaller six-string *tzouras* and much smaller *baglamas* (I buy one and it fits easily inside Casey as another good travelling companion). These are the instruments of the old songs; the traditional music.

It is a long and interesting conversation and I tell the folk in the shop how much I liked not only the fact that I had seen a young man playing one, but that all the people with him knew the songs, the words. The past integrated into the present.

Lesiba in Lesotho

As you now know, I am particularly interested in stringed instruments and Lesotho's *lesiba* is, in many ways, the most unusual of all. It has long been said to be extinct.

It is a slightly bent hardwood stick, about as long as a man's arm. Plaited horsehair is fixed around one end and then run down its length, the other tied through a hole in the end of a piece of quill, and then it is blown, to make reverberating notes. It is the only stringed musical instrument in history that has not been plucked, hit or bowed.

It was first described to the wider world in 1719 by German Peter Kolb, and is sometimes called the *t'Gorrah* or *goráh*.

H. Lichtenstein, in his *Travels in South Africa, in 1803–1806*, said it was dying out, and that only the older men could play it with any skill. He wrote that it was often played lying down. Some seemed "scarcely able to play but amid the tranquillity of night.

"They wrap themselves up comfortably in their skin, lay one ear to the ground, and hold the *t'Gorrah* commodiously before the mouth. Heard at a distance there is nothing unpleasant in it, but something plaintive and soothing. Although no more than six tones can be produced from it, which do not besides belong to our gamut, but form intervals quite foreign to it, yet the kind of vocal sound of these tones, the uncommon nature of the rhythm, and even the oddness, I may say wildness, of the harmony, give to this music a charm peculiar to itself."

John William Burchell, in his *Travels in the Interior of southern Africa*, wrote, "The *goráh*, as to its appearance and form, may be more aptly compared to the bow of a violin, than to any other thing; but in its principle and use, it is quite different; being in fact that of a stringed and wind instrument combined, and thus it agrees with the Aeolian harp.

"But with respect to the principle on which its different tones are produced, it may be classed with the trumpet or French horn while in the nature and quality of the sound which it gives, at least in the hands of one who is master of it, this strange instrument approaches to the violin.

"It consists merely of a slender stick or bow, on which a string of catgut is strained. But to the lower end of this string, a flat piece of about one and a half inches long, of the quill of an ostrich, is attached, so as to constitute a part of the length of the string.

"This quill being applied to the lips, is made to vibrate by strong inspirations and expirations of the breath; each of which ending with an increased degree of strength had always the same effect of forcing out the upper octave; exactly in the same way as produced in the flute, an instrument, therefore, which may be made to imitate the *goráh* sufficiently near to give some idea of it.

"The old musician seating himself down on a flat piece of rock, and resting his elbows on his knees, putting one forefinger into his ear, and the other into his wide nostril, either as it so happened, or for the purpose, it might be, of keeping the head steady, commenced his solo, and continued it with great earnestness, over and over again. The exertion which it required to bring out the tones loudly was very evident; and, in his anxious haste to draw breath at every note, our Orpheus gave us, into the bargain, intermingled with his music, certain grunting sounds which would have highly pleased the pigs; and if any had been in the country, would indubitably have drawn them all round him, if only out of curiosity to know what was the matter."

Burchell wrote down the music as it was played and adds: "I find a difficulty in conceiving how an instrument, having its tones on the principle above described, can produce either the *tonum majus* or the *heptachordon.* The crotchets of that part which is in triple time, were exactly of the same length as those in the common time preceding and following, consequently the time reckoned by bars, was there accelerated. The whole piece played once through occupied just seventy seconds, and was repeated without variations. There is sufficient in these few notes, to show that he possessed an ear capable of distinguishing musical intervals, and they are besides remarkable under all circumstances as a specimen of natural modulation."

And so, the *lesiba* is something extraordinary to me, and something thought extinct.

I am standing in a stone hut, talking to Aleni Sebilo, trying to find out a little more about this instrument.

And when her father, Tseko Sebilo, comes in, wrapped in a blue and cream blanket, and I ask him too, he just gets out his *lesiba*, encrusted with years of smoke and hand-dirt, and plays it for me.

I am shocked to see it; astounded to hear it.

Perhaps he can see this.

He just holds it out in the palm of both hands, and gives it to me.

I was a child who wanted to be a writer, not an astronaut.

I look around the bejewelled walls of my writing study, at the musical instruments from around the world; the ukulele, the *baglamas*, the *lesiba* – that greatest of gifts. Then at fabrics; the *bangdian* bought in a monastery in Tibet, silk from Cambodia, cotton from India that was hand printed with wooden blocks. I glimpse the backs of the denim jackets, with panels from Vietnam, Sri Lanka, South Africa; Nepal and New Zealand now complete.

I was a child who wanted to be a writer, not an astronaut, and who went out and discovered a most remarkable planet.

Acknowledgements

We are nothing without family and friends, and my heartfelt love and appreciation to all around me, particularly Virginia and Max Ward. They not only allow me creativity – I feel they create it in me. They are in me and part of me every moment of every day, wherever I am.

Some of these stories have appeared in other forms, in the Travel supplement of *The West Australian* in Perth, Australia, but the words that make this book what it is were largely written on the back patio of my mother's house in Worcester, England, just a few miles from the house in which I grew up, on the Malvern Hills.

I was staying with my mother, Shirley, for her eightieth birthday celebrations, rising around 4.30 am and out there in the warm English summer morning; quite literally up with the sparrows, watching these amusing and endearing little birds teem from the hedge at the end of the garden to the bush by the back door. Hearing a chip-chip-chip and looking round to see a robin, red breast and all, staring back, head cocked. One morning a goldfinch, with the flash of yellow on his wings and his scarlet mask. The garden is neatly lawned, full of fuchias, the greenhouse door open.

My brother Rob drops by, sometimes with his son Scott and daughter Gemma. My sister Sally with her children Jack, Adam and Becky, and Becky's daughter Ella. And there we are in the back garden, with mother's friends Ron and Beryl "from over the road".

As counterpoint and counter balance to my life in Australia and its broad landscape, it connects me to all I was growing up, and all I have grown up to be.

It is a pleasure being a University of Western Australia Publishing author. My thanks to UWAP director Terri-ann White, publisher Kate Pickard, Kiri Falls, Britt Ingerson and Katie Connolly.

Among the organisations that have kindly supported my travels are Emirates airline, Singapore Airlines, South Africa Airways, Thai Airways International, Garuda Indonesia airline, Malaysia Airlines, Air Asia, Qatar Airways, Air Canada, Travel Directors, Wildlife Safari, Cox and Kings, Peregrine Adventures, World Expeditions, Travel Tree, Orion Expedition Cruises, Unique Tourism, David Baker & Associates, India Tourism, South Africa Tourism, Sultanate of Oman Tourism, Tourism Authority of Thailand, Tourism Malaysia, Sabah Tourism, Canadian Tourism Commission, Tourism Yukon, Australia's North-West and Australia's Coral Coast.

I appreciate the help of many others who help me.

My colleagues at West Australian Newspapers, and particularly my colleagues in Travel, Niall McIlroy, Jan Bromilow and Gemma Nisbet, offer the fellowship of the like minded.

Other Titles by Stephen Scourfield

As the River Runs
Other Country
Unaccountable Hours

Stephen Scourfield's works of fiction can be bought from bookshops or direct from the publisher, with free postage and handling to anywhere in Australia, or A$10 to anywhere else in the world. They can also be bought as Kindle eBooks.

As The River Runs

As The River Runs is a powerful ode to one of Australia's most stunning regions, from an author who writes with red dust in his veins.

A secret plan is being cooked up to bring water from the monsoonal north of Australia to the south. But Government minister Michael Mooney needs to find out what opposition he might face around the river valley. He sends Kate Kennedy, his young, career-minded Chief of Staff, and political fixer Jack Cole on a 'fact-finding' trip.

Ex-greenie Dylan Ward is their guide. Respected by both the mining industry and Aboriginal elder Vincent Yimi, Dylan is unaware that he has been compromised until their journey takes some unexpected turns. But as they travel through the wild river country, Kate begins to see Dylan and the world around her in a new light.

"Scourfield plots neatly: there is intrigue, romance and bold, well-kitted-out adventure. There is also, intermittently, a good deal of comfortable didacticism. As the River Runs *is a fable for our times, a robustly related piece of literary advocacy for ecological and indigenous interests. He hangs his vivid examinations of the journey and the country on a page-turning narrative line."*
The Australian

"Where Other Country *was a very masculine breathing out,* As the River Runs *is a more feminine breathing in. In that sense, both are not only gripping, but enriching, life-enhancing reads. Ultimately it is in the descriptions of landscape, flora and fauna – unsurprisingly, given Scourfield's extensive experience as a travel editor, writer and photographer – that one finds the most musical and heartfelt passages."*
West Australian Newspapers

The printed book is available worldwide, through the UWA Publishing online shop, www.uwap.uwa.edu.au. It is $A26.99, with free postage within Australia and a flat fee of $A10 for every country other than Australia. (International orders have Goods & Services Tax subtracted.)
ISBN: 978-1-74258-4904
Download for Kindle at www.amazon.com/Kindle-eBooks

Other Country

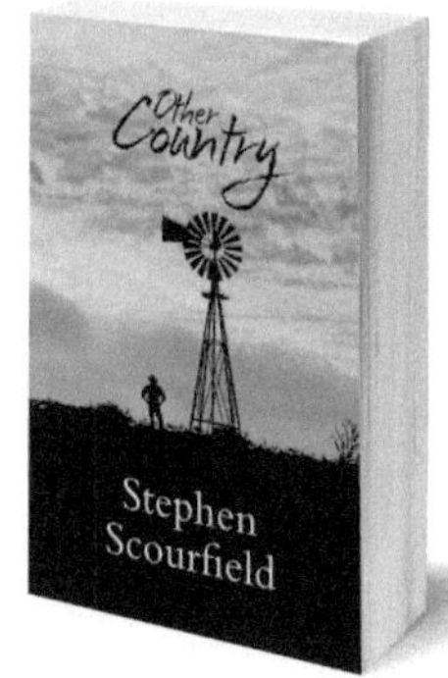

Other Country has been described as "raw, forceful and intensely masculine". The author has been called "a wholly new, striking and original voice in Australian fiction."

Set in the mythic, remote country of the Top End, *Other Country* tells the story of two young brothers, The Ace and Wild Billy, and their struggle to overcome the bitter legacy of their brutal father. Bound by blood and memories and trust, they are destined to clash – one bound by the past, the other straining towards the future. "And out of it all lead only two paths, to end up mean and empty like the Old Man, or not."

Written with an authentic grittiness and an understated, dry humour, it is also an unforgettable story of the 'the other country' of the Top End, the implacable and unforgiving moods of the landscape and the laconic and tough characters who make this unforgiving country their home.

Other Country is republished in its third edition. It was the fiction winner in the WA Premier's Book Awards 2007, shortlisted in the Commonwealth Writers Prize and longlisted for the 2009 International IMPAC Dublin Literary Award.

"The success of Other Country *is also largely due to its voice, which is immediate, dramatic and stark. Poetic as well as vernacular, it suggests Proulx, McCarthy and other US writers for whom voice is, in many ways, story. Scourfield's evident intimacy with the landscape and subject that have inspired him percolates through every page of this impressive novel."*
The Weekend Australian

"… an engaging novel that has flashes of pure poetry and a resonant, deeply affecting ending."
Australian Literary Review

The printed book is available worldwide, through the UWA Publishing online shop, www.uwap.uwa.edu.au. It is $A22.99, with free postage within Australia and a flat fee of $A10 for every country other than Australia. (International orders have Goods & Services Tax subtracted.)
ISBN: 978-1-74258-5031
Download for Kindle at www.amazon.com/Kindle-eBooks

Unaccountable Hours: Three Novellas

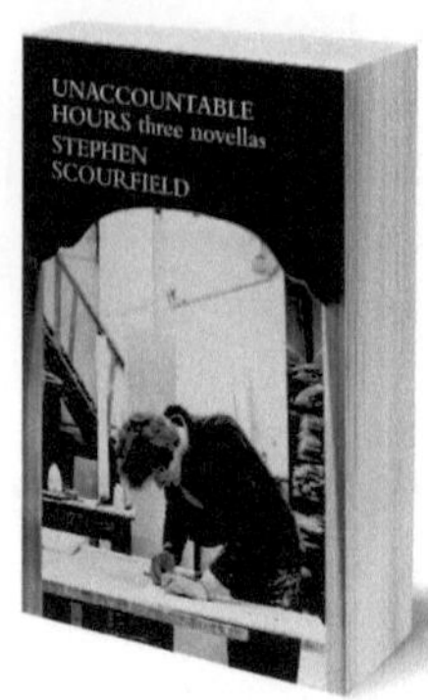

Unaccountable Hours is a collection of three novellas that follow the fortunes of a maker of musical instruments, the ethical dilemma of a biologist and birdwatcher, and the romantic friendship between a young man and an aged woman – all firmly set in and defined by the surrounding landscape. In 'The Luthier', musician Alton Freeman devotes his life to crafting a violin that will reproduce the perfect sound of Bach's Partitas and Sonatas, as played by his idol, musician Monica Erica Grenbaum. 'Ethical Man' follows the biologist and birdwatcher Bartholomew Milner, who lives stringently according to his 'Milner's Ethic', and is put to the ultimate ethical test whilst on a research expedition in the Australian outback. 'Like Water', tells the story of an unlikely friendship and subsequent romance that develops between two kindred spirits, Matthew and Beatrice – two soulmates born generations apart.

"There's a creative intelligence at work in this book, diligently crafting the narrative intensity to nourish literature and help sustain cultural cohesion."
Canberra Times

"Unaccountable Hours *is a powerful, evocative collection of three novellas that together explore many of Scourfield's concerns; familial relationships, ethics, the concept of tradition, the transition from adolescence to manhood – and, of course, nature and the landscape."*
The West Australian

The printed book is available worldwide, through the UWA Publishing online shop, www.uwap.uwa.edu.au. It is $A32.95, with free postage within Australia and a flat fee of $A10 for every country other than Australia. (International orders have Goods & Services Tax subtracted.)
ISBN: 978-1-74258-291-7
Download for Kindle for $A9.99 at www.amazon.com/Kindle-eBooks

About the Disk

We are pleased to include a disk with this book, to take the stories further. The disk, to be used in a computer, contains photographs, videos and audio by Stephen Scourfield, to accompany and enhance the stories in this book.

There are more than 500 photographs in 20 galleries:
Armenia
Athens, Greece
Borneo
Myanmar (Burma)
Dubai
London, England
Malvern Hills and region, England
Georgia
Greek Islands
India
Kenya
The Kimberley, Western Australia
Lesotho, southern Africa
Madagascar
Nepal
Ningaloo Reef, Western Australia

Oman
South Africa
Sri Lanka
Tibet

In them you will see the places, but also many of the people featured in the book – Willis Muirimi in South Africa, Pramod Pandey in India, Paul Dimus in Borneo, Glen Chidlow in the Kimberley, Lucy Wanjiru at the spinning and weaving workshop in Kenya and many more.
You will see Tseko Sebilo playing his *lesiba.*

You will see the food and the fabrics.
You will see the Hajar Mountains in Oman and a whale shark swimming along Ningaloo Reef in Western Australia.
For the photographs also give glimpses of many situations and moments in *Beautiful Witness.*

The photographs are presented in PDFs, for ease of viewing on all computers.

The podcasts include the author reading from the book, and some material not in the book – an introduction to "Australia All Over" and more particularly to Western Australia.

The audio is presented as m4a, mp3 and wav files, for installation and playing on any device.

The videos are in mp4 and mov formats, to play on PC or Mac operating systems.

www.ingramcontent.com/pod-product-compliance
Ingram Content Group UK Ltd.
Pitfield, Milton Keynes, MK11 3LW, UK
UKHW041445070726
13610UKWH00009B/19

9 781742 585833